ALLAN
BROWN
not well drawn by Gray

15
June
2012
Alasdair

THE **GLASGOW** SMILE

Allan Brown was born in Glasgow in 1967 and attended the city's university. A former Scottish Journalist of the Year, he is the author of *Inside the Wicker Man* and *Nileism: The Strange Course of The Blue Nile*. He lives in Partick.

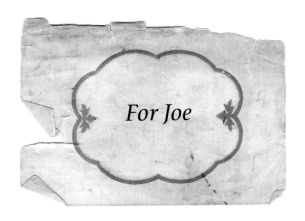

For Joe

THE GLASGOW SMILE

An A–Z of the Funniest City on Earth

ALLAN BROWN

BIRLINN

First published in 2013 by
Birlinn Ltd
West Newington House
10 Newington Road
Edinburgh EH9 1QS

www.birlinn.co.uk

ISBN: 978 1 78027 062 3

Designed and typeset by Mark Blackadder

Printed and bound in Britain by T J International, Padstow

ACKNOWLEDGEMENTS

Johnny Beattie, Wattie Cheung, Gavin Docherty, David Flynn, Jonathan Melville, Tony Osoba
and Kirsten O'Neill. Particular thanks to Alison Kerr for use of her John Byrne, Emma Thompson
and Robbie Coltrane interviews; and to Kevin Pocklington, Alison Rae, Andrew Simmons and
Kenneth Wright. Thanks also to Julie, Jim and Scott, Brian McFie, Hugh Hood, Craig Mann,
Edwin Moore and my mother and father for photographs. And to Lavinia Blackwall, Michael
Hastings, Simon Shaw and Alex Neilson, the constituent members of Glasgow's (and Yorkshire's)
own Trembling Bells, whose wondrous music soundtracked the writing of this book.

PICTURE CREDITS

Every effort has been made to trace copyright owners. Where this has not been possible, no
credit is given. The Publisher will be happy to include appropriate credits in future editions.

viii Wattie Cheung; 7 Allan Brown; 16 Hugh Hood; 20 Edwin Moore; 22 Edwin Moore; 25 Brian
McFie; 32 Arnold Brown; 35 Chris Close; 41 Edwin Moore; 42 John Byrne; 44 Allan Brown; 45
Malky McCormick; 54 Andy Scott; 59 Scottish Screen Archive; 60 Jeremy Cutler; 64 The Daily
Mash; 68 Tony Osoba; 73 Edwin Moore; 75 Corbis; 84 Carol Foreman; 89 Hugh Hood; 90 the
Glashan family; 91 Malky McCormick; 93 Allan Brown; 97 Chris Adkins; 106 Linda Nylind; 116
Knowle West Media Centre; 117 Claire Pendrous; 118 Gillian Kyle; 125 Wattie Cheung; 133–35 Joe
McGrath; 141 Scottish Film Archive; 147 Hugh Hood; 148–50 Annabelle Meredith; 151–2 Ranald
McColl; 155 The Herald; 156 Harry Papadopoulos; 162 Ian Dickson; 165 Edwin Moore; 169 Brian
McFie; 176 Edwin Moore; 177 Brian McFie; 179 Newquest; 181 David Shrigley; 188 Corbis; 190
Wattie Cheung; 192 Hugh Hood; p. 195 Alan Harrison; pp. 197–200 Edwin Moore; 202 The
Torrington family; 205 Jean-Christophe Beaumarchais; 212 John Byrne; 215 John Byrne; 220 Craig
Mann; 227 Craig Mann; 229 Brian McFie; 236 Brian McFie; 240 Craig Mann.

CONTENTS

INTRODUCTION

In a 1980s diary column, the *Glasgow Herald*, as was, ran a most instructive item. It told of a German tourist to Glasgow encountering a harassed mother smacking her errant child. The tourist interrupted: 'In Germany,' he announced 'we do not hit our children.' 'Is that right?' replied the mother. 'In Partick we don't gas our Jews.'

Reflect upon this remark. Consider its aggression, its swift, rhetorical kick to the tender regions. It is defensive, yet offensive, to extents that border on the sociopathic. It takes no prisoners, gives no quarter, bars no holds. It is a boxing kangaroo of a comeback, up on its hind legs instantly, lashing out. It invokes, almost casually, what is perhaps the darkest hour in human history, the Holocaust, merely to disoblige an impertinent stranger – an impertinent German stranger at that, who, being so, was probably a mite sheepish about the matter anyway. Such is the humour of Glasgow – if not at its best then certainly at its most refractory and oppositional, which is to say at its most typical. The retort contained all one needs know about the temperament of this vital, restless, charismatic and, above all, unyielding city. Truly, the humour of Glasgow is a formidable thing. No place in the kingdom has anything to compete or compare with it.

In fact, when it comes to wit, the entirety of Scotland is but Glasgow's colonial outpost. There is no Scottish comedy that is not Glaswegian. Subtract Glasgow from the comedic equation and Scotland becomes the square root of nothing much; a wasteland, an eternity spent in Ronnie Corbett's anecdotal armchair. To identify a Scottish comic figure of consequence who is not Glaswegian is like naming an American map-maker or a great Welsh painter. It can't be done.

You're welcome to try, of course. You might point out that Alastair Sim, star of the St Trinian's films, hailed from Edinburgh, as did Muriel Spark, whose early novels were exquisitely comic. Aberdonians would cite *Scotland the What?*, the dusty stage revue decipherable only by Aberdonians. Sir Harry Lauder came from Portobello. Neil Munro, writer of the Para Handy stories, was an Inverary man. Will Fyffe, author of the music-hall standard 'I Belong to Glasgow', came, wouldn't you know it, not from Glasgow but Dundee.

But the exercise is pointless. North of Carlisle, only Glasgow can do humour. For a nation of 6 million souls over the span of more than a century Scotland has proven pitifully deficient in the provision of wit, a calamitously unfunny place. When people speak of the Scottish sense of humour, what they mean is the Glasgow sense of humour. It needs admitting that, really, there is no Scottish sense of humour, no funny bone running from Gretna Green to John O'Groats. There is simply Glasgow, and the wit it lends out like a library book. Glasgow's humour is what linguists term a synecdoche, a part that stands for a whole. In this respect, as in so many others, Scotia is merely the chaff around the grain that is Glasgow. The comic productivity of the entire nation was outsourced to the city by the Clyde.

It can even be argued that Glasgow's standing in this regard is global, that this is the funniest city on the planet. You'd assume such a designation would belong somewhere grander: New York, for example, with its history of club comedy and cabaret, the city of Woody Allen and Joan Rivers; or to Los Angeles, centre of film and television production; or to London, which has given us Chaucer, Noel Coward and Monty Python. Yet each of these cities is essentially just a hub, a magnet, pulling in talent from hundreds of miles around. As a rule they have not given birth to the stuff.

Glasgow has. Pound for pound, per head of population, no city on earth has produced such a ceaseless torrent of comedy, created by and for its own folk, though enjoyed across the globe. As the Irish sociologist Sean Damer wrote: 'Glaswegians are among the best talkers in the world, the most articulate debaters, the wittiest story-tellers, the best one-liners, the best purveyors of what they themselves call the "lightning repartee".' A close analogue in this is Jewish humour. The wit of Glasgow, also, is less a type of entertainment than a philosophy, a prism, a telescope, a way of seeing the world – or, to be more exact, a means by which Glaswegians can 'see' Glasgow better.

This comedic prowess, however, is not immemorial; the mastery is modern and post-industrial. We have little way of knowing if the Glaswegians of yore were amusing or otherwise. Mass literacy was yet to come, and anyway the market in conspicuous cleverness was being cornered in Edinburgh, by Hume and Boswell, by *Blackwood's Magazine* and the *Edinburgh Review*. In Glasgow there was no paper trail of tradition, nothing much written down. The Presbyterian hierarchy had set its face against theatre, believing it redolent of the pageants of Catholic times. In 1754, for instance, a playhouse at the top of the High Street was demolished on the orders of George Whitefield, a Methodist preacher, who'd labelled the structure 'a limb of Satan'. Edinburgh, then, had the Enlightenment; Glasgow had the Endarkenment.

But then came industrialisation and with it an explosion in Glasgow's population, few of whom were to be mollified with Bible stories. Instead came the era of the 'penny geggies', wild, illicit jamborees which turned streets into open-air theatres. There were four such in the Saltmarket alone, with the street's length divided up by concentrations of collapsible canvas booths. Inside them were presented historical dramas, songs, storytelling, though the gatherings were also hotspots of pickpocketing, drunkenness and brawls, which often had to be calmed by performers.

Their popularity saw some Glasgow publicans convert their premises into makeshift mini-theatres, where performances were given by gymnasts, jugglers and comics. From the 1850s, such adaptations gave rise to concert halls, their attendances swollen by the depressing fact that domestic dwellings of the period were too grim to be lingered in. Soon it was estimated that

Glasgow's city centre contained 26 theatres, purveying cleaned-up versions of the bacchanals offered in the penny geggies. These mutated into the Victorian music-hall, followed eventually by the advent of cinema. By the early 1900s a Glaswegian in search of distraction was spoilt for choice; between the penny geggies, saloon shows, cinema, variety theatre, concert halls and any number of museums of curiosity, or freak shows, such as the one in the Britannia Music Hall on Argyle Street, enhanced by a rooftop carnival and a waxworks. And this inventory omits the pantomimes, operas, miscellaneous concerts and Shakespearean productions staged in 'legitimate' theatres such as the King's and the Theatre Royal.

This was happening as the city itself changed. In the decade after 1841 the Irish community in Scotland increased from 4.8 per cent of total population to 7.2 per cent, compared against 1 per cent in England and Wales. As workers were drawn by naval engineering Glasgow absorbed a third of the population of the west Highlands. Jews arrived too, fleeing Russian pogroms and, later, the rise of National Socialism: by the end of the First World War 9,000 Jews were living in the city, almost the entirety of their population in Scotland, employed mainly in tailoring. Glasgow became home also to the UK's third-largest community of émigré Italians. And few of the incomers could afford to settle anywhere but the Gorbals, the notorious slum district just south of the river.

'The streets were slippery with refuse and often with drunken vomit,' recalled Ralph Glasser in his memoir *Growing Up in the Gorbals*; or as Jeff Torrington wrote of Crown Street in *Swing Hammer Swing!*: 'We came now to a thorough-fare that blitzed the senses with its sudden blitz and uproar. Here, there were many shops doing business: bakers, fruitshops, fishmongers, banks, dairies, butchers. Above these thronged premises there were dental surgeries which shared their common stairs with tenanted flats from between the curtains of which faces could now and then be glimpsed. On the pavements, shoppers' feet churned the slush to fine black mud.' The squalor and violence were delineated most famously in the novel *No Mean City*, by Alexander McArthur and H. Kingsley Long, with a vivid grimness that ensured the book's infamy has never faded. The Gorbals grew to be among the most overcrowded areas in Europe, a sump of dereliction and despair, where the ethnic poor competed for survival in a Colosseum of

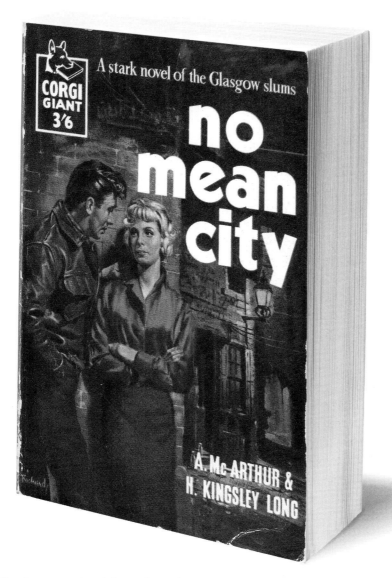

On the cover:

A stark novel of the Glasgow slums

CORGI GIANT 3'6

no mean city

A. McARTHUR &
H. KINGSLEY LONG

disadvantage. In shipyards and railway yards, or in pubs, jails and pawnshops, or in the shadow of the hellish Dixon's Blazes ironworks, where five vast blast furnaces belched smoke and ash unceasingly, the character, the tenor and timbre, the very identity of modern Glasgow was being forged, in literal and metaphoric fire.

For comfort and distraction the city wrapped itself in the patchwork of its people, began to see itself through the kaleidoscope of its citizenry. Glasgow absorbed the fatalism of its Jews, the vigour of its Highlanders, the verbal ingenuity of its Irish, and the machismo of its Italians. The Glaswegian dialect and mindset came defiantly to stand apart. In contrast to Cockney rhyming slang, say, this was not a patois made to alienate the outsider or to help criminals confound the police. Neither was it the lobster pot of nautical allusion and country wisdom heard around the sea coasts. Rather, Glasgow was breeding a mongrel argot: from the flinty consonants of the Doric and the whispery poetry of the Gaels; from the fragranced expressions that floated over from Edinburgh; from the glottal weaponry smuggled in from Ulster; from American songs and cinema – but, most of all, from the contingencies of hard, industrious lives, in which each word was galvanised, stressed and tempered until it flashed the keenest edge.

Hardly surprising, then, that the new audiences began to look beyond the theatrical fare of the day: the soppy romances of Victorian music hall, the kailyard entertainments of Harry Lauder et al. In Glasgow, the demand was for entertainment that described and reflected these tempestuous surroundings. The first significant figure in this was Tommy Lorne (1890–1935), whose face paint, long gloves and high strangulated voice owed much to the European clowning tradition. Lorne's catchphrase – 'In the name of the wee man!' – is common Glasgow parlance yet. The city's sense of itself deepened with the popularity of 'I Belong to Glasgow', Will Fyffe's ditty of well-refreshed bravado. But the comic who did most to legitimise the local tongue was Tommy Morgan (1898– 1958). To the modern ear Morgan's comedy is impossibly quaint but he is remembered in the city, by those old enough to remember him, with deep fondness: 'A man and his wife are going to the air raid shelter,' went one routine. 'The wife shouts, "Ah hiv tae go back tae the hoose, Ah forgoat my teeth." The husband says, "For Goad's sake, wumman, it's bombs they're drappin, no' sandwiches."'

In the 1960s Lex McLean (1907–1975) was anointed Morgan's spiritual successor, though by now the genie was out of the bottle. The humour of Glasgow was living its life beyond the shipyard and the variety stage. It was becoming a fixture of radio and television, of books and newspapers, beginning on radio in 1939 with The McFlannels, a couthy, homely BBC Scotland sit-com. Soon after, entertainers began to return from active service. To keep theatres and performers busy the year round, summer seasons were introduced. These begat lavish revues like the *Five Past Eight Show*, which in turn produced *Francie and Josie*, still perhaps the most consequen-

The statue of Lobby Dosser, Rank Bajin and El Fideldo in Woodlands Road, Glasgow.

tial stitch in the tapestry of Glasgow comedy. In 1949, meanwhile, the *Evening Times* had introduced Lobey Dosser, a strip by Bud Neill in which the Wild West became the adopted home of Glasgow characters and scenarios. BBC Scotland was launched in 1952; STV arrived five years later and launched The One O'Clock Gang. In 1959, Stanley Baxter debuted The Professor, the sketch that would develop into *Parliamo Glasgow*. Also flourishing was a distinctively Glaswegian style of pantomime which became in time the kind of training academy once furnished by variety theatre. In the 1970s the floodgates opened, ushering in *Scotch & Wry*, Billy Connolly, Ivor Cutler, *The Slab Boys*. The years since have added countless others: *Tutti Frutti*, Victor and Barry, *The Steamie, Gregory's Girl*, Susan Calman, *Still Game*. Today, Craig Ferguson sits at the summit of American network television. Armando Iannucci is British comedy's puppetmaster. Billy Connolly is named regularly the world's favourite stand-up comic. Frankie Boyle and Kevin Bridges perform in stadiums and arenas to tens of thousands. It is all some distance from Tommy Lorne in clown make-up in the back room of a spit-and-sawdust pub.

Documenting the humour of Glasgow, then, is akin to measuring a coastline – to merit inclusion, how big need a bump be? The corpus of the city's humour swells by the day, as writers, comics, cartoonists, councillors, footballers, police officers, publicans, cab drivers and even concerned German tourists play their parts in the sketch show of Glasgow street life. As William McIlvanney's novel puts it: 'Laidlaw said to Harkness, "That's what I love about Glasgow. It's not a city, it's a twenty-four-hour cabaret."'

This all legislates, I'd argue, against a history recounted chronologically. Glasgow's wit is disruptive; it bursts through unbidden. It can be funny when least expected, or intended. It is peripatetic, al fresco and extra-mural. Could there be another city in which a police squad hunting a serial killer in local dance halls dubs itself the Marine Formation Dance Team, after the nickname of its headquarters? Where else would a future Lord Provost retail a necktie bearing the slogan 'Ya Bass' above a heraldic shield of crossed swords? And surely Glasgow is alone in producing a churchman whose autobiography recounts his dealings with mass murderer Fred West as he operated his Mr Whippy ice-cream van? Each of these incidents occurred in Glasgow and illustrates as effectively as any bit of show business the city's raw and fearless levity. Hence the nature of this survey: equal parts encyclopaedia, miscellany, anthology and treasury – a study of the Glaswegians who have made us laugh, and of the gloriously fractured milieu whence they have sprung.

This is not to argue that Glasgow's humour is fully achieved. It clearly isn't. It comes up short in many areas. The novel, for one. The Glaswegian comic novel is difficult to find. Certainly, many Glasgow novels are funny, but inadvertently, because they are so relentlessly, proudly grim and take themselves so seriously. In terms of intentional comedy there is only really *Swing Hammer Swing!* by Jeff Torrington; bits of Alasdair Gray; Anne Donovan's *Buddha Da*. And, basically, that's it. Prior to the 1970s, comedy featured seldom in the works of the city's playwrights; 7:84 and Wildcat redressed this, and today we have D.C. Jackson, Johnny McKnight and Douglas Maxwell. Glasgow's comic theatre is still largely a kind of pantomime for grown-ups, whether it's a nostalgic confection like *Paras over the Barras*, the history of a football club or a musical about the heyday of the Apollo concert hall. When Glaswegians visit the theatre they're happier, it seems, if the ghosts of variety and music-hall stay close at hand.

Neither has the city tackled smut or innuendo of the Benny Hill or Whitehall farce kinds (excepting, perhaps, Jimmy Logan's appearances in *Carry On Abroad* and *Carry On Girls*, in the latter as a character named Cecil Gaybody). With the exception of Ivor Cutler, Glasgow has attempted only rarely the absurdist humour of a Monty Python or Spike Milligan type, or touched upon the macabre, like *The League of Gentlemen*. It has never really done surrealism or slapstick, or the comedy of embarrassment, as typified by *The Office*. Unlike *Dad's Army* or *Yes, Minister*, it has little interest in the peculiarities of the British social order. Stanley Baxter aside, it prefers to avoid camp. It barely does satire, excepting the work of Armando Iannucci. It wouldn't touch racial issues; it barely does whimsy of the kind found in, say, the cartoons of Heath Robinson or in the humour of Stephen Fry (though the work of John Glashan is an exception here).

Put like this, there doesn't seem much Glasgow humour does do. Which is sort of the point. The comedy of Glasgow is a mirror, not a window. It considers the world outside Glasgow of limited interest. The purpose of its humour is to reflect for the benefit of Glaswegians what it is to be Glaswegian. It is local humour for local people. Any appeal it might hold for those outwith Glasgow is a bonus, but it is scarcely the point. The point is to forge an ongoing oral autobiography, a sociological celebration of a city and its people: their speech, their rituals, their joys and despairs. The mission is predicated upon a confident, happily immodest, assumption: that Glasgow is simply a place apart, altogether a different calibre of city, with qualities as disparate and contradictory as its ethnic make-up; tough but tender, warm but wary, blunt but philosophic. You may say these claims are arguable, but, then, that's precisely what we want you to say – so we can argue with you.

Allan Brown,
Glasgow, 2013
allanbrown@mac.com

A sense of humour is a serious business; and it isn't funny, not having one. Watch the humourless closely: the cocked and furtive way they monitor all conversation, their flashes of panic as irony or exaggeration eludes them, the relief with which they submit to the meaningless babble of unanimous laughter. They are handicapped in the head. The humourless have no idea what is going on and can't make sense of anything at all.

Martin Amis,

The War against Cliché

The energy that otherwise would have been used to repress a desire is saved by joking which allows aggression to be released.

Sigmund Freud,

Jokes and Their Relation to the Unconscious, 1905

The trouble with Freud is that he never played second house at the Glasgow Empire on a Saturday night.

Ken Dodd

"It's very real, isn't it?" said Claire, with a tremulous whisper'

AA GILL

ALADDIN BY MICHAEL PALIN AND TERRY JONES
(pantomime, 1971)

In 1971, a version of *Aladdin* written by Michael Palin and Terry Jones of the absurdist BBC series *Monty Python's Flying Circus* appeared at the Citizens Theatre in the Gorbals. The theatre's artistic director Giles Havergal had commissioned the production while running the Palace Theatre in Watford and had brought it with him on moving to Glasgow, staging the first pantomime the Gorbals had seen in many a decade. Palin recounted the experience in his 2006 volume *Diaries 1969–1979*.

Our rooms had been booked in the Central Hotel which adjoins the station. It is a railway hotel built in monumentally impressive proportions in the great age of railway expansion. The walls were about three foot thick, with about fifteen foot width to play with on each step of the mighty staircase. After leaving our bags we decided to walk in the direction of the Citizens Theatre.

We never did reach the Citizens but we did find a bar with very old brown, varnished tables and a wooden floor, and we did meet three shabby men, one of whom told us at great length why he was an alcoholic, and then asked for one of our empty whisky glasses. With elaborate furtiveness the rather sad-eyed, younger man of the three took the glass towards his flies, unbuttoning his coat at the same time. I watched amazed, and then a little relieved, as he produced a surreptitious bottle of what looked like sherry and filled the alcoholic's glass with it.

We walked back to the hotel, bathed, and took a taxi across the river to the Citizens Theatre where Aladdin by Michael Palin and Terry Jones was the first pantomime the Gorbals had seen in years.

The theatre is a neat size, with a circle and a balcony. We were met at the door and ushered into the Manager's office. The Artistic Director, Giles Havergal, we learned was in Tangier. After seeing the pantomime, we understood why. None of the cast seemed to be able to act too well – they certainly didn't seem to be enjoying it – and, despite the enthusiastic support of the kids, they hurtled through it. What few gems of wit there are in the script were lost forever, and the creation of atmosphere, which is perhaps something the script does best, was spoilt by the speed and incomprehension of the line delivery. The principal boy had been taken ill and the girl playing her looked marvellous, but acted like a Canadian redwood. The love scene with the princess was one of the most embarrassing I've ever witnessed – combining, as it did, her extraordinary lack of acting ability and the princess's extraordinary lack of charm.

Afterwards, we met Phil McCall, the Widow Twankey of the pantomime. He regarded us cautiously at first, as though he felt rather guilty about the way the pantomime had been done – but when he realised that we didn't hate every minute of it, he became quite friendly, and we went next door, to the Close Theatre Club – a student-run club with a bar and homemade food. We ate plates of chilli and drank a bottle of Scotch which Phil McCall produced, surreptitiously, from his coat. We parted on very convivial terms, and walked back across the bridge to our hotel. In one of the huge high-ceilinged rooms, we watched the Marx Brothers film *Duck Soup* on TV. Sank, happily, into bed at about 1.00

Michael Palin, *Diaries 1969–1979*
(Phoenix, 2007)

ANCESTRY

BLIND ALICK
(poet, 1771–1840)

Born Alexander Macdonald, Blind Alick was, indeed, blind, lending him the soubriquet of 'Glasgow's Homer', even though the Greek poet in question, we now know, was not actually blind. A character from the city's pre-Victorian *galère* of destitute and toothless eccentrics, Blind Alick would not detain us long were it not that his poetry was so catastrophically amusing and deserving of the delighted pity more commonly thrown the way of William Topaz McGonagall. The latter wrote infamously, for instance, of the Tay Bridge disaster of 1879: 'Beautiful railway bridge of the silv'ry Tay/Alas! I am very sorry to say/That ninety lives have been taken away/On the last sabbath day of 1879/Which shall be remembered for a very long time.'

Nearly a century earlier, though, in 1797, Blind Alick was penning this:

> Good news I have got, my lads,
> For country and for town;
> We have gained a mighty fight
> On the sea at Camperdown,
> Our cannon they did rattle, lads,
> And we knock'd their topmasts down;
> But the particulars you will hear
> By the post in the afternown.

ALEXANDER WYLIE PETRIE
(barber and publisher, 1853–1937)

Some Westenders in Glasgow might recall a fellow who in the mid-1980s was a constant presence on the streets. Wearing full Culloden regalia and an expression of infinite cosmic resentment, he trudged a grim circuit of local bars attempting, usually fruitlessly, to sell copies of the SNP newsletter he carted round like a leper's bell.

Alexander Wylie Petrie was his spiritual forebear. An iconoclastic individual, Petrie edited and published a late-Victorian civic scandal sheet entitled *The Clincher*. Verbally and in print, he waged a one-man war against the city corporation and its police service, lambasting both for their principles and their practices. Launched in 1897, the publication was sold on the streets by Petrie personally, rendering him highly identifiable, both to his readership and to those he criticised.

He was so persistent a thorn in officialdom's side, in fact, that in time he was arrested and committed to Woodilee Lunatic Pauper Asylum near Lenzie – a touch extreme, you might say, though it's to be remembered this was an era when a man could be sectioned for glancing at an uncovered piano leg. Happily, Glasgow rebelled and a public outcry was raised against the treatment of Petrie. Before his release, however, he underwent one final examination. Passing with distinction, Petrie requested its conclusions be stated explicitly on a medical certificate. For years afterwards, Petrie insisted he was considered the only man in Glasgow to have been officially declared sane . . .

ALBERT ERNEST PICKARD

(theatre owner and impresario, 1874–1964)

PICKARD'S WAXWORK, Trongate, Glasgow

THE HUMAN SPIDER

PICKARD'S MUSEUM

The Human Spider Now Showing—ALIVE

History has not recorded whether A.E. Pickard set out to be screamingly funny. It may have been that his comic value was a by-product of the latitude provided by his enormous wealth. Either way, he was one of the last great variety-hall showmen, a dynamo of flamboyance. Born in Bradford and trained as an engineer, Pickard moved to Glasgow in 1904 and soon developed an ambition to dabble in property. Starting with the Gaiety Theatre in Clydebank, Pickard assembled over the following six decades a mammoth portfolio, to the point where he knew neither how many buildings he owned nor how vast his fortune truly was.

More certain was the wilful levity with which Pickard comported himself. One early purchase was the Britannia Music Hall in the Trongate, soon to become the Panopticon, where the comic who would become Stan Laurel made his stage debut. Packard had a singular approach to the role of proprietor, sitting atop a ladder by the side of the stage to hurl screw-nails at rowdy audience members. He wielded also a long pole with a hook, for removing unsatisfactory acts. At his home, Golden Gates, Pickard kept 18 Rolls-Royces in the drive, only one of which was functioning. Neatly, he required 18 attempts to pass his driving test; when he finally did so the news was reported in the *Daily Telegraph*. Cars loomed large in Pickard's life, as might be expected of a very wealthy man living in a very damp climate. As a Francie and Josie routine had it: 'Aboot twinty year ago there was a famous explorer in Glasgow called A.E. Pickard. Ye mind o' A.E. Pickard?'

PRINCESS CRISTINA. PICKARD'S MUSEUM, GLASGOW.

PICKARD'S GREAT SHOW.

THE HUMAN FRESCO.

'Aye, he used to have a lotta old bangers up wan side o' his driveway.'

'That's right. And a lot of old motor cars up the other.'

The first person in Glasgow to be booked for a parking offence, he once famously parked in a rush on Platform 8 of Central Station; the £1 fine he paid with a £100 note. During the Second World War he built in his garden an air-raid shelter, cone-shaped and decked in neon lights. 'The Nazis wouldn't dare bomb A.E. Pickard,' he commented. He died in a fire at his home, aged 90.

WIT

'The citizen of Glasgow is not, generally speaking, a very witty person, but he possesses in some degree that dry humour which is to be found in most Scotsmen. Everyone is aware that all Englishmen believe, or at least say, that Scotsmen are devoid of humour and are unable to see a joke; but recently one writer has been found courageous enough to assert that all the inhabitants of Scotland are humorous.

This seems a fairly strong claim; but it is not very wide of the mark so far as dry and caustic humour is concerned. The shallow wit which appeals to the average Londoner is conspicuously absent in Glasgow. But despite an unfavourable climate and a smoke-laden atmosphere, the Glasgow Scot occasionally manages to make a joke, even if it is made 'wi' deeficulty' ... the idea has been to illustrate the types of humour which are perhaps most frequently to be found in Glasgow, and, generally speaking, the dry and caustic is principally in evidence.'

from *The Book of Glasgow Anecdote*, Donald Macleod Malloch, 1913

APPETITES
(diet and lifestyle, 17th century onwards)

It is meretricious, perhaps, to describe the history of health and nutrition in Glasgow as a black comedy. Yet anyone planning to crack wise at the city's expense knows the subject is a safe bet. For an equivalent number of years, Glasgow's citizenry and their physical dereliction have served honourably as the punchline that comics can use between jokes without ruining their appetites.

The city takes this ribbing in good part, mainly because it doesn't care particularly, it just wants its chips and a half with which to wash them down. When it comes to diet and lifestyle, Glasgow is happily, wilfully resistant to any suggestion that its collective innards are mutating into time-bombs. Glaswegians believe the entire matter is out of their hands. A complex tangle of reasons explain this native craving for alcohol, nicotine and battered carbo-hydrates, proceeding from climate, budget and habit. But unambiguous are the consequences. In 2008, the World Health Organisation reported that in some areas of Glasgow life expectancy was as low as 54, less than in Colombia, Albania or North Korea. If you wish to die with greater expedience than someone from the Calton you would require to hail from Burma, Nepal or Somalia. Glasgow is, as *The Economist* put it, no city for old men. In September of 2012 the television documentary series *Extreme World* examined poverty in Glasgow and found a man subsisting on hamburgers priced at £2 for 20, resulting in a constitution so compromised he had snapped off five of his own toes.

All the horrors of the Glasgow diet await within Gerry's Snack Bar, 1974.

Even so, some natives derive from all this some measure of impish glee; diet is the joke Glasgow tells against itself. The diet features the culinary equivalents of pantomime villains: the deep-fried Mars bar (conceived in Sussex but annexed by Glasgow); Buckfast tonic wine; battered pizza; square sausage – and the Scotch pie, considered by the humorist AA Gill in this column in the *Sunday Times* from June 2012.

So a friend called to say he'd got a spare ticket and a seat on a private plane. We were off to Munich for the Champions League final. Oh cruel fate. Oh cruel Scottish fate. I couldn't. Much as I'd love to be able to chant 'Two world wars and one World Cup' over and over, I'd already committed myself to an altogether higher Corinthian contest. I was heading north in economy for the Scottish Cup final at Hampden, betwixt Hearts and Hibs. You effete Sassenach muckle-faced blathershites won't understand the significance of that. Hibernian and Heart of Midlothian are the two Edinburgh teams. Hibs are Catholic, from Leith, started by poor, mouth-breathing Irish immigrants, and Hearts are supported by upright, hard-working Protestant Scots. The twa live in the sporting shadow of Rangers and Celtic, and have not met in a final since before the Clearances. This was a big one, and mah friend Dougray Scott has been a lifelong Hibs fan, and, at a push, if I'd stayed in Edinburgh and if I liked football, I'd probably have been a Hearts fan. It was enough. We went up with Dougray's missus, Claire, and his lad, Gabriel, for what they were calling the salt'n'sauce final. On the west coast, they eat their fish and chips with salt and vinegar. On the east coast, the condiments of choice are salt'n'sauce. That is, broon sauce, epicureanly cut with vinegar and a little water to get the consistency right. And it's just as tongue-scouringly, moreishly vile as it sounds.

The march of the two east coast armies through the lowering Glasgow day was cacophonous. Glasgow always feels like a bungalow. The sky hangs so low. The lads shouted with a guttural, furry-tongued fury. Swaggering loons, naked to the waist, with painted faces, gaped their black-toothed, plosive roars. Mostly they walked with hunched shoulders, bent heads, the stance of men habituated to rain and blows. There is something movingly pessimistic about large groups of Scotsmen. You just know this is all going to end badly. It has always ended badly. The great Caledonian strength is humour and resolve, spat in the stony face of repeated defeat. 'It's very real, isn't it?' said Claire, with a tremulous whisper. Life does seem more real here. There is no stylish cushion, no prophylactic of irony, no soft and sweet words. The reality is granite and cold. The game was like a kids' after-school kickabout, 22 mottled-thighed lads running after the ball in a shin-hacking, scowling huddle, taking swipes at each other and falling over. It was the characteristic rout. The Hibees were put to the stud not prettily but relentlessly. The army of fans, like so many Scottish armies before them, melted away. By the time the fifth goal had gone across the line, half the stadium was empty. Just blowing programmes, and a handful of die-hard teuchters, keening for a tearful vengeance. Dougray took it hard, nursing his head, but I told him it was just another historic defeat to be filed away in the great lexicon of Scottish shortcomings and disappointment.

The high point for me was the half-time pie in the press room. One in three Scottish football fans eats a pie at a match. Pies are far more the national dish than haggis. They're made with mutton and heavily spiced with pepper and onion, encased in a hot-water pastry crust with a lid that sits half an inch below the side, brilliantly making a small plate to add your mash, beans or gravy. Scottish pies are like Hinduism. You can't convert. You have to be born to them. I offered a bite of mine to Claire. She made a face like someone whose dog has inadvertently dug up a mass grave.

The best pies are full of steaming, dark, unctuous, silky, pungent meat, but you never get the best pies. What you get is a pie that has a layer of slag at the bottom, a sticky puddle of textureless effluvia, and a space between this meat and the pastry roof. It's in this space that the flavour seems to live as a miasma of something that might have been. The waft of dreams. The soul of a pie that never was. The hole in the hope and the emptiness in the heart.

There is something very football and very Scots about pies, and I love them, despite myself. I love their gawky, pale, unkempt look, their mottled edges, their goitred bellies, and their lifelong ability to be simultaneously welcoming and disappointing. The Scotch Pie Club's motto is 'Say aye tae a pie'. Which I think would make a bonny tattoo. A man travelling from Chelsea to Glasgow reduces his life expectancy by 14 years. Drop that in batter and fry it.

A.A. Gill

ATLETICO PARTICK
(aka Partick Thistle aka The Jags, football team, 1876–)

'I used to live by the dockside near Partick,' said Billy Connolly on his acclaimed *An Audience with . . .* TV show in 1985, 'as in where Partick Thistle FC come from. I say Partick Thistle *FC* as most Englishmen think they're called Partick Thistle Nil.'

One half of this remark isn't strictly accurate – as most Glaswegians know, it has been more than a century since Partick Thistle was based in Partick. The club is associated now with the area of Maryhill, where its stadium, Firhill, is located. This imprecision arose because the club, founded in 1876, had its Partick ground bought from under it during construction of the hulking Meadowside Granary building. A nomadic period followed before the club settled on Firhill in 1909.

The second half of Connolly's claim does hold water; it is held widely that Thistle are especially prone to not scoring goals. This anti-talent is now something of a running joke. In Scotland and beyond, and particularly over the past two decades, Thistle have become synonymous with a brand of plucky, heart-warming ineffectuality. No other football team, foreign or domestic, can provoke the same indulgent sigh. In Bill Forsyth's film *Gregory's Girl*, the blithe foolishness of Gregory is alluded to by a Partick Thistle scarf on the wall of his bedroom.

It isn't easy to identify why the club is so associated with failure, though it certainly didn't help that Thistle were the first British team to play in a pink strip, as they did in 2008. Many British football teams are conspicuously less competent than Partick Thistle. And the team has on occasion achieved truly great things, most notably humiliating Celtic 4–1 in the 1971 League Cup final. The club is commended to glory also by a remark made by manager John Lambie on hearing that his striker had sustained concussion and didn't know who he was. 'That's great,' Lambie barked at his assistant. 'Tell him he's Pele and get him back on.' (Lambie has earned a place in the Malaprop hall of fame too, for describing a Thistle goal as 'pure textile', as opposed to 'textbook'.)

Nonetheless, the die was cast and Partick Thistle were installed in the public's mind as the canonical gaggle of semi-pro blunderers. Billy Connolly underscored the point in the tour film *Big Banana Feet* when he said: 'I support Partick Thistle. We'll be in Europe next year . . . if there's a war.' In his 1981 book Glasgow photographer Douglas Corrance put it like this: 'In Glasgow the Huns support the Bears. A small but indomitably faithful crowd of eccentrics support Partick Thistle.' A similar insinuation was made in the title of *Atletico Partick*, a 1995 BBC Scotland comedy series concerning a hopeless Sunday league team. Or consider Partick Thistle Las Vegas, an amateur side in the city's Platinum Division, founded in the

PREMIER LEAGUE CHAMPIONSHIP JANUARY 1, 1977

v

PARTICK THISTLE

CHAMPIONSHIP CUP: HOLDERS: RANGERS

SCOTTISH CUP HOLDERS: RANGERS

GLASGOW CUP HOLDERS: RANGERS

THE LUCKY PROGRAMME IS WORTH £50

1990s by ex-pat devotee Billy Smith. The joke seems to be that the shiny, sunny, energised culture of Las Vegas could have no more amusing contrast than the drab and thwarted environs of Firhill.

Thistle supporters have learned to bear the cross of ridicule manfully, though a quasi-ironic masochism lies inside each supporter of a small club. At heart, though, Thistle supporters believe themselves to be on the side of the angels. Football in Glasgow is divided along rigorously sectarian lines, with the Protestant Unionist majority of Rangers on one side and IRA-sympathetic Irish Republicans on the other. Those who prefer to be unaligned know they have a home at Partick Thistle, or as a club song puts it: 'There's a well-known Glasgow football team/They don't play in blue and they don't play in green/Red and yellow are the colours we love/The colours of Partick Thistle Football Club.'

This has resulted in the team garnering a rather particular sort of support. Disavowing the bitter quarrels of sectarianism, the Thistle fan tends to come from a better social station and, commonly, to possess some acquaintance with further education. The club's physical location – on the fringes of the West End, where the city's principal university is found – only enhances this. One school of thought argues it is the very refinement of Thistle's support that has landed the club with its semi-comic reputation. The prejudice has it that Thistle's support isn't a 'real' football support; isn't a gathering of ordinary blokes kicking back with a pie and a Bovril after a hard week's manual labour; the type of supporter who might follow, say, Motherwell or Hamilton.

Rather, the Thistle support is a more selfconscious group, whose members relish the proletarian authenticity that only football can bestow: university lecturers, trainee doctors, actors, those of the media and the professions; the type of people who were first in their families to make it to university. Essentially, Thistle is a club supported by those who, in a hilariously prim fashion, believe themselves above the quarrels of the Old Firm, which is doubly rich given the bitterness of relations between supporters of Partick Thistle and Clyde FC. Think of Thistle less as a football club, in fact, than as the athletic wing of the Tron Theatre.

Firhill, home of the much-maligned Partick Thistle.

'A maddening chanting in an unspeakable eldritch tongue that would drive you insane just to hear it'

BURNISTOUN

'THE BARLINNIE HOTEL'
(traditional song)

As well as serving as the temporary postal address of several notable persons – disgraced politician Tommy Sheridan, tycoon Duncan Bannatyne (for a teenaged resisting of arrest) and Lockerbie bomber Abdelbaset al-Megrahi, to name a few – HMP Barlinnie is legendary in Glasgow folk mythology as the destination guaranteed to all who risk the city's disfavour. Part netherworld, part snake pit, the Bar-L is comic, also. To Glaswegians the Bar-L isn't merely a prison, it is a judgement set in stone; the last word in loss of face; a threat whose power borders on the supernatural. Accordingly, the place is the punchline of a thousand sitcom sketches and variety routines; the place so serious it is almost amusing. The fact is commemorated in the following traditional ditty:

In Glasgow's fair city,
There's flashy hotels,
They give board and lodgings
To all the big swells.
But the greatest of all now
Is still in full swing –
Five beautiful mansions
Controlled by the king.
There's bars on the windows
And bells on the door,
Dirty big hard beds
Attached to the floor.
I know 'cause I've been there
And, sure, I can tell
There's no place on earth like
Barlinnie Hotel.
I was driven from the Sheriff,
And driven by bus –
Driven through the streets,
With a terrible fuss.
Drove through the streets,
Like a gangster in state.
And they never slowed up,
Till they got to the gate.
As we entered reception,
They asked me my name,
And asked my address,
And the reason I came.
As I answered these questions,
A screw rang the bell – It was time for
my bath,
In Barlinnie Hotel.
After my bath, I was dressed like a doll.
The screw said, 'Quick march,
Right into E-hall.'
As I entered my flowery,
I looked round in vain –
To think that three years, here,
I had to remain.
For breakfast, next morning, I asked
for an egg,
The screw must have thought
I was pulling his leg.
For, when he recovered, he let out a yell –
'Jailbirds don't lay eggs,
In the Barlinnie Hotel!'
The day came for me,
When I had to depart.
I was as sick as a dog,
With joy in my heart.
For the comfort was good,
And the service was swell,
But I'll never return
To Barlinnie Hotel.

STANLEY BAXTER
(entertainer, 1926–)

Were you to nominate Stanley Baxter as the father, the true progenitor, of modern Glasgow comedy you might be treated sceptically, especially by anyone who ever saw him wearing a fruit bowl and the bulk of the Max Factor autumn range. But a progenitor is how Baxter must be considered, despite his years as drag artist and Hollywood parodist in a series of expensive London Weekend Television specials.

What Baxter (and his co-writer Alex Mitchell) did at the dawn of the 1960s was seismic. From early days, Glaswegians had treated their comedy as a means of showing to them how they spoke and carried themselves. Not for Glasgow the humour prevailing in the music halls of Cockney London, romantic and wryly reflective about class and social status; nor the interest in political theatre and burlesque of Dublin. What Glasgow demanded was the reflection of Glasgow: *comedy vérité*.

It received it to an extent in the work of Tommy Lorne, Tommy Morgan and Lex McLean, comics whose routines made a point of foregrounding local idioms and colloquialisms. Again, this had been the case elsewhere, with the likes of Frank Randle in Lancashire or Charlie Williams in Yorkshire. It was wholly to be expected that entertainers would mine the stuff of everyday life, in the provinces especially. Humour rarely works without recognition.

For the humour of Glasgow, however, the deal would be sealed by television, or rather television would help construct a wholly new deal. In the late 1950s a comic in, say, Macclesfield or Halifax could not reasonably expect to appear on television – their accent would be regional, while television was rigorously metrocentric. Yet, in the north, the division was less decisive. BBC Scotland had been introduced in 1952, STV five years later. Both had their headquarters in Glasgow. To fulfil their charters, each was required to screen a given quantity of home-grown material. Suddenly, the conditions that kept local entertainers off the national airwaves were, in Glasgow, courtesy of devolved broadcasting, singularly advantageous.

And Stanley Baxter was among the first to benefit. He had been a beloved entertainer in Scotland since the 1940s, in

pantomime and on radio. But, as a man of a thousand faces and of *risqué* sensibility, he would find his natural medium to be television. He started as a writer and performer on the now obscure BBC Scotland sketch show *On the Bright Side,* from which sprang *Parliamo Glasgow,* a series of mock tutorials in the local patois, launched in 1960.

The show was a watershed for the humour of Glasgow. Its popularity revealed the true depth of the city's self-fascination. It demonstrated that Glaswegians wanted more than basic outlines and broad brush-strokes; they were invested in the minutiae, the nuts and bolts, the dots and commas of being Glaswegian. Half a century later, they still are.

JOHNNY BEATTIE
(entertainer, 1926–)

Like the living equivalent of an Easter Island statue, Beattie is the last man standing, the final link to an ancient civilisation. Unlike Stanley Baxter, who relocated to London, Beattie remained. Age has not withered him, and we shall not see his like again. He made his stage debut at Ayr's Gaiety Theatre in 1952 and there is scarcely a lively art in which he has not since involved himself (he even made an appearance on the silver screen, in the 1990 adaptation of William McIlvanney's *The Big Man).* If the humour of Glasgow were represented *à la* Mount Rushmore, the face of Beattie would feature on its higher reaches. Or you could settle for the animatronic Johnny Beattie that stands in the Winter Gardens, Rothesay, reciting the history of Scottish variety theatre.

Beattie is associated with three showbiz specialties; with pantomime – for many years he was the doyenne of the dames at the Pavilion and the King's; with television (in the BBC Scotland soap *River City* and, much earlier, the STV game show *Now You See It*); and he appears, even yet, on the variety stage, where when occasion demands he dusts off the old *schtick* for testimonials and anniversaries. 'Do you know, in 2011 there wasn't one summer show in Scotland,' he says. "When I started there were at least nine summer shows on the Clyde coast alone – Largs, Gourock, Rothesay, Millport, Dunoon, Saltcoats, Troon, Girvan, Ayr. It was like the old

George Burns line – they were places you went to be lousy. If you did a show and it died the death you just thought, Well, I'll no' do it like that again . . . And now, it's ta-ta Bella, they're all gone.'

Even for the time, Beattie always had something stridently wholesome to him; something cheerful and kilty: 'I was known as the Mary Whitehouse of Glasgow comedy at one point, though I don't think it was meant as a compliment.' In such theatres as the Alhambra, the Pavilion and the Glasgow Empire he operated squarely within the respectable Scottish variety mainstream, his style foregoing the raciness of a Lex McLean or the cheek of a Rikki Fulton. As Glasgow forged its humour in the 1960s Beattie stood to one side. 'I had a rule for playing Glasgow,' he recalls, 'I always wore the kilt. I wanted to tell the audience straight away, I'm one of you!' He was, he admits, a technical performer, a cog within productions possessing many moving parts. 'I was what they called a production comic,' he recalls. 'You had your big opening, then I'd go on and do warmup, six minutes or so, then I'd introduce the first act, maybe an accordionist, then I'd do a sketch, then another act, then I'd do a big comedy scene at the end of the first half. The second half began with the dancers, then I'd do a few quickies, then an act, then a sketch, then another act, then a single act at the end, then a finale.'

Accordingly, a conversation with Beattie can resemble delving into a heap of yellowing theatrical directories as he recalls acts that never made it into the footlights of posterity: 'Charlie Stewart and Ann Matthews, Ivy Carey, Eric V. Marsh (he was a great act), the Fol de Rols, Alice Dale, Wee Jimmy Fletcher – every one of them was just fabulous.' But Beattie came right up to date in 1974 by taking a hand in the career of the young Billy Connolly, watching as the comic floundered at a Rotarian function in the Golden Lion hotel in Cumbernauld, then hiring him as his warmup act during a run at the Pavilion. 'Billy was a hairy monster then and his audience came from the folk clubs, of course,' Beattie recalls. 'They were sitting in the stalls with their cans of beer. I remember the theatre manageress showing me that they'd used the stairs from the stage door as a toilet.'

Now in his ninth decade, Beattie celebrated his

Last man standing – variety veteran Johnny Beattie.

showbusiness diamond jubilee in May 2012 with a gala charity show at the Citizens Theatre, featuring Alan Cumming, Andy Cameron, Una McLean and the cast of *River City*, the continuing drama in which Beattie plays Malcolm Hamilton, the amiable patriarch of the Rossi clan. 'The producer came to me recently and said, "We're thinking of giving Malcolm Alzheimer's." I said, "Is Alzheimer's no' a bit grim, a bit heavy?" He went away, came back and said, "OK then, Johnny . . . how'd you feel about a touch of dementia?"'

BLACK HUMOUR

When out of the earshot of the general public any police officer will tell you a ghoulish sense of humour is an occupational necessity, as will those in the criminal arena or in emergency medicine. When death, injury or imprisonment are near such customer-facing roles tend to assume a certain piquancy. Officers claim that an appreciation of the grimly comedic is a kind of pre-emptive post-traumatic stress counselling, a crucial mechanism of psychiatric self-repair. In the coining and sharing of inappropriate remarks a camaraderie is implied, a sense of perspective is fostered; or, with the habitual miscreant, a sense of the absurd.

The criminal underworld of Glasgow is replete with black humour, attaching usually to nomenclature. The late Arthur Thompson, son of the equally late criminal overlord, was distinguished from his paternal namesake by the addition of the soubriquet Fat Boy. With a wit recalling the cartoons of Bud Neill, the compound of knocked-through villas in which the Thompsons lived was known to all as the Ponderosa. Gangster Ian 'Blink' McDonald was so dubbed in recognition of a facial tic. Thomas McGraw, the late gangster, was nicknamed the Licensee in rueful recognition of the 'arrangement' he enjoyed with Strathclyde Police (he was known also as Wan-Baw McGraw, for reasons we shall not dwell upon; the same applies to the late Kevin 'Gerbil' Carroll). The mobster Paul Ferris, meanwhile, won much scandalised admiration in 1994 when he told a court that the crack cocaine with which he'd been apprehended was for treating his psoriasis.

As for those opposed to crime, two examples of Glaswegian police mordancy have been commended to posterity. In 1968, a manhunt was launched in Glasgow for a murderer dubbed Bible

John. Known to have quoted scripture to one of his victims, Bible John haunted the Barrowland Ballroom, a dance hall in the East End. The venue became a focus of such intensive police scrutiny that the squad assigned to investigating regulars at the hall became known in the press as the Marine Formation Dance Team, after the name of the local police division.

Similarly, in the 1980s, the so-called Ice Cream Wars raged through the city's bleak housing schemes as gangs vied to supply narcotics by means of mobile confectionery vans. To gather intelligence Strathclyde Police established and sent out a fleet of fake ice-cream vans staffed by undercover officers. It was quickly awarded a nickname – the Serious Chimes Squad.

THE BOGIE MAN
(graphic novel, written/illustrated by John Wagner, Alan Grant and Robin Smith, 1989)

Like *Your Cheatin' Heart* and *Charles Endell Esquire* on television, *The Bogie Man* traded on Glasgow's spiritual kinship with modern urban America, particularly its film and music. Turned down by DC

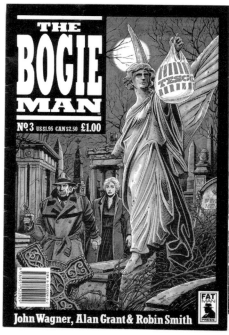

Kenneth Wright marks the publication of the first adult Glasgow comic with a survey of the latest cult reading matter, *The Herald*, 7 June 1989.

Bathed in the cinematic lamplight on that mean street he's just gone down, our hero hunches deeper into his trenchcoat under a dingy snap-brim and takes another draw, waiting to meet the next development in the sordid little noir B-movie in which his is the starring and heroic role. This urban knight in slightly soiled armour is *The Bogie Man*, authentic bottled-in-bond gumshoe hero of the first big-production adult comic to be set in Glasgow. Out of all the cities in all the world . . . he walked into mine?

Well, why not? Not for nothing has Glasgow been called the easternmost city of the USA. Always a big, tough, dirty town, or so its fans like to think, Big G has lately been picking up the kind of tacky glamour – real as well as media-made – that makes it a fit home for a down-at-heel shamus with a shaky licence and an adventurous taste in customers.

It's easy to see him killing a few imported lagers at a waterfront nightclub with a tough door policy, asking the barman if he recognises the dame in the picture or buying information from an ex-employee with a grudge. Glasgow nowadays has a nightlife, a café society, and a lot of fast and funny money flying around. It could use a good cheap detective. Heck, this guy's so tough he's already (to give his CV a romantic interpretation) made New York too hot to hold him. That's the beat he worked when the idea was turned down by Marvel Comics, proprietors of a whole pantheon of superheroes, who felt he wouldn't fit into their marketing strategy with the boys who wear their drawers outside their tights.

So his creators, John Wagner of Greenock and Alan Grant from Edinburgh, dumped him on a shelf, where he lay for some time until the entry into the game of John McShane, part-owner of Glasgow bookshop AKA Comics, who came up with the idea of moving *Bogie Man's* seedy operations to Culture City.

And here he is, or will be in a fortnight, courtesy of Fat Man Press, the imprint set up by McShane and his friend and business partner George Jackson for the purpose. No penny-ante up-a-close production, this: Fat Man are looking at a print run of 70,000–100,000 copies at a quid a shot, with mainstream distribution in Britain, Canada, and the US. Plus a book-format graphic novel release in full colour if the four planned bimonthly episodes go well. Nor are the talents behind the Clydeside private eye any raw hands at this racket. One writer, John Wagner, is the co-creator of cartoon cop hero Judge Dredd, a sort of cybertronic Dirty Harry ('in the 21st century, he is the law") whose gonzo satirical adventures are Britain's biggestselling comic. The other, Alan Grant, is the present bubbles man for Batman, now in his fiftieth year of caped crusading. Artwork comes from Robin Smith, former art editor of *2000 AD*, award-winning original home of the noble Judge. About the storyline the publishers are as yet almost suspiciously coy, but hints have been extracted, in a teeth-like sort of way, over a few beers in a dirty little deadfall not a .45 calibre shot from these offices. '*The Maltese Falcon* meets *Tutti Frutti*' is one of John McShane's descriptions of what is promised to be 'a hilarious romp through Glasgow on the heels of a hard-bitten private eye . . . an irreverent black comedy with a startling twist in the tale'. A preview of some early pages of the harsh, 50s-style artwork sets the opening scenes at a New Year staff party at sinister Spinbinnie Hospital, an institution for the very highly strung. The time is about ten minutes into the future; tattered posters for Culture City Year flap forlornly around the corners of later frames.

Perhaps the best manifesto yet for *The Bogie Man* is the episode titles, knowing cod-Hollywood gems like 'The Big Neep' and 'Treasure of the Ford Sierra'. Glasgow fit for cheap fiction may just be about to meet a cheap fiction fit for Glasgow. Here's looking at you, Bogie.

Comics, the strip was taken by writers John Wagner (creator of *Judge Dredd* for 2000 AD) and Alan Grant (previously a writer of Batman strips) to an independent publisher in Glasgow, Fat Man Press. The strip remains an admired but well-kept secret among comic buffs.

Distinguished by ingenious Glaswegian variations on hard-boiled scenarios and dialogue – the hero pursues his fantasy woman, soup kitchen operative Lauren McCall, for instance – the stories concerned Francis Forbes Clunie, a schizophrenic who escapes Spinbinnie Hospital convinced he is the incarnation of the gumshoes played by Humphrey Bogart. Pastiching the plots of such Warner Bros films as *To Have and Have Not* and *Farewell, My Lovely*, *The Bogie Man* followed Clunie's movements through a comically hopeless Glasgow underworld as the city prepared for its stint as the European Capital of Culture – for example, a tramp begs for £20 to buy himself Scottish Opera tickets. The quality of the writing garnered *The Bogie Man* generous coverage during 1990, but a Christmas television adaptation two years later, starring Robbie Coltrane, was received badly, despite sharing much of its creative nucleus with the team behind *Tutti Frutti*.

BOOING

In 1906, the English anthropologist Sir Francis Galton, cousin of Charles Darwin, hit upon a theory he was to dub the Wisdom of Crowds. Galton was attending a country fair where a prize was offered for guessing the weight of an ox. He reasoned, correctly as it turned out, that if each guess made was added up and averaged the total resulting was more likely to be accurate than any one individual guess. The implication of Galton's theory was that, somehow, crowds are greater than the sum of their parts and develop an enhanced collective intelligence. Throw some unwarranted aggression into the mix and we have a working definition of the Glasgow crowd. The infamous Riot Act, for example, was read at the Red Clydeside battle of George Square in 1919, or it nearly was; rioters tore it from the hands of the city's sheriff.

This waywardness has been witnessed more recently. As 1989 became 1990 the comic and actor Robbie Coltrane was hosting a Hogmanay celebration, televised live from the same George Square. He incurred the crowd's wrath, however, though perhaps illogically, by displaying unmistakable signs of seasonal cheer, culminating in his failure to draw attention to the bells at midnight, a cardinal error in the Glaswegian mind. A similar spirit of mass derision manifested later that year when the singer Sheena Easton insisted on addressing an audience at Glasgow Green in a mock-American accent and received for her considerations a hailstorm of bottled urine. And it was present in September 2012 when the oily and opportunistic Alex Salmond, First Minister in the Scottish Executive, was booed in George Square at a reception for British Olympians, having demonstrated little interest in same prior to their winning a haul of medals.

It was present, too, in the ABC cinema in Sauchiehall Street in 1995 at a screening of *Dr Jekyll and Ms Hyde*, a female-friendly Hollywood update of the Robert Louis Stevenson classic. The film's heroine is leafing through a family scrapbook with her grandmother when she comes upon a snap of a fearsome, snaggle-toothed man. 'Who is that?' she asks her grandmother. 'That's your Great-Uncle Henry,' the old woman explains. 'He was from the Glaswegian side of the family.' Immediately, something arced through the darkness of the theatre; a can of Coca-Cola, which emptied itself messily as its flight was halted by the cinema screen.

THE BRITANNIA PANOPTICON
(venue, 1857–)

Stepping into the Britannia Panopticon, the world's oldest surviving music hall, is an exquisitely spooky experience. In 1938 this wooden theatre – sited then as now in the floors above an amusement arcade, slap in the middle of Glasgow's busiest shopping street – pulled down the curtain and became storage space for a tailor. When that business folded, the space was sealed off and forgotten about. And there it slept for sixty years, until it was chanced upon by one Judith Bowers.

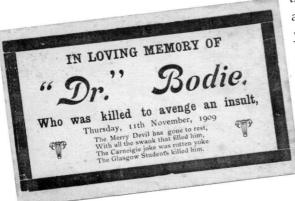

What she found was remarkable: a theatrical time capsule, unaltered since the earliest years of the twentieth century – a ghost theatre, lost in time. Since then, Bowers and a charitable trust have worked heroically to preserve the fabric and

TINY TIM

HAROLD PYOTT,
THE ENGLISH MIDGET.
Age 43 years.   Height 23 inches.   Weight 24 lbs.
THE LIVING DOLL.
Twelve inches smaller than the renowned
TOM THUMB of BARNUM FAME.

fixtures of the Panopticon, and to return to it with film shows and performances a measure of the life that made it a pillar of Glasgow's showbusiness history. 'The Britannia is of such rarity and interest in a national context,' concluded the Theatres Trust, 'that a full physical and documentary investigation needs now to be undertaken.'

TOM THUMB,
At PICKARD'S MUSEUM, Trongate, GLASGOW.

PICKARD'S LATEST ENTERPRISE.
The Smallest Man in Existence.

None of this is to say that visiting the Britannia Panopticon is necessarily a salutary experience. Although the theatre is intact structurally, decades of dereliction hang in the air, giving the place an ambience bordering on the melancholic, like any place that holds the distant echo of laughter. Nevertheless, minor is the act of imagination needed to visualise the theatre as it once was; when the rambunctious shop and shipyard workers of Victorian Glasgow crowded the compact balcony, the young Stan Laurel trembled in the wings and A.E. Pickard perched atop his on-stage ladder to aim screw-nails at the less decorous members of the congregation. This latter aspect persists into the present day: in 2012 the theatre was pressed into service as a principal location for series two of the tittersome Sapphic psychodrama *Lip Service*.

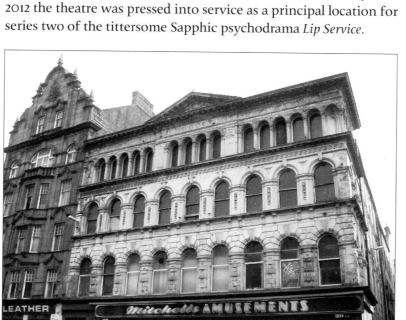

The fading grandeur of the Panopticon conceals a theatrical time-warp.

ARNOLD BROWN
(comic, 1936–)

Rather by accident, Arnold Brown played a momentous role in comedy history. As the first act to take the stage on the opening night of the Comedy Store in London, he was in at the birth of the movement that changed British humour forever. Like being the chap who introduced Ringo to John, Paul and George, then, Brown was at close quarters as all was redefined and the nation's sharper comics rose against all that was represented by the likes of Bernard Manning, Benny Hill and Jim Davidson. The coup went mainstream, and Brown's pioneer status meant that, in the resultant television and cinema projects, he was often to be spotted in the background, retained as some kind of lucky mascot. Nearly 35 years later, he's still on the go, too straight to be hip and too odd to be big.

A chartered accountant until middle age, and hence at one remove from what he terms 'the comedy', Brown is seldom a vital proposition. Slow and ruminative, he is unafraid to say not very much, not very quickly. His material is scraped together from man-at-the-bus-stop kvetches, abstract thoughts, impractical suggestions and autobiographical whimsy, rendering it practically unquotable beyond Brown's catchphrase 'And why not?' The cumulative effect rather resembles confinement with a tentative and quietly spoken egomaniac.

BURNISTOUN
(sketch show, BBC Scotland, 2009–)

At first glance, this sketch show, written and performed by Robert Florence and Iain Connell, owes much to *Chewin' the Fat* (to whose scripts Florence and Connell contributed). Like the earlier show, *Burnistoun* is an assemblage of sketches hinged around everyday, blue-collar street life, its characters, cabals and catchphrases – pub life, petty feuds and spoof TV adverts – abound. *Burnistoun*, though, retains one point of difference, or a point of difference to anyone who missed its debut appearance in *The League of Gentlemen*: the sketches all take place in the same fictional town, the titular Burnistoun.

Hence, Paul and Walter, a pair of eccentric brothers, squabble while piloting their ice-cream van around the town; two constables cock up their investigations repeatedly while still insisting they are 'quality polis'; a cheerful family are secret diabolists ('In your dark name/Christians we will kill!'); at North Burnistoun Housing Association a resident complains he is being disturbed by a 'maddening chanting in an unspeakable eldritch tongue that would drive you insane just to hear it'; and a single-issue local politician rises to the office of prime minister on the back of his campaign against 'the needless installation of traffic lights at the Dekebone roundabout'.

Though broadly similar, *Burnistoun* grows to reveal itself as several shades darker than *Chewin' the Fat*. One of the show's implications is that a madness or compulsive disorder has seeped into the Burnistoun gene pool, presenting in the locals' nonsensical staccato conversations and their intimations of the supernatural, like the suitor who curtails a relationship because he's able to read the minds of cats, or the four uncles who tremble constantly on the brink of inflicting extreme violence upon a harmless boy who wishes to take their niece to the cinema ('Are you squarin' up tae me, in ma ain hoose?').

Grace Dent was so taken with the show that, inadvertently, she opened one of Glasgow comedy's oldest cans of worms, access to the national television network, or, rather, the continuing lack of it: 'Due to the unique way in which it is funded,' Dent wrote in the *Guardian* in March 2010, 'the BBC produces a diverse range of excellent telly, then promotes it in such a piss-poor manner that no one ever sees it. Take, for example, the brilliant BBC 2 Scotland comedy *Burnistoun*. This assumption that Scottish comedy is of niche appeal rankles me hugely. Iain Connell and Robert Florence's imaginary landscape of demented ice-cream van owners, petty single-issue local MPs and hapless husbands deserves a much wider audience.' The debate is time-honoured. In one sense, *Burnistoun* comes from the same place as Tommy Morgan and *The McFlannels*, presenting a heightened version of the world that Glaswegian audiences were familiar with, replete with routines about the pub, local loonies, bottled soft drinks and the citizenry's constant and comically doomed attempts to

Town called malice – BBC Scotland's sketch show Burnistoun.

triumph over circumstance. At the same time, the series was – alongside *The Limmy Show* and *Gary: Tank Commander* – among a raft of new comedies created in 2009 by the Comedy Unit, addressing BBC Scotland's historical reliance upon proleporn. With *Burnistoun*, an agreeably twisted start has been made.

JOHN BYRNE
(artist and playwright, 1940–)

John Byrne is bohemian to the toes of his burgundy, lace-up winklepickers. The very day I met him, in fact, his debit card was rejected in Tesco and he says there's a summons from the Bank of Scotland lying in his studio. By his own admission, Byrne 'doesn't have a bean', a situation more or less constant throughout his life, commencing 73 years ago in the drear barracks of Ferguslie Park, Paisley. Sustained, nonetheless, by a set of consummate talents, the

painter, playwright and set designer lives in a world not wholly aligned with our own, yet in a house that's only slightly smaller than Kingussie. The mystery could be resolved, though it would be vulgar to ask, by factoring in Tilda Swinton, the A-list Hollywood star and mother of Byrne's children Honor and Xavier. That mystery, though, is surpassed only by the mystery associated most commonly with his name: why did *Tutti Frutti* disappear for nearly three decades?

The six-part BBC comedy drama grew legendary in the Scottish psyche, a Rosetta Stone of deathless one-liners and whiplash putdowns. The tale of a washed-up 1960s rock group, the Majestics, reuniting for their silver jubilee tour of Scotland, *Tutti Frutti* follows the has-beens through the cabaret club cesspits of Buckie, Largs and Dunoon. 'Oh God, I heard a hundred different stories about why it vanished,' sighs Byrne. He was told one of the leading actors refused to give their permission. Another theory was that the BBC wouldn't pay for the rights to the vintage music in the series. Byrne was told that the executive in charge would see it released 'over my dead body'. Byrne diverts his attention to the next in a never-ending series of roll-ups. 'That's weird, isn't it? That sounds kinda personal to me. What's this guy's dead body got to do with anything?'

Byrne has a studio in a little back room on the third floor of the house, a castle-dimensioned new-build close to the coast in Nairn. Above the artistic detritus, the word Tadpole is painted along one wall, next to an electric guitar for Byrne's son. Byrne has been up here a lot lately, painting. His break as an artist came via a typically Byrnesian curlicue of whimsy when he passed off several of his paintings as the work of his father, Patrick, a newspaper seller in Paisley, a prank that led to the phantom painter becoming a *cause célèbre* of the 1960s London art scene.

The Glasgow Smile: Is it difficult to live with the persistence of the legend of *Tutti Frutti*?

John Byrne: No, because I'm so fond of it, too. I enjoyed it hugely, though it's not like it fell off the pen and wrote itself. I had a deadline of eight weeks to write six episodes or I didn't get paid. That was me working round the clock, with only the premise of a rock'n'roll band that was still playing. The premise came from Bill Bryden (then head of drama at BBC Scotland). Bill said to me, 'There was a band called the Poets. Do you remember them?' I said, 'I do remember them.' 'Well, imagine there's a band still going today and they had a hit twenty years before.' And he went on to say that one member could be a garage mechanic, they could end up going to Nashville and so on. I said, 'Stop there. I'll take away the premise, that there's a bunch of rock'n'rollers still playing who had a minor hit twenty years ago, right – that's enough.' Bill said, 'The conditions are: it's to be called *Tutti Frutti*, it's to have a star of Michael Grade's choice, and it's to be on Michael Grade's desk eight weeks from now.'

TGS: So, how did you assemble the skeleton?

JB: Well, there's a logical process. I think, What's going to move the story along? A tour. What's Danny's background? He went to art school, he plays in piano bars, he's skint. So I got a map of Scotland and sent them to places I'd never been – including Buckie, places like Methil. The only place I'd been was Glasgow, the Pavilion in Glasgow, which is where they had to end up. So, I drew the map, I had all the characters' names and I'd draw them as I wrote, because I'm in there from eight in the morning till three or four the next morning. Getting up at seven, start at eight, seven days a week – for eight weeks. I'd said to Bill Bryden, this was another condition, I will deliver the scripts two at a time. I don't want any comments, I don't want any advice, editorial input, anything. I don't want any praise. I just want you to tell me you've received the scripts.

TGS: Where did the character names come from?

JB: Suzi Kettles – there were the Kettles who lived across the road from us in Ferguslie Park. Very interesting name. But I have to get the first name. Suzi with a 'z' and an 'i' at the end. Great name.

McGlone – there was a boy McGlone in our class. I'll spend enough time on the names because I can't start until I have the name. Fud O' Donnell. Francis O'Donnell was a boy in our class. There's a painter and decorator in Cardonald called Clockerty. And what's his first name? It has to be a racy name – Eddie. Eddie Clockerty. There was a guy called Toner in our class: Willie Toner. There were great names in our class. They always had a ring to them. I love names. I'd never make names up. So what's her first name? Janice. Janice Toner. Miss Toner – that's how Eddie addresses her. People have asked me what the relationship is between Mr Clockerty and Miss Toner. I say, I don't know, how should I know? It's none of my business. You're taking dictation from the characters; they're sitting in the back of your head, or the front of your head. It's like you're taken to town – they say 'I wouldn't put the remark that way' and then you've got to rewrite it. You get so involved in it, you cannae do anything else, you cannae think about anything else.

TGS: And the process was . . . pleasurable? Tortuous?

JB: It was absolute pleasure *and* torture, all the way through. It was everything that is worthwhile in life: love, death, agony, everything, delight, joy. There's a bit you get to called the hump – well, I call it the hump – and it's just a slog, till you bring yourself up and see the summer and it's a joy thereafter. And rewriting is a joy. You need to get over the hump and then it's plain sailing, you've got your second wind and you're through the tape. But you can't get there unless you do the slog; nothing's worthwhile unless you do the slog. Somebody somewhere thinks they can cut out that slog, but you don't want it cut out: you need it.

TGS: There was *Tutti Frutti* and *Your Cheatin' Heart* – any temptation to attempt a musical trilogy?

JB: I wanted to do another one, but not one person has asked me since. I wanted to do one on Scottish country-dance music. That would have been nice. There was the hint of a commission and then Bill Bryden left, and it all fell into abeyance. I've no idea whether I'd like to do another – nobody's asked. I'd need to be asked and then I'd consider it seriously.

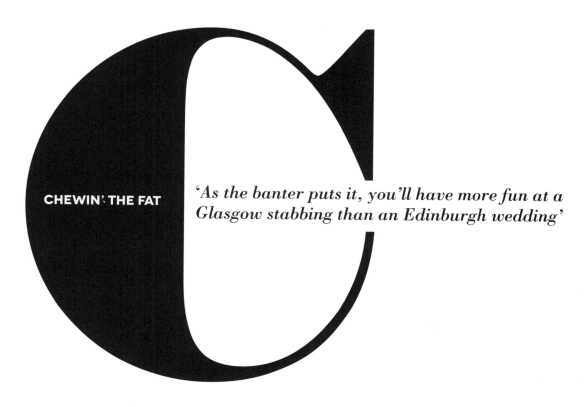

CHEWIN' THE FAT

'As the banter puts it, you'll have more fun at a Glasgow stabbing than an Edinburgh wedding'

SUSAN CALMAN
(comedian, 1974–)

Calman is notable for being, as well as a stand-up of no small charm, one of the few Caledonian performers to have penetrated the inner circle of the Oxbridge-dominated panel game nexus, appearing frequently on *The News Quiz*, *Have I Got News For You*, *Eight Out of Ten Cats* and any other confection requiring a quick-fire sideways look at the passing scene. Her prominence has derived from a winning ability to combine whimsy, self-deprecation and a certain tempered aggression. Having forsaken a career in law for comedy, Calman was something of a late starter but her likability and her singularity as a sarcastically cuddly lesbian slacker has seen her become one of Glasgow comedy's most accomplished and conspicuous exports.

The Calminator, Live

Sometimes people are afraid of Glaswegians, it's the way we can make even a compli- ment sound quite threatening. For example (rolls neck) *That's a pretty baby*...

I'm a lesbeterian. I like to call us that, it makes us sound more like a union. Men think I hate you. I don't, I don't hate you – I just find you all physically repulsive...

I'm a very short person, I'm 4ft 11in, exactly the same height as Kylie Minogue. And that's where the similarity ends. I have one talent being this short – I can stand up completely straight in the back of a black taxi-cab. There's not a lot else you can do when you're this short, except sneak into schools …

My nickname is the Calminator. I gave it to myself, because I noticed how celebri- ties when they change their names become more sexually attrac- tive. Like Harry Webb became Cliff Richard; Barry Bulsara became Freddy Mercury; Gary Glitter became Prisoner 943454 …

I love eating. If you ask me what I'm doing tomorrow I won't tell you what I'm doing, I'll tell you what I'm eating, that's how I plan my day. I'll have a snack with *Diagnosis Murder*. And if you do that it's rude not to have something with *Murder She Wrote*...

ANDY CAMERON
(comic, 1940–)

In the late 1960s the few remaining variety comics moved out of theatres and became club comics, dropping a rung to play a circuit of British Legions, Miners' Welfares and football socials. Their stage names are blasts from a spangly, if budget, showbiz past: Clem Ashby, Mr Abie, Allan Stewart, Dean Park *et al.* The most successful and conspicuous of them was Andy Cameron, perhaps because his appeal covered the age range. In tuxedo and bow tie, Cameron could fire out with the best of them jokes describing the hormonal volatility of his dear lady wife. Equally, he could pull off the cuddly-uncle bit for audiences of children, leading to a fifteen-year stint as a family-favourites disc jockey on Radio Scotland.

Cameron will be known always, however, for three things. He inherited upon the death of Lex McLean the mantle of number one celebrity supporter of Glasgow's principal football club, Rangers F.C.; he had a number six chart hit during the 1978 World Cup with 'Ally's Tartan Army', a novelty record that soon took on tragicomic overtones as Scotland capitulated pitifully; and, following a joint appearance at the Oxford Union, he recommended Armando Iannucci to his bosses at BBC Scotland. He also tells at every possible opportunity a joke describing a phone call from a young listener, asking Cameron to name a vegetable that makes us cry. 'I replied, "Onions,"' Cameron recalls. 'The wee boy said, "Naw, a turnip." I said that a turnip does not make you cry. The boy said, "It does if it hits you in the testicles." And he did not say testicles . . .'

CASINO ROYALE
(film, 1967)

In 1967, audiences were flocking to *Casino Royale*, a movie offering a star-studded and satirical take on the James Bond phenomenon. While not belonging to the Bond series officially, the movie did at least feature a cameo from the much-loved local comedian Chic Murray and had been directed, nominally at least, by a local boy, Joe McGrath, producer of a television hit of the day, *Not Only But Also*, with Peter Cook and Dudley Moore.

At one point during the film, Bond points a rifle at an on-screen grouse. When it was shown at the Odeon Cinema in Renfield Street, as Bond fired, a pigeon flew across the screen, provoking from several viewers the cry of 'You missed!' Cinema manager John Murray told newspapers he'd been trying to catch the same pigeon for a week. 'I nearly caught him the other night,' he told reporters. 'There he was, sitting in one of the best circle seats.'

CHEWIN ' THE FAT
(sketch show, 1999–2005)

Starting life on Radio Scotland, *Chewin' the Fat* attached jump-leads to the comedy of Glasgow, and the patient twitches to this day. Particularly in its televisual incarnation, *Chewin' the Fat*, written by and starring Greg Hemphill and Ford Kiernan, was the first properly popular Scottish sketch show since *Scotch & Wry* twenty years earlier, a reminder that what Glaswegian audiences found *truly* laughable was any suggestion that Glasgow humour could be too particular or parochial. Few television shows have worked with such

a delimited view of their intended audience. *Chewin' the Fat* sketches were written for a precisely calibrated identifiable constituency, the Glaswegian upper working class, particularly those with some experience of further education, all the better to penetrate the show's broad pop-cultural palette of allusion, film and television parody, and in-joke. There was one concerning thespian preciousness, courtesy of the hopeless actor Ronald Villiers; Scottish ruralism, in the shape of Alistair and Rory or the Foul-mouthed Fishermen; sexual grotesquerie, with Betty the Auld Slapper; sink-estate thuggery courtesy of the Big Man; and middle-class pretension, as practised by the Banter Boys. For the first time, a Scottish television sketch show had been fashioned for an audience beyond the mild, the elderly and the suburban.

Characters

The Big Man
Impossibly foul-mouthed Glaswegian hard man whose stated role as a Good Samaritan hides darker intentions.

'Listen, I'll put my boot so far up your arse, people'll be thinking Doc Marten started making hats.'

'If I wasnae such a gentleman I'd batter her into so many shades of purple she'd resemble a Dulux colour chart.'

'Ah bet if the Big Man stuck his hand doon yer trousers he wouldnae find any hair, just traces of your old man's lipstick.'

The Banter Boys
Two camp older gents in thrall to the colourful colloquialisms of Glasgow gone by, and constantly in pursuit of surviving examples.

'Edinburgh? Scotia's midden seat. Capital in name only! One dirty great big wet blanket o' a place. Full of tacky rock shops and saunas puntin' hand relief. As the banter puts it, you'll have more fun at a Glasgow stabbing than an Edinburgh wedding.'

'The taxi driver, well, what a Glesgae man, full of the banter, sittin' in the back there I could hardly make a word oot. But the ebb and flow of his phrasing was absolutely delightful . . .'

The Lighthouse Keepers
A pair of seamen trapped in a desolate and isolated lighthouse, where one relieves the boredom by playing increasingly elaborate practical jokes on the other, prompting the rejoinder 'Gonnae no' dae that?'

Jack and Victor
Two squabbling pensioners, spun off into the affecting sitcom *Still Game*.

The Lonely Shopkeeper
Conceived by Sanjeev Kohli, who played Navid in *Still Game*, this was a character driven to madness by solitary confinement, with only passing trade for company.

Betty the Auld Slapper
Recounting her wartime memories for a local history project, Betty reveals the racier side of life in the air-raid shelter.

Ronald Villiers
Blithering actor and serial auditionee, unable to carry out satisfactorily the most basic request.

Glasgow neds arrange their next square-go.

COLLINS DICTIONARY
(1979–)

Established in 1979, the Collins English Dictionary brought lexicography into the modern age, compiling its definitions with the aid of computer databases, as opposed to relying solely on the weird, retentive knowitalls who typically work in this field. With Collins, entries were on a hard disk (this was quite swizzy in 1979) and could be fleshed out instantly with reference to newspaper sources from around the globe. This might help to explain what happened in June 2005, when the editors of the dictionary announced, to wholesale incredulity, that the next edition would take account of Glaswegian street slang, notably the words *ned*, *chib* and *square go*.

The definitions left much to be desired, though. A *ned* was described as 'a young working-class male who dresses in casual sports clothes'. So much nuance was absent from this summary. It neglected to mention the ned proclivity towards offering to keep an eye on parked cars at busy football grounds; their keening nasal voices; their habit of tattooing themselves with ballpoint pens; their Buckfast; their sports socks; their sisters named Beyoncé and so much more. *Chib* was classified only as a verb, as in 'to stab or slash

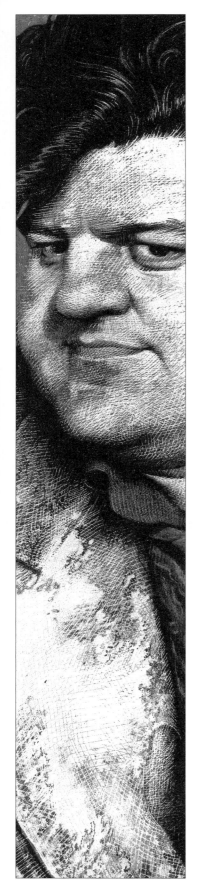

with a sharp weapon', when everyone knows *chib* can also serve as the noun that denotes the implement with which the act of chibbing is perpetrated, as in 'I got my chib and I chibbed him', a statement that is syntactically correct even if it is a terrible indictment of modern parenting. *Square go* – 'a fair fight between two individuals' – is also a lazy definition and could equally well describe the world heavyweight championship. *Square go*, used properly, carries all kinds of connotations, mainly of brave impatience from the party proposing the square go.

'It was about time these words went in,' said Justin Crozier, an editor of the dictionary. 'One thing that has been difficult traditionally for dictionary publishers to do is include a lot of regional dialects and vernacular language, simply because it doesn't appear in print very often. But we have a dedicated team of lexicographers and editors, and when we come across a word which we really think should be in, then we just have to fight for it to go in.' Or propose a *square go*, preferably deploying *chibs* in both senses of their usage.

ROBBIE COLTRANE
(actor, 1950–)

The son of a GP and a piano teacher, Coltrane stands as the strongest bond Glasgow has forged with the well-spoken comedy scene that germinated at Oxbridge and in the 1980s and 1990s grew to dominate British light entertainment. His first appearances on television – if we discount the kids' comedy *Metal Mickey* – were in a Granada TV sketch show entitled *Alfresco* with Stephen Fry, Hugh Laurie and Emma Thompson. He went on to work frequently with the *Comic Strip Presents . . .* team, fighting the cause of progressive/liberal alternative comedy by spoofing film genres. Thus he found himself drawn into a nexus where appearances on charity telethons alternate with voice-over cameos and Sunday-evening documentary series on hobby-horse subjects such as *Robbie Coltrane's B-Road Britain* (2007), *Coltrane in a Cadillac* (1993) and *Coltrane's Planes and Automobiles* (1997).

As a performer, meanwhile, Coltrane has honed three specialities: bulky, combustible Glaswegians (*Tutti Frutti*, *Cracker*, *A Kick up the Eighties*, *The Bogie Man*); bulky, combustible Americans who sound as though they might have Glaswegian roots (*The Adventures of Huck Finn, Message in a Bottle*) and character parts predicated upon his size (*Boswell & Johnson's Tour of the Western Isles,* Hagrid in the *Harry Potter* franchise).

COMFORT AND JOY
(film, 1984, directed by Bill Forsyth)

In a perfect world it would be *Comfort and Joy,* and not *It's a Wonderful Life,* that served as our default Christmas television movie. However, it is not a perfect world. This is rather the argument of Forsyth's beguilingly bittersweet comedy. His fourth film concludes on a note that is obligingly festive and harmonious yet it is preceded by much that is ambivalent. Like the ice-cream fritters the film's hero Alan 'Dickie' Bird develops to pacify two warring Italian catering clans, *Comfort and Joy* is dualistic and Manichean, its warmth coming from Forsyth's signature comedy, fond and absurd, and its cool from the film's prevailing tone of mid-life *ennui.*

As with the Yorkshire pudding and penicillin, the movie was born of a misapprehension. The Ice Cream Wars of the early 1980s had been infamous features of Glasgow's peripheral housing estates. These titanic settlements on the northern and eastern flanks of the city had been built with few amenities, particularly shops, nearby. Billy Connolly famously dubbed Drumchapel, the estate on which he grew up, a 'desert wi' windaes'. Private enterprise stepped in, and ice-cream vans that had previously offered confectionery and soft drinks were selling stolen goods

and narcotics (*see* Serious Chimes Squad, p. 27). Traders competed for the most lucrative territories, leading in 1984 to a house fire in which six members of one family perished. As David Bruce, former director of the Scottish Film Council, put it in his 1996 survey *Scotland: The Movie*: '*Comfort and Joy* was to some extent the victim of one of those accidents of history where life and art imitate each other to nobody's benefit.'

Many years later, Forsyth admitted he'd skipped some finer points in the news coverage of the Ice Cream Wars and had created his own story inspired by the colourful phrase. The film concerns itself more with emotional than literal carnage. Dumped during Christmas week by his volatile, kleptomaniac girlfriend Maddy, breakfast disc jockey Bird (Bill Paterson) takes to driving round Glasgow to reflect upon his life's shortcomings. During one excursion, with the bruised atmosphere of the city caught perfectly by cinematographer Chris Menges, Bird becomes embroiled in a feud between rival families in the business of ice-cream supply. Glad to have his mind taken off Maddy, whose memory is now provoking a series of daydreams, and to have a chance to get closer to the alluring Charlotte (Clare Grogan), Bird sets about reconciling the warring clans of Mr Bunny and Mr McCool. In the process he learns how unfathomable the heart, and the family, can be.

BILLY CONNOLLY
(comic, 1942–)

The Scotia Bar has changed little in the past 40 years, though the area surrounding it has. Stockwell Street, running south from the city centre to the River Clyde, has had its face washed and its teeth capped. The tenements have been replaced by business hotels built from beige brick, or they have been swept away entirely to create cheerless acreages of car parking. But the bar itself persists, still a close-packed little place, with oak-panelled walls and a rough clientele with faces like melted candles. There is just one trace of the bar's best known customer, a small, curling snapshot sited, perhaps with a mordant eye for the allegorical, right next to the cash register.

The Scotia has long been considered the foundry of Billy Connolly's career, the place where he learned to turn the growling banter of howff and shipyard into a style that would conquer the

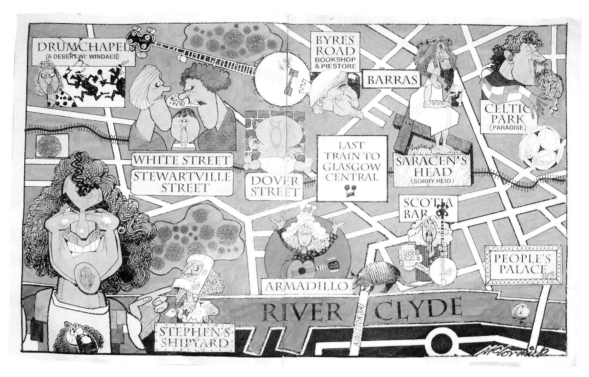

The yin and yang of Billy Connolly's Glasgow, as visualised by Malky McCormick.

comedy world. Peter McDougall has been a friend of Connolly's since those days, and was the writer of three television dramas in which Connolly appeared. 'See, if this was a pub in Dublin there'd be paintings and posters of the guy everywhere,' he notes. 'There'd be tea-towels with his face on them. They have a deep reverence for talent over there. They honour the people they love. In Glasgow, they don't. There's an unconscious hostility towards anyone who gets away. Billy's suffered that from day one.'

Well, up to a point, Lord Copper. The relationship between Connolly and his home city has always been more nuanced: dysfunctional yet co-dependent. And not just with Glasgow. As Connolly's first biographer Jonathan Margolis put it in *The Big Yin: The Life and Times of Billy Connolly* (Orion, 1994): 'He provokes a peculiar reaction in Scotland, in America, Canada, New Zealand and Australia. Young people think he is a has-been, the middle-aged that he is a never-was. The elderly think he is too filthy; alternative comedy fans that he is too clean; while hippies insist he is a sell-out. Journalists have a distinct downer on him, as do churchmen, local politicians in Glasgow, posh Edinburghites, TV critics in the USA . . .'

The case against Connolly lies in several charges. As soon as the comic appeared, in the early 1970s, folk wisdom quickly had it that Connolly lacked comic invention and merely polished up what he'd heard on street corners, in the process depicting his own people as scowling, unlettered drunks. 'Glasgow has a problem with Billy, it feels he's that bit too perspicacious,' McDougall says. 'He's like a really good novelist. He says things people have known all their lives but didn't know they did. The city almost feels Billy has stolen a bit of its soul.'

That particular argument was put to one side as Connolly became feted by the light entertainment establishment in London, though this was to create difficulties of its own. From being considered too close to his roots Connolly was then judged too distant, certainly as the 1980s progressed and he underwent the personality boil-wash that saw him emerge as a vegetarian Buddhist teetotaller in a linen suit, performing material about reiki healing and baby alarms.

The Scottish media, principally its newspapers, became the dynamos of this friction, rendered queasy by Connolly's growing acquaintance with the royal family, his baronial indulgences and his tolerance for being lavishly psychoanalysed by his wife, Pamela Stephenson; the pair became quickly the worst thing in the world, a couple which never finished reminding us how intelligent the other one is. Connolly retaliated by claiming that the press would feel the 'black sperm of my vengeance', a threat that certainly warranted some thinking about, regardless of its genito-urinary practicalities. As with the Hollywood stars of yore, Connolly retreated.

He was protected by one of the most famously disobliging management teams in show business, Ticketyboo, a company whose answerphone message might as well consist of the single word 'No'. On the rare occasions Connolly gave a personal audience it was invariably to Michael Parkinson, an old friend and a toothless acolyte. His authorised biographies, *Billy* and *Bravemouth* – books with all the objective rigour of a Valentine's card – were written by his wife; at one point Stephenson even describes the infant Connolly as a 'future enemy of the bourgeoisie'.

Airports became the sole chink in his armour. It was in an airport, Heathrow, in 2004, that Connolly was called to account for one of the most regrettable episodes of his career. On stage at the Hammersmith Apollo the week previously Connolly had discussed the plight of Ken Bigley, an English engineer taken hostage in Baghdad, commenting on the man's young Thai wife and saying of his threatened execution: 'Don't you wish they [the abductors] would just get on with it?' Connolly claimed he'd been quoted out of context. Few believed him and the row rumbled on until the moment Connolly was departing for his (then) home in Los Angeles. 'I've got nothing to say. Why the fuck would I want to talk to you? I don't give a fuck if you are asking me a question. I don't know who you are. You're the enemy.' Pressed on whether he was sorry for the joke, he added, 'Never mind. I don't want to talk to you. You're a prick. Go and hassle Elton.'

And, so, we find Connolly deep in his imperial period. Nowadays, he is merely a lightning rod for whichever random notions strike him; he is the verbal diarist of a life whose substance is determined by its own celebrity. He speaks the awkward truth of how it feels to bump into Jack Nicholson twice in the same afternoon. Locating the Connolly of 40 years ago – folksy and demotic – in today's portentous and splenetic Connolly is no easy task. Yet he's a habit his home city can't seem to kick. Consider the comedian Gary Moir. Like Connolly himself, Moir was a product of the Clydeside shipyards. He now works as a club comic. His material is the standard bran-tub of quips and observations, but they're performed in an approximation of Connolly's rough, drawling delivery, in the style of Connolly's mid-1970s heyday, with Moir tricked out in leotard and banjo. It all seems to suggest that Connolly is, to all intents and purposes, dead, particularly when Moir explains he handles subjects Connolly would 'if he was still around'.

The contemporary Connolly show, meanwhile, is one long digression on how it feels to be Billy Connolly. The audience is pulled along by that compelling blare of a voice and by the mesmerising force of the performer's self-fascination. These days Connolly performs not comedy but a kind of spoken autobiography. The only truly funny thing about him is the degree of seriousness with which he is prepared to take himself.

Amid the polishing-up Glasgow has undergone over the past two decades, a surprising amount of Connolly's old city remains. Even the Saracen's Head, where he set his 'Crucifixion' sketch, survives despite several threats to demolish it. The Citizens Theatre, where he made his debut as a musician in a typical piece of 1970s agitprop entitled *Clydesiders*, remains. Connolly's various homes in the city – in Stewartville Street and White Street – are now in the heart of Partick's property explosion. On Connolly's 69th birthday a twenty-foot steel mural showing him in his 1970s incarnation was unveiled on a wall near Connolly's birthplace in Anderston. 'Billy's comfortable with Glasgow now,' says McDougall, 'though I don't know if that's true the other way round. He wanders around without minders all the time, goes into pubs, minds his own business. He's viciously funny in pubs, more so than on stage, but you still get these guys who want to compete and tell a funny story about their Auntie Mary. I don't know how Billy suffers it; he has tremendous patience with these people. He gets more patient the more famous he becomes.'

Connolly's friends speak of him with a fierce loyalty and acknowledge his kindnesses. When McDougall's electricity and telephone were cut off, Connolly arranged for the bills to be paid, even though he and McDougall were then in conflict over a cancelled film project. Nobody could expect his friends to agree that Connolly is an increasingly troubling figure, whose audience is principally the offspring of his original audience, now grown prosperous and keen to flirt with social roots from which they've been estranged. 'In one sense,' the late trade union leader and journalist Jimmy Reid told me, 'Billy *is* Glasgow. The city has changed and Billy has changed, but both have a core that cannot change.'

We must accept that a quantity of romantic tripe will always be spoken about Connolly. Increasingly, his name provokes in Glaswegians a certain lightness in the head, the combined effects of nostalgia, pride, envy and uneasy class awareness. The old-fashioned, respectable working classes grew to dislike him for his embrace of the rich and the royal; for the knowledge that he bruises easier than a ripe peach; for his wife's psychobabbling biographies. Meanwhile, the offspring of that audience knows little and cares less about the back-story; to them Connolly is just a sweary pensioner, Frankie Boyle's dad.

What those audiences won't know is a more edifying Connolly entirely: the audacious and terrifyingly funny hippie prole of the 1970s who, as Gary Moir's tribute notes, is sadly no longer with us, having found himself supplanted by a bumptious, purple-bearded, ceaselessly self-absorbed bully, now the comedy equivalent of awaiting a bus on the unlovely wind tunnel outside the Scotia Bar.

1942

Connolly born at 6 p.m. on 24 November at 69 Dover Street, Anderston, 'on the linoleum, three floors up', to Mary and William Connolly, respectively a housewife and an engineer. 'My father was in clean engineering – he came home the same colour he left.'

1946

Mary Connolly abandons the family home, remarries and settles eventually in the Clyde resort of Dunoon. 'I don't like her much, but I don't blame her for going. There was a war raging. She was 21, living in a real slum area with two kids.' Connolly and his elder sister Florence are left in the care of William Connolly and his sisters Margaret and Mona. 'I was beaten up a lot by my aunt [Mona]. I am still working on the stuff she did to me. There are other things that disturb me greatly. I will get round to it eventually.'

1952

The commencement of a five-year period during which Connolly is abused sexually and physically by his father. 'The most awful thing was that it was kind of pleasant, physically. That's what nobody tells. I remember it happening a lot, not every night – but every night you were in a state thinking it was going to happen, that you'd be awakened by it.' Playing truant from school, Connolly attends several performances of *The One O'Clock Gang* at the Theatre Royal.

1957

Connolly leaves St Gerard's Secondary School in Govan with two engineering qualifications, one awarded to him erroneously (it belonged rightly to a classmate named Connell).

1958

Works as a van driver for John Smith's Bookshop and Bilsland's Bakery, where a colleague is Tony Roper, who later becomes author of *The Steamie*.

1960

Connolly signs on for a five-year welding apprenticeship at Stephen's shipyard in Linthouse, at £20 a week. 'I became a welder and I'm glad. Because if I'd become an engineer I would have gone to sea and that would have been the end of that, or I'd be working up on the oil rigs. But I became a welder and I loved it, because they called us the Black Squad – the welders, cokers, platers, riveters and other guys that get dirty.'

1962

Following a spell in the Drumchapel area of the city, the Connolly family move to a tenement flat in White Street, Partick. Connolly undergoes a brief flirtation with homosexuality: 'I went through a phase when I fancied men. There was a kind of androgyny going on – high heels and perfume for men – and I thought it was a bit of OK. I was a chrysalis on the point of becoming a moth. I had an actor friend whose feelings were much stronger than mine and he put me right about a few things. I thought, What's happening? This isn't my department at all.' Inspired by Pete Seeger and the bluegrass movement, Connolly takes up the banjo and takes lessons at the Glasgow Folk Centre on Montrose Street.

1965

Meets Iris Pressagh in Glasgow's Polish Club. They wed four years later at Martha Street Registry Office in Glasgow. Connolly's father's strict Catholicism means he refuses to condone any marriage held outwith church and he does not attend. The legend has it that, while performing a folk show, Connolly forgets a song's lyrics and launches himself into an extended anecdote. In reality, the Scottish folk scene at the time featured many acts who laced their shows with comic storytelling.

Forms the Humblebums with guitarist Tam Harvey. 'My name's Billy Connolly, and I'm humble. This is Tam Harvey, he's a bum,' he tells audiences. The pair are augmented later by Gerry Rafferty, a singer/songwriter from Paisley. The expanded Humblebums play the Metropole Theatre in Glasgow, formerly managed by Arthur Jefferson, father of the Hollywood film comedian Stan Laurel. Connolly's routines between songs expand in duration: 'I just had to get funny. You can't go on singing about dead lifeboatmen forever.'

1969

Birth of Jamie, Connolly's first child. The debut album from the Humblebums, *First Collection of Merry Melodies*, is released in February. Tam

'I just had to get funny'

Harvey leaves the band and *The New Humble-bums* is issued in September.

1972

Tours Scotland with his debut solo show *Connolly's Glasgow Flourish*. Lands a contract with Polydor Records. Works with writer Tom Buchan and artist John Byrne to create *The Great Northern Welly Boot Show*, a rock musical based around the Upper Clyde Shipbuilders work-in, led by shop steward Jimmy Reid. One of Byrne's designs is a banana welly, which Connolly adopts as the banana boot. The show travels to the Edinburgh Fringe and the Young Vic in London. Inspired by a quip heard in the Scotia Bar, Connolly devises 'The Crucifixion', one of his best-known and most contentious routines, in which the Last Supper takes place in the Saracen's Head bar in the East End of Glasgow: 'Oot aw mornin' daein' they miracles. Ah'm knackered! Gie's a glass a' that wine. See the miracles Ah've dun this mornin' . . . Take a look oot that windae, there's nuthin' but deid punters walkin' up and doon . . .'

1973

Connolly opts to devote himself to comedy: 'I got a wee bit frightened, the only thing left was to do it all again. I've got a wife and two kids and I'd hate to end up a 40-year-old folk singer and somebody's father.' He makes a crucial break-through on the STV chat show *Dateline Scotland* as the last-minute replacement for an errant guest. 'I set out to be a cross between Lenny Bruce and Robert the Bruce. My main thrust was the body and its functions and malfunctions – the absurdity of the thing.'

1974

Tours Canada, plays the King's Theatre in Glasgow and releases two live albums, *Solo Concert* and *Cop Yer Whack for This*. Receives a request from Willie Ormond, manager of the Scottish football squad, to entertain the team as it prepares for the finals of the World Cup in West Germany. While in Munich Connolly is spotted

by a passing Scotland supporter who shares a joke involving a murdered wife and a bicycle. In the same year his daughter Cara is born.

1975

The Sunday Mail newspaper in Glasgow launches *The Big Yin*, a weekly comic strip drawn by Malky McCormick, outlining the duo's fictional gallus adventures in Glasgow. The strip ends three years later when Connolly objects to its treatment of the royal family. Connolly makes his first appearance at the London Palladium, embarks on his debut solo British tour and acts in *Just Another Saturday*, a play by Glaswegian writer Peter McDougall. The swiftness of Connolly's rise sees him secure a coveted booking as guest on the Saturday night BBC chat show hosted by Michael Parkinson. Against the advice of his manager, Connolly tells the joke gifted by the Scotland supporter in Munich. The effect is explosive and the appearance makes Connolly a star overnight.

1976

Connolly's first play *And Me wi' a Bad Leg, Tae*, featuring future *Taggart*, *Gregory's Girl* and *Comfort and Joy* star Alex Norton, opens at the Third Eye Centre in Glasgow. It transfers later to a sold-out run at the Royal Court Theatre in London. He and Iris move from the West End of Glasgow to a house in Drymen, Loch Lomond-side. His wife's drinking escalates. He publishes a whimsical 'autobiography' – *Billy Connolly: The Authorised Version* – and embarks on a disastrous American tour supporting Elton John. 'I would go on first and they would all throw bottles at me for a while. Then when they're knackered the band comes on. So you're a victim of the audience all the time.' *Big Banana Feet*, Murray Grigor's film documenting a short tour of Ireland, premieres at the Edinburgh Film Festival. Connolly tours Australia and America.

1977

For the second time Connolly plays a straight dramatic role in a television play by Peter McDougall, *The Elephants' Graveyard*, in which two men dodge their work to wander the hills. Connolly embarks on his Extravaganza tour of the UK, taking in Oban, Largs, Arran, Ayr and Skegness. Connolly's management ask the Fyffes banana firm if they would be interested in using him and his big banana boots in commercials. Fyffes reply that they do 'not want a family fruit associated with Mr Connolly'.

1978
Another American tour and another straight dramatic role, this time in the cinema feature *Absolution*, written by Anthony Shaffer and starring Richard Burton. Connolly played a drifter embroiled in a murderous plot hatched at a boys' school.

1979
The Big Wee tour of the UK. Plays Bogul McNeep in an episode of *Worzel Gummidge*.

1981
Separates from Iris and provokes a tabloid storm when he becomes involved with Pamela Stephenson, then a star of BBC sketch show *Not the Nine O'Clock News*. Becomes embroiled in a number of skirmishes with press photographers he deems unnecessarily intrusive.

1982
Connolly makes significant inroads into American acceptance when a film of the benefit show *The Secret Policeman's Other Ball* becomes a hit there. Appears on stage in *The Beastly Beatitudes of Balthazar B*. Publishes the travel memoir *Gullible's Travels*.

1985
Before an invited celebrity audience, he makes *An Audience with Billy Connolly* for London Weekend Television, a studio performance so successful it reignites wider interest in his performing career. The show features such routines as 'Glasgow Parties' and 'Incontinent Disco Dancer' ('I'll be with you as soon as I've emptied my underwear').

1988
Connolly's father dies following his eighth stroke. Immediately, Connolly confesses to Pamela Stephenson he was abused sexually in his childhood.

1989
Connolly wins custody of his children Jamie and Cara. Marries Pamela Stephenson on a Fijian beach. 'Marriage to Pam didn't change me; it saved me. I was going to die. I was on a downwards spiral and enjoying every second of it. Not only was I dying, but I was looking forward to it.' He shaves off his beard.

1990
Appears as star of US sitcom *Head of the Class*, though the series is cancelled during his tenure.

1991
Connolly, Stephenson and family win their Green Cards and relocate to Los Angeles. Their home overlooks a Universal back-lot featuring the house where Norman Bates lived in *Psycho*.

1992
Performs his 25th-anniversary concert in Glasgow.

1994
The World Tour of Scotland is made into a six-part comedy travelogue for the BBC.

1997
Appears as ghillie John Brown in the Queen Victoria drama *Mrs Brown*. He is nominated for a BAFTA award.

1999
Completes a 25-night sell-out run at the Hammersmith Apollo in London.

2001
Publication of Pamela Stephenson's biography *Billy*.

2004
Pilloried for encouraging the captors of Ken Bigley to 'just get on with it'.

2005
Connolly buys Candacraig House in Aberdeenshire from Body Shop founder Anita Roddick. He thus becomes head of the Lonach Games and a laird.

2007
Tops poll in the Channel 4 show *100 Greatest Stand-Ups*.

2010
Connolly confirms he and his family are resident in New York City.

2011
Hosts a four-part series for ITV detailing a journey along Route 66 from Chicago to Los Angeles. Appears with Brian Cox in *The Quest of Donal Q*, a Christmas radio play for BBC Scotland. A massive steel mural depicting a banjo-playing Connolly is unveiled on a building in Anderston, Glasgow.

2012
Criticised widely for curtailing shows in Scarborough and Blackpool after being heckled for using old material. A remastered edition of Connolly's 1975 film *Big Banana Feet* is shown at the Glasgow Film Festival. Plays the King of Scotland in blockbuster Pixar animation Brave.

2013
Press stories claim Connolly has shown memory problems while performing on stage. In September he puts his Candacraig estate on the market for £3 million amid speculation he plans to retire to Australia.

'I set out to be a cross between Lenny Bruce and Robert the Bruce': Billy Connolly in conversation

The Glasgow Smile: Your comedy underwent a blossoming in the early 1990s as you explored, with startling candour, your childhood in Partick; your work never again got so dark and personal.

Billy Connolly: The death of my father [in 1988] was the thing that sparked it – all those painful experiences that had scarred me very deeply and that made me anything I've become, inasmuch as they drove me to become a performer, you know – that fucking quest for approval thing. I realised this before I ever saw any therapists. I'm a classic case of the nutter who needs help; all that self-medication, the whole shooting match. So the death of my father awoke in me all those things I hadn't confronted. I brought them up on stage, I tidied them up through comedy. Because, when my father was alive, I was too keen on making him love me to do it face-to-face. I didn't want to rock the boat by bringing up stuff that might have put that project back.

None of it worked, though; I fucked up, I was in disarray. So I worked it out on stage. And it was a painful thing. But funny – because pain and comedy are so closely related. I'd be on stage pretending to cry as part of a routine and I'd be actually crying, I'd get caught up in the rhythm of the thing. The audience could see a real tear now and again. But it worked well as comedy, it was immensely funny. But it was a dark, dark period for me. It was fulfilling and cleansing, though, it had this great ring of truth to it. It was comedy of a type that no comedian had done before. I knew that if I hadn't heard this kind of stuff before the audience wouldn't have.*

I remember Gerry Rafferty came to a show. He said, 'God, I love the dark stuff, it's brilliant.' Because he knows that from songwriting; if you don't get in there you don't write good. That's what it's all about, really. As I change in my life or confront things in my life it all shows up on stage. I don't know it's happening. If you don't want anyone to know anything about you, never write a song. You'll give away something about yourself, even if the song's about how you like bananas. You'll let go a secret, you can't not do it. Now, the comedy is lighter, more anecdotal. It's just another phase, another shape I'm enjoying.

TGS: Do you regret the rather torrid phase when you constantly assaulted photographers? You've sustained perhaps the most attritional campaign against the media in showbusiness history . . .

BC: The thing about hitting photographers is this: it's a joyous thing to do. They've had decades of going for me, so it's my turn now. They've made a cunt of me, they made an arse of my mother, they made an arse of my brother, they've had a pretty good time for decades, so now it's my turn. They will feel the black sperm of my vengeance!

They've got twenty fucking years of it coming. And then it's eachy-peachy. They could end it pretty smartly, by apologising. Because, for about twenty years, it was hard, on my fucking own, being really savagely attacked in my own country all of the time, being called unpatriotic. When I moved out of Glasgow they talked about me as if I was insulting Glasgow, complaining that I was a friend of the Queen, that I didn't like Scotland. So I fucking loathe the bastards. They all get treated better than me – Sean Connery, Robbie Coltrane. I'm the sweary one, I'm the welder, I'm the Celtic supporter. That rankles, that fucking rankles. They're a pretty nasty fucking bunch of Alistairs, you know.

TGS: You suspect the Scottish press single you out for harsh treatment for sectarian reasons?

BC: Yes. Of course. It's true. What do you think the numbers are in the Scottish press? Is it weighted in any one direction, do you think?

TGS: That might have been true thirty years back but . . .

BC: That's not what I asked you – do you imagine the bias is weighted on any one side?

TGS: It could be . . .

BC: What do you mean, 'it could be'? *Yes or fucking no*?

TGS: To the extent that I've thought about it, I really don't think the claim is as true as it once was.

BC: *Like it's never crossed your fucking mind? With all these Freemasons around? Don't give me that shite!*

TGS: How much does your comedy owe to your Glasgow upbringing?

BC: I don't really like talking about Glasgow now because I don't really know it any more, and I've been proved wrong so many times in the past. I feel really dodgy about saying* anything about Glasgow, I'm always fucking wrong. I end up talking about the Glasgow I used to live in and it doesn't really exist. I wasn't yearning for a different, better Glasgow; I was yearning for my own youth. I'm becoming that guy, who thinks kids played better in his day and were fairer and fought cleaner. I'm more sentimental about the Appalachian mountains than I am about Glasgow, and I couldn't find the Appalachian mountains in a taxi.

It's like, do you know Drury Street, where the Horseshoe Bar is? I used to go there on Friday nights, my pals would go to the Barrowland Bar. I'd go to the Horseshoe then meet up with my pals. And I always remember Drury Street in the rain. I was in my pointy shoes and my wee white sporty coat. So, I always remember Glasgow as cobbles in the rain, and I miss that. It had an amazing look, Glasgow, the shiny cobbles and the tram cars, you see it in the paintings of the 1940s and 50s. It was a Victorian look, a cracking look, a seriously good look. And the pub lights and the street lights shone on the cobbles – that's what I miss. But apart from that . . .

Glasgow is Glasgow is Glasgow. It's like Liverpool or Belfast, it'll go on and on. Glasgow will have the same soul after a nuclear explosion. It's got a *thing*, it's got a noise that I love. But I can't see it the same any more, because I'm not anonymous. I can't go to the Barras or to football in the way I used to. I can't be in the merry throng in Argyle Street, just listening to the noise it makes.

TGS: Does living with your colossal global fame get easier with time?

---

* In 2001 Connolly revealed that as a child he had been physically and sexually abused by his father.

BC: It's strange and traumatic for a few years and then it becomes invisible. People with you say, 'How do you do this?' But you haven't noticed it. Because it mostly happens behind you. Recognition is like an arrow that you're at the point of. People notice you as soon as you've gone. People who're walking six feet behind you see it all, they see the whole reaction process.

And when people write about you, it's not that they lie but they ignore that fact that you're a decent guy; they always take the worst interpretation of things. If you're confident you're a bighead. You're supposed to creep around and apologise for your success and say, 'Oh, I don't know how that happened to me, other comics are just as good.' No, they're not! They're not as fucking good as me. That's why I'm the biggest – because *I'm the best*! And once you realise that you can sleep at night.

TGS: How do you feel about the Big Yin archetype that still attaches to you?

BC: It means nothing to me, although, I do like it if it's said to me properly. If I'm in, say, California, and especially if an older man says it to me, 'How's it goin', Big Yin?' There's something awfully friendly and nice and warm about it that I really like. But when people shout it across the road or when they say it wrong – 'Ladies and gentlemen, please welcome The Big *Yin*' – I get

kind of nauseous. I feel about it the way Vera Lynn must feel about 'We'll Meet Again'. You think to yourself, I wish that bit would pass, painlessly, into the ether.

I don't play the Scottish card at all, I don't hang out with Scottish people, I don't go to Scottish community centres and talk about how nice Scotland is. My idea of a good time isn't hanging about at three in the morning with drunk Scottish guys. I used to go to a fish and chip shop in Santa Monica because my daughter liked it, but it wasn't fun doing it. I love the possessiveness of the audiences in Scotland, it's a great thing, it's done me no harm at all. It paid my rent for a few years. You feel like you've married their daughter.

TGS: How do you assess your career and achievements?

BC: The Scotland I came from had that kilty element. Then I brought that freak element, though I was a freak on my own for many years. And now it's acknowledged that there's a beauty in swearing, in the world of the arts, at least. I look at James Kelman or Irvine Welsh and I have a little party in my heart. Because I know, without waving any flags or putting up any standard for myself, that I'm a pretty essential part of that. When I hear announcers on television with Glasgow accents I know I had a great deal to do with that, I know it.

Andy Scott's mural of Connolly in Anderston, Glasgow.

In March 2001, Billy Connolly's grownup daughter Cara gave birth to her first child, Connolly's first grandchild. The author was asked by *The Sunday Times* to picture the scene.

Bairn To Be Wild: At Home with Clan Connolly

Cara: Dad, Pamela, I'd like you to meet (unwraps swaddling clothes) your grandson — Walter Valentine Connolly-Wilkes.

Billy: (brushes curtains of hair back from his face with both hands, peers into the bundle with startled look, points thumb and forefinger in the air for no apparent reason): *A baby!* A wee person. That's . . . that's . . . well, there's no other word for it. That's *brill-yint!* (breaks down into uncontrollable laughter, places both hands on knees, tries to speak then breaks down in uncontrollable laughter again)

Pamela: (coldly) Mmm. Walter. That's an interesting name.

Cara: Yes, he's named after my husband's grandfather.

Pamela: You didn't go with my suggestion then? You didn't like Bruce? Or Shane? What about Crocodile? Crocodile's a lovely name for a boy.

Billy: (looks up from tuning his banjo) Aye. Crocodile Connolly! Ah love it! Wooh-hooh! Make way for Crocodile Connolly, boys!

Cara: No. Hubby wasn't happy with Crocodile. (Pamela rolls her eyes and ripples a set of red enamelled nails against a table-top) He didn't like Dad's suggestion either . . .

Billy: (suddenly serious) No offence, love, but your husband's a bampot by the way. A total tube. Ah said to him, Listen, matey, I'll be paying for the christening: you know, the dancing Zulu warriors. When the time comes

I'll be paying for the kid's place at the Santa Barbara Educational Facility for Taxidermists and Clairvoyants. I'll be buying the kid his first banjo . . . (drifts off into reverie) . . . and what a banjo it'll be . . . utterly *brill-yint* . . . twenty foot high, studded with diamonds and rhinestones . . . with strings spun from molten gold . . . (shouting at the top of his voice) . . . The Most Beautiful Banjo The World Has Ever Seen! (someone coughs loudly) Sorry. Where was I? Oh aye, I'm the one with the deep pockets here. So, if I wanted the kid to be called Bumface McGonagall the Third I think I should have been listened to. It's a *brill-yint* name. It's windswept and interesting.

Pamela: Your father has a point, Cara.

Euphemia, the family nanny: (brightly) Now then, now then. Let's not argue. In this house, I think we all agree, the boy will always be known as . . . the Wee Yin!

Billy: (with icy self-possession) Euphemia, you are reminded that 'The Big Yin', herein known as the 'trademark', is the sole copyrighted property of Tickety-boo Enterprises. Any infringement of this intellectual design or device, either in part or whole, is deemed a violation of the Copyright and Patents Act 1988 and will render the third party liable for damages, in the instance of any complaint made by Tickety-boo Enterprises being upheld in an appropriate court.

   (An awkward gloom descends)

Pamela: (recovering) Cara, you got the christening present we sent?

Cara: Yes, thanks. It was very . . . *unusual*. Where did you find a pram in the shape of a giant phallus?

Billy: (laughs uproariously for no apparent reason, gasps for breath, breaks banjo over head and collapses on the floor in sobbing paroxysms) You think that's good? Wait till you hear what I've got planned for the circumcision!

(laughs so hard a small trickle of blood appears from left ear)

Cara: The what?

Billy: Aye, Robin Williams told me about it. All the Hollywood big shots circumcise their kids. Steve Martin'll be there. Whoopi Goldberg. Judi Dench, Michael Palin, Jimmy Logan. It'll be fan-dabi-splendido! The dancing Zulu warriors will sing 'Tie Me Kangaroo Down, Sport'. Then Jimmy Reid, Gerry Rafferty, Elton John and twenty of his young friends, dressed as gay Beefeaters, come down a glittering staircase. I'm having the word *Brillyint* shaved into my head specially, and we've got a live satellite link-up to Clive James in Brisbane, and . . .

Cara: (exploding) Dad, for God's sake, you're almost sixty and a grandfather! Isn't it time you grew up? Don't you get sick of the endless wackiness? Of the nipple rings and the monocles and the streaking round Piccadilly Circus? Of the obsession with flatulence and the relentless showbiz glad-handing? Are you going to end up an eighty-year-old man in a tartan frogsuit and bowler hat, shouting at traffic lights? Does this little baby mean anything to you? Well, does it?
   (A guilty silence fills the room. Everybody gathers round the child making apologetic noises. Cara beams proudly, cradling the baby in her arms)

Billy: (humbly) Ah'm sorry, love. I know you're right. (to baby) Hello there, hello wee Walter, welcome to the family. You'll love it, it'll be *brill-y—* it'll be smashing. Coochie-coo, coochie coo (turns to Pamela, voice lowers to a whisper) Hey, and see if you can find me one of those tartan frogsuits the lassie was talking about.

Pamela: (taking out mobile phone) I'm already on it . . .

ELVIS COSTELLO
(songwriter, 1954–)

At a concert in Glasgow in May 2012, the prolific singer and songwriter recalled for his audience an anecdote involving his late father, the well-known bandleader Ross MacManus. In the 1970s, MacManus was touring with his cabaret band. The troupe were booked to play a miners' club in Lanarkshire, an area renowned for the extremity of its loyalism. Being something of a showman, MacManus travelled always with a wardrobe of flamboyant stage outfits. The fact that he was profoundly colour-blind had never proven a problem before. Now, however, he was in Glasgow. Moments before showtime MacManus donned the waistcoat he intended to wear for the show, a waistcoat that to him appeared grey-brown but, actually, was a deep, strobing emerald green. He stepped into the wings and was readying himself for the stage, when the club secretary hurried over in an evident panic.

'Are you intending to go on stage in that?' he spluttered, pointing at the waistcoat.

'Certainly!' the confused bandleader replied.

The secretary's expression turned to one of pity. 'And, tell me, do you intend coming off?' he asked.

CUMBERNAULD HIT
(film, 1977, directed by Murray Grigor)

Something of a cuckoo in the context, *Cumbernauld Hit* is included a) because so is *Gregory's Girl* and b) because the film is a genuine, carpet-chewing oddity, allowing us to overlook that it was made thirteen miles outside Glasgow. Almost nothing in the chronicles of comedy readies the unsuspecting viewer for *Cumbernauld Hit*. In its affectionate and cosy weirdness it is beyond everything.

The film was commissioned as a promotional fanfare for the New Town of Cumbernauld, shot in the year it marked its twentieth birthday. Murray Grigor (1939–) was engaged as director. Formerly a filmmaker at BBC Scotland, Grigor is renowned for his documentaries on architecture, such as the 1968 film which helped resurrect the reputation of Charles Rennie Mackintosh. More pertinently, Grigor was known also as a director of distinctive vision, as evinced by his early 1970s film *Clydescope*, a tourism short which featured performances from Billy Connolly and animations by John Byrne.

Civic war – Fenella Fielding in the outrageous *Cumbernauld Hit*.

It's easy to imagine what the burghers of civic Cumbernauld were expecting of Grigor: a conventional summary of the town's bounties, with inventories of its many recreational facilities and footage of happy families admiring the ample parking. Grigor did deliver the aforementioned, after a fashion, but it was folded into a bizarre James Bond spoof in which a high-camp lady baddie, played by Fenella Fielding, the plummy star of *Carry On Screaming* (1966), pursued a fiendish plot to defraud the New Town of £200m. Shot on the finest 16mm film stock that money could ignore, *Cumbernauld Hit* followed a young female journalist on the *Cumbernauld News* as she strove to thwart the plot. Amid crane shots of the town centre's modular architecture and chase sequences past branches of Templeton's supermarket, the reporter did battle with jive-talking American henchmen and lavishly bearded heavies as kinky, campy farce was compounded and a voiceover tried to talk town councillors off the nearest high ledge: 'The people of Cumbernauld . . . none better anywhere.'

IVOR CUTLER
(schoolteacher, poet and absurdist, 1923–2006)

Those who know *Life In A Scotch Sitting Room Vol. 2* – sadly, a constituency still quite stunningly meagre – tend to regard Cutler's 1978 monologue, recorded at the Third Eye Centre, in one of two

Ivor Cutler, patron saint of the sideways look.

ways: as either an hilariously bewitching ramble through a mind addled by herring, toilets and antimacassars, or, conversely, as perhaps the most sizable quantity of bubonic marzipan they have ever heard.

The same debate attaches to Cutler's legacy overall. To the tiny confederation of arts-centre liberals who loved him, Cutler, who died in London aged 83, was the poet laureate of drab whimsy, the patron saint of the sideways look. Nothing could thrill his devotees like the hollow rattle of that tiny voice as it recollected grim family outings during which he'd hug walls 'to escape the worst effects of the fresh air' and his father would point out thistles. 'Mother was also informative,' Cutler would drone, with affectless misery. 'Look, she would say, a patch of grass! And we dutifully twisted our heads.'

Like no other could – or would wish to – Cutler catalogued the doleful oddities of life and the debilitating after-effects of a 1930s Scottish childhood. Attending his performances felt like being trapped on a train with someone who'd kept every scrap of paper they'd handled in the previous four decades. The shows were séances in which Cutler attempted to contact the living: 'I'm like a liquorice strap,' he said, attempting to summarise his strange appeal. 'Those who like it are always guaranteed that the same flavour will be running through.'

Often this gave Cutler's work a sad and eldritch beauty, or a charming childish innocence, such as on his almost listenable album track 'Good Morning! How Are You? Shut Up!'

Throughout his long and modest career Cutler was so resolutely odd and culty he became a kind of cultural shortcut – many affected to appreciate him solely because he was so clearly the last word in eccentricity. This rather made Cutler catnip to tastemakers and hipsters, each convinced they'd find the joke hilarious the instant they'd worked out what it might actually be. That ghastly old groover John Peel claimed to be a huge fan; Alan McGee, the Svengali behind the band Oasis, reissued several of his albums. At EMI, George Martin was his record producer.

Cutler's most illustrious patrons, however, were the Beatles, who in 1967 featured him in their disastrous television film, *Magical Mystery Tour*. Cutler played tour guide Buster Bloodvessel, who compounded the charabanc jollity with announcements delivered in a lifeless, speak-your-weight brogue: 'I am the courier. Good morning, men. And women. Welcome. I am your friendly courier. Mr Bloodvessel is my name. Buster Bloodvessel. I am concerned for you to enjoy yourselves. Within the limits of British decency.'

Cutler's friend Roger Kohn recalled a contemporaneous visit from Paul McCartney. 'Ivor saw Paul cutting his fingernails in the wash-basin, so he took one of the larger cuttings down to his local butcher and said, "This is Paul McCartney's fingernail!" The butcher, used to Ivor's eccentricities, humoured him. "Yes, of course it is, Ivor." Ivor returned to his flat, collected Paul McCartney and returned to the butcher's shop. Matching the cutting to the living digit, Ivor repeated, "This is Paul McCartney's fingernail!"'

Born a hundred yards from Ibrox Stadium, the home of Rangers F.C., Cutler was the son of prosperous Jewish immigrants. He became an engineer with Rolls-Royce. Later he was decommissioned from the Air Force, for dreaminess, he claimed. Until he could sustain himself by his art – there never really was a noun for what Cutler did – he did several things, developing a portfolio on the fringes of progressive education, teaching music and drama at the innovative Summerhill School, writing poetry, broadcasting on the Home Service and working on *Life In A Scotch Sitting Room*.

In his later years Cutler chose to become something of a curmudgeon, joining the Noise Abatement Society and plastering the lampposts near his London flat with absurdist stickers ('To remove this label, take it off' one read). The older he became the more he proved his own point, that age is an illusion; that mentally and psychologically speaking the toddler changes little in its journey towards becoming a pensioner. For Ivor that particular journey is now at an end. He is sorely missed, but by a very small group of people. You sense it is what he would have wanted.

'*Queen Sets Attack Dogs on 'Ghastly Salmond Fellow''*

THE DAILY MASH

THE DAILY MASH
(satirical website, 2007–)

Following the model patented by American site *The Onion*, *The Daily Mash* was founded by Neil Rafferty and Paul Stokes, two veterans of the Edinburgh/Glasgow journalistic nexus. One of the few satire websites to be genuinely amusing, *The Daily Mash* takes a more acerbic and jaundiced view than *The Onion*, very much in the mould of *Private Eye*, that legendary organ of satirical comment. The *Mash*, though, is crueller and more attuned to modern phenomena. The typical *Daily Mash* story identifies the unspoken truth within a given news event, then assumes the truth deserves formal coverage in its own right, as in 'Bank Holiday Fun To Be Outweighed by Hassle' or 'Is The Celebrity Diet We Recommended Last Week Killing You?'

Over its lifetime the site has expanded to lampoon every facet of the daily, middlemarket tabloid, including page leads ('Glasgow Launches Bid For Swearing Olympics'), news features ('Are Our Seagulls Being Radicalised by Foreign Clerics?'), lifestyle ('The Magic Fox Vintage Smoothie Boutique Urban Forest Pop-Up Chill Retreat

Alex Salmond according to *The Daily Mash*

Queen Sets Attack Dogs on 'Ghastly Salmond Fellow'

Alex Salmond was forced to flee for his life yesterday after the Queen set a pair of dogs on him at the end of their first official audience. According to royal insiders the Queen and the First Minister were cordial to each other for much of the meeting at the Palace of Holyroodhouse. But after fifteen minutes the monarch grew visibly bored and restless and looked at her watch continually.'

Scotland to Ban Swearing in Public Places

The Scottish Parliament is drawing up plans for a wide-ranging ban on swear words in public places. Concerned at the effects of passive swearing on children, MSPs are compiling a list of words and phrases that will be banned in pubs, hospitals, police stations, art galleries, farmyards and the front – but not the back – of Transit vans. The proposed legislation has the full support of First Minister Alex Salmond, a reformed swearer with a particular hatred of the phrase 'smug prick'.

Independent Scotland Could Be Exactly the Same, Warn Experts

As Scottish First Minister Alex Salmond set out his timetable for an independence referendum, he was dealt a devastating blow after research showed separation from the UK would make absolutely no difference whatsoever.

Ein Reich, Ein Volk, Ein Salmond

The Scottish National Party has registered the name of its leader Alex Salmond as an election brand so it will appear on ballot papers all across Scotland. SNP activists said the tactic would entice voters to support lesser-known SNP candidates, such as the 128 other people it has standing in the forthcoming Scottish elections.

Salmond: I'm Bigger Than Jesus Now

SNP leader Alex Salmond provoked religious fury last night after announcing he was now more popular than Jesus Christ. Salmond told reporters: 'It's getting really crazy now. Women are screaming at the sight of me. People are giving me insane amounts of money. There's even a village in Lochaber where I'm worshipped as some kind of supernatural astronaut.'

Salmond to Generate Electricity by Rubbing Himself Against Shereen Nanjiani

First Minister Alex Salmond plans to satisfy the nation's energy needs by rubbing himself against a variety of high-profile Scots. Following the Executive's decision to oppose nuclear power the First Minister said: 'If this country is to be nuclear-free it will require a great national effort, involving wind, wave and rubbing. I am prepared to give up two hours of my day for some very vigorous rubbing. Are you?'

Salmond's Face to Be Projected on to Moon Night Before Election

The SNP election campaign will reach a spectacular climax this week when the face of party leader Alex Salmond is projected on to the surface of the moon. An SNP spokesman said: 'With around 40 per cent of voters undecided, what could be more impressive than Alex Salmond beaming down at you from space?'

As bank-holiday Britain heads for the seaside…

ARE OUR SEAGULLS BEING RADICALISED BY FOREIGN CLERICS?

Is to Be Britain's First 100% Twat-friendly Festival'), sport ('Irishman Hot Favourite To Be Drunkest Person at Cheltenham'), politics, opinion, an agony aunt and a horoscopes page ('Leo, 23 July–22 August. The only way you will reach your holiday weight is if that holiday is to take place on Mercury.') Particularly enjoyable are the satires on the Scottish National Party project to create around leader Alex Salmond a messiah cult, and also the site's über-cool futurologist and fashion victim Dermot Jaye, Stylish Masturbator: 'Despite the protestations of my long-legged spouse,' he writes, 'for sheer edgy cool you cannot top masturbating in a disabled toilet in the provinces.'

GAVIN DOCHERTY
(journalist, 1952–)

One of the most admired and oft-repeated exit lines ever used in the world of Glasgow journalism – a realm, regrettably, where exit lines are becoming more necessary by the day – fell from the lips of Gavin Docherty, then of the short-lived title the *Sunday Scot* (1991). Docherty was, and remains, a well liked fixture of the city's fourth estate, an entertainment correspondent often more entertaining than those he is canvassing. Docherty had made himself a comfortable nest at the *Evening Times*, Glasgow's breathless evening title, a paper with two real and abiding interests: the city's underworld and Glasgow showbiz stars who might play members of the city's underworld. In 1991, a new paper was mooted to rival national Sunday tabloid the *Sunday Mail*. The paper was to be bankrolled by Sir David Murray (1951–), an educated, bullish construction tycoon who yearned to achieve a station in Scottish society. The title didn't prosper: issue one led with a weak story about naval dockyards while rival the *Sunday Mail* was uncovering the errant mother of Billy Connolly in Dunoon. Week on week the *Sunday Scot's* circulation dwindled. As part of an attempt to halt the slide Docherty was lured over. He found immediately, though, that he and the *Sunday Scot* were not a comfortable fit. The journalist began to suspect he had made a major mistake. The *Sunday Scot* closed after fourteen weeks. But not before Docherty had stepped into the office of editor

Jack Irvine and delivered a line that has assumed a cherished place in the memory of every Glaswegian journalistic colleague: 'I think I'm in the wrong movie, man,' he told his employer.

'DRUMCHAPEL MIST'
(traditional song, unknown author and date)

Gallagher's famous home-made wine
Will easily get you pissed
If you wake up in the morning and you rue the day
You drank Drumchapel Mist
Brewed in the sun at Partick Cross
Made of napage of fungus-mould
Fermented underneath an unmade bed
Drunk when it's nine months old
Made from deadly nightshade and laced with dross
Castor oil added for taste
If it trickles down your chin it'll singe your beard
So don't let it go to waste
A purple flush comes over your face
And it spreads down to your jaw
Your teeth play castanets inside your mouth
And your tongue comes down your nose
Gallagher fled when he heard the news
Of the damage that his wine had done
He left behind some unfermented booze
And we know 'cause we drank some.

'*Here's your copy of* The Bizarre History of Plastic Knickers,*sir, and would you like Green Shield stamps with that?*'

CHARLIE ENDELL

SHEENA EASTON
(vocalist, 1959–)

On the morning of 3 June 1990 Sheena Easton awoke as one thing and by bedtime was another thing entirely, as through the evening skies plastic bottles filled with urine arced towards her. That day the singer didn't blot her copybook so much as immerse it in a big bucket brimming with the city's blood, sweat and tears.

Born in the dolorous north Lanarkshire town of Bellshill, Easton had paid her dues on the club circuit of industrial Scotland then lucked into becoming the subject of a BBC documentary on her attempts to make it big. The programme had a self-fulfilling effect and in 1980 Easton was signed to EMI Records. She enjoyed a series of British chart hits, sang the theme to the 1981 James Bond movie *For Your Eyes Only* and won that year the Grammy for Best New Artist. After relocating to America, Easton released a series of successful albums, broadened her stylistic range and established an alliance with Prince, the highly respected funk and soul performer. For the singer, all was going swimmingly. And then she returned to Glasgow.

The Big Day was to be the highpoint of Glasgow's year as the European Capital of Culture with a series of free pop concerts held over four city-centre stages. Local heroes were the theme of the day, with appearances from Deacon Blue, Love and Money, Hue and Cry, Texas, Wet Wet Wet and many others. Easton was to perform on a stage sited on an area of Glasgow Green known as Flesher's Haugh. The medieval name translated as 'The Meadow of Butchery', which did at least turn out to be curiously appropriate.

Yet it had all begun so auspiciously. Arriving in the city Easton discharged her celebrity obligations happily: 'This morning a sparkle-eyed Sheena Easton stepped off the London shuttle, sporting a new hairstyle and a big smile,' trilled the *Evening Times*. On stage, however, Easton made what Glasgow audiences consider a cardinal error; she comported herself as though she hailed from somewhere other than Glasgow. The first obligation of every Glaswegian performing in the city is to acknowledge their origin, humbly and decorously. This was what Easton had failed to do, as the *Glasgow Herald* of the day noted: 'Could Sheena Easton be less without disappearing?' it wondered. 'Her watery funk, feebly raunchy gyrations and painfully thin voice failed to convince, as did her assertion that she was glad to be back amang us once mair after ten years, her ain folk. "Eff off back to America," sections of the crowd around me shouted. Others pinged paper cups at the stage. A lot left, numbed either by Sheena or the cold.'

When it was discovered afterwards that many of the bottles with which Easton was pelted contained urine, the singer vowed never to perform in her home city again. And, more than two decades on, she never has.

CHARLES ENDELL

(TV character in *Budgie*, London Weekend Television, 1971/1972, and *Charles Endell Esquire*, Scottish Television, 1979)

Although conceived by writers from Yorkshire (Keith Waterhouse and Willis Hall) and incarnated by an actor who'd attended Aberdeen Grammar (Iain Cuthbertson), Charlie Endell somehow ended up the definitive Glaswegian comic creation, the ultimate embodiment of the city's id, psyche and super-ego. As with Malcolm Tucker in *The Thick of It*, Endell was a shiver looking for a spine to run down yet he was no mere thug or bully-boy.

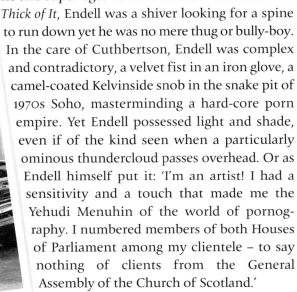

In the care of Cuthbertson, Endell was complex and contradictory, a velvet fist in an iron glove, a camel-coated Kelvinside snob in the snake pit of 1970s Soho, masterminding a hard-core porn empire. Yet Endell possessed light and shade, even if of the kind seen when a particularly ominous thundercloud passes overhead. Or as Endell himself put it: 'I'm an artist! I had a sensitivity and a touch that made me the Yehudi Menuhin of the world of pornography. I numbered members of both Houses of Parliament among my clientele – to say nothing of clients from the General Assembly of the Church of Scotland.'

Hence, each episode of *Budgie* became a tango of imminent violence, as Endell endured with fraying patience the players in his sordid psychodrama: his hapless gofer and patsy 'Budgie' Bird (Adam Faith), a Cockney hustler whose biggest blag turns out, pathetically, to be a box containing 24,000 government-issue ballpoint pens. 'There are two things I hate in life,' he tells Budgie, 'and you're both of them.' Or his motley band of henchmen: Laughing Spam Fritter, Careless McDavitt, Starting Handle Harry and Peter the Pastry. Or his never-speaking wife Mrs Endell, who on no account is to hear word of her husband's various enterprises: like the Strip Strip Hooray Club; the Sex Boutique; Endell's Turf Accountants; or Hers Personally, Charlie's chain of pregnancy testing centres. Where Tucker served as a bully for the state, Endell was driven by motives more complex: by the need to be his family's breadwinner; to set an (admittedly terrifying) example to his three sons; to protect his naive wife; and to do it all while maintaining the fiction that he is a decent, upright member of the business community.

Crucial here was the quality that made Endell such a convincing archetype of the Glasgow social climber: his affectations of gentility. Whether battling Maltese competitors, upbraiding incompetent hoods or expanding into porn by mail order ('Here's your copy of *The Bizarre History of Plastic Knickers*, sir, and would you like Green Shield stamps with that?') Endell was first and foremost a lounge-bar prig. He was fastidious, sometimes dainty in his habits, and, when necessary, his growling diction would smooth itself into elongated vowels and sugar-tongued felicity ('In the course of a slight disagreement I bent a crowbar around a person's skull.')

It remains mysterious how two writers from West Yorkshire, Willis Hall and Keith Waterhouse, creators of Budgie and hence of Charlie Endell, glommed onto this particular characteristic. It might be sensible to conclude they didn't. Charlie Endell was truly Cuthbertson's creation. 'Waterhouse and Hall had written this part for the first episode then the character was to disappear,' recalled Verity Lambert, producer of *Budgie*. 'Iain Cuthbertson at that time was on television, playing rather middle-class people like bank managers or lawyers. But I had seen him at the Royal Court in a production of *Serjeant Musgrave's Dance* where he was absolutely terrifying. So I said, 'Please see this actor because I believe he can surprise people.' Iain absolutely saw it as an opportunity to do something very different. He had this thing that Charlie would speak with this Scottish accent overlaid with these kind of Americanisms. That came from him, and Willis and Keith loved what he did with it. So they wrote him in as a running character.'

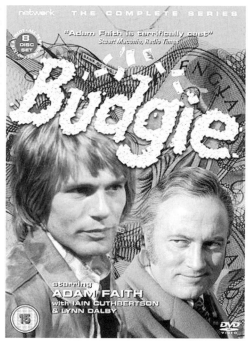

As displayed repeatedly during his tussles with the Soho underworld, Endell had an instinct for survival. It saw him outlive even the show that spawned him. In 1973, Adam Faith sustained serious injuries in a car crash and a third series of Budgie was abandoned. Charlie Endell was dead. But he wouldn't lie down. Six years later Scottish Television launched Charles Endell Esquire, a primetime Saturday night show for the ITV network. Written by the well-regarded Robert Stewart

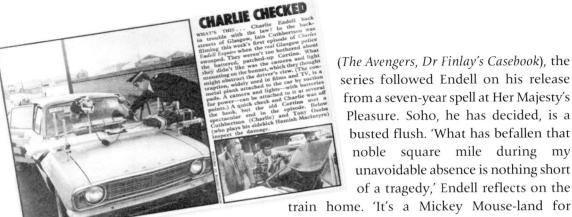

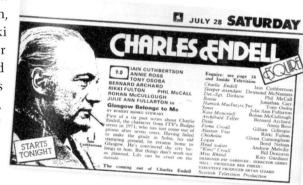

(*The Avengers*, *Dr Finlay's Casebook*), the series followed Endell on his release from a seven-year spell at Her Majesty's Pleasure. Soho, he has decided, is a busted flush. 'What has befallen that noble square mile during my unavoidable absence is nothing short of a tragedy,' Endell reflects on the train home. 'It's a Mickey Mouse-land for cheating the tourists – instead of selling them good, honest dirt.'

But the Glasgow to which Endell returns is changed too. His favourite hotel is now the Strathclyde Region Hostel for the Homeless. There's a new set of gangsters in town, headed by Vint (Rikki Fulton). Endell's solicitor appears to have misplaced £180,000 of his client's cash. While pursuing it, Endell diverges into any new scam he can find: football management, pop music, illicit whisky.

By this point, the character was cosily comic and some considerable distance from the volatile snob seen in *Budgie*. But the new series was not to prosper. A strike by technicians took the ITV network off air for three months, a gap that separated the first two episodes of *Charles Endell Esquire* from the final four. By the time that normal service resumed, a new series was leaping up the ratings, concerning a lovably comic criminal also-ran in a camel-hair coat. That series was *Minder*. And who would have thought the fearsome Charlie Endell would be seen off finally by Arthur Daley?

EUROPEAN CAPITAL OF CULTURE
(event, 1990)

There are two schools of thought – or *académies* – concerning Glasgow's tenure as the European Capital of Culture in 1990. Many believed that in the years preceding the city had made a decent fist (if such is the proper metaphor) of living down its violent heritage and of adapting to its new service economies. Perhaps the honour was in recognition of this? Or was it, as Alasdair Gray suggested conspiratorially, a Westminster payback for the 'reluctance' of Glasgow City Council throughout the 1970s and 80s to pursue increases in public housing subsidy?

Whichever it was, the accolade was duly bestowed, and few in the city were about to walk past such a comedic open goal. The very notion of an A&E inpatient like Glasgow raising its pinkie and going all cultural, with concerts by Luciano Pavarotti and Frank Sinatra, and drama by Dario Fo starring Robbie Coltrane, provoked a steady, lukewarm stream of waggish hilarity. Largely, of course, the stuff was historically ignorant, self-loathing and aggressively lowbrow, from parties who chose to overlook the city's formidable artistic and cultural back-story. A serial culprit was the horrifying *Rab C. Nesbitt*, a show which appeared to consider any kind of self-betterment tantamount to civic treason. If any danger existed of audiences feeling deprived of jokes concerning diddies sipping cappuccino in Royal Exchange Square *Rab C. Nesbitt* challenged it. But there was no shortage of alternative jokes, many making the point that in Glasgow culture was something found more normally growing up the wallpaper in damp council housing. With greater charity, the subject was touched upon frequently in Tom Shields' Diary in the *Glasgow Herald*, in the later routines of Francie and Josie, and in *The Crack*, Michael Munro's follow-up to his popular Glasgow lingo-guide *The Patter*: 'How do you spot a Glaswegian intellectual?' it asks. 'When he chooses "Delilah" on a karaoke machine, it's the Alex Harvey version he prefers.'

Perhaps the best laugh of the year, however, was provided by Glasgow's Glasgow, subtitled 'A City Within a City', a sprawling multi-media extravaganza held in the 22 arches beneath Central Station. Part museum, part theatre, Glasgow's Glasgow strove to relate the history of the city, its people and its architecture, and was one of the tent-peg events of the year. However, Glasgow's Glasgow was not its original title. Its original title, until the show opened in April, was *The Words and the Stones*. And then someone pointed out what its acronym was . . .

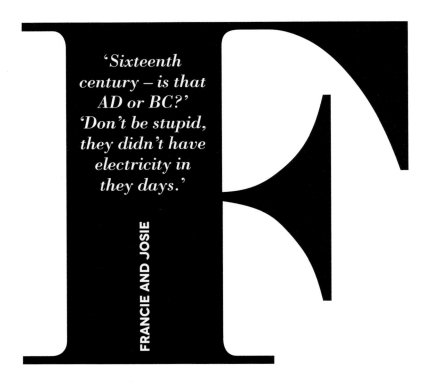

'Sixteenth century – is that AD or BC?' 'Don't be stupid, they didn't have electricity in they days.'

FRANCIE AND JOSIE

FAGS, MAGS AND BAGS
(radio series, 2007–)

Imprisonment is at the heart of the British sitcom: Tony Hancock failing to convince the world he deserves better than a bedsit in East Cheam; Harold Steptoe trapped in the rag-and-bone yard with his appalling father; Basil Fawlty in his Alcatraz of doomed snobbery. From *Porridge* to *The Office*, few things are funnier than a protagonist ruing the shackles of their own miscalculation.

Fags, Mags and Bags continues the tradition, depicting the labours of Ramesh, proprietor of a convenience store in the Glasgow suburb of Lenzie. Thirty years of milk, rolls and newspapers have earned him a tan Mercedes, but his sons crave something beyond the world of low-return retail, setting up the central conflict of the show. 'My thinking was, let's not hide from the fact that a disproportionate number of Asians keep shops,' says its co-creator and star Sanjeev Kohli, 'or that the guys who end up driving Mercs are the same guys who're prepared to accept 0.1 pence from every chocolate tool they sell. The shop is a real weight round your neck and you can't trust anybody but family. For Asians, the corner shop is basically a prison without slopping out. It has to be family, because who else is going to sit on a crate for eight hours a day? I know one family where the daughter is a doctor but she still has to do shifts in her dad's shop. Nothing sums up the Scottish immigrant experience like a shop van picking up the kids from Kelvinside Academy.'

With a dim-witted assistant played by Donald McLeary, *Fags, Mags and Bags* clearly owes something to the classic shop sitcom *Open All Hours,* but it stays in strict Glaswegian tradition for its fascination with the city and the very specific obsessions of its citizens. It is significant, though, that the programme was made not in Scotland but by the national network, appearing on Radio 4. 'It would be nice to think that the people who run BBC Scotland kept an eye on the Petri dish of talent that's out there but they clearly don't,' says Kohli. 'The stuff on Radio Scotland now is just woeful. I actually can't listen to it because it's so pedestrian and monochromatic. It just doesn't have any comedy sensibility. It can be quite crippling to work in comedy here.'

The confinement of the corner shop, addressed in *Fags, Mags and Bags.*

THE FALL OF KELVIN WALKER
(novel, Alasdair Gray, 1985)

Subtitled 'A Fable of the Sixties', Gray's tale is a sourly hilarious study of the wrong man in the wrong place at the wrong time: Flower Power London, as viewed by the fearsomely exacting son of a Highland minister. Like the hero of Jerzy's Kosinski's novel *Being There* (published, incidentally, years after Gray conceived Kelvin Walker), Gray's protagonist rises without trace as his rural openness is taken by the hip and credulous as a new kind of profundity. Before long, Walker is a television interviewer and newspaper columnist, through little more than his disarming honesty and his monolithic self-belief, allied to a love of the teachings of Nietzsche. 'Kelvin turned and walked towards a doorway with a young woman in it. Before going through he stopped and looked back, saying "Sir Godfrey! It is good that we discovered so soon how impossible it would be to work together. I want you to remember this afternoon. A moment ago I called you a man of vision. I no longer believe that. In less than a month you will realise how shortsighted you really are. Good-day!"' In the end, having experienced the easy glamour and social mobility of England, Walker returns to the village of Glaik and a life in Scotland that is every bit as grim as anything in the work of Ivor Cutler. To be born Scottish, the story appears to conclude, is to be born cursed.

BASIL FAWLTY
(Donald Sinclair, hotelier and model for Basil Fawlty in Fawlty Towers, BBC Television 1975, 1979)

It is some considerable distance from the rain-slicked streets of Glasgow to the palm-fringed boulevards of Torquay, jewel of the English Riviera. Taking the journey, however, ensured that Donald Sinclair would live forever in the pantheon of British humour. As co-proprietor of the Gleneagles Hotel, Sinclair unleashed over several days in 1970 an ice-storm of Glaswegian brusqueness so appalling it lives forever in comedy history. For from this onslaught was born Basil Fawlty – snob, sycophant, grotesque and emblem of the service industry maxim that the job would be a hell of a lot more bearable if only it weren't for the customers.

Sinclair's personal biography was scarcely the stuff of levity, though. Born in 1909, he served commendably in the Royal Navy during World War Two, though he did have the misfortune of being sunk twice, first off Greenland in 1941 then Algeria in 1942, a recurrence that might have rendered anyone grouchy. In 1940 he married Beatrice, an outgoing Aberdonian who worked as a dance hostess in Glasgow's Piccadilly Club. The couple had one child, Ann, in Glasgow, then moved to Torquay to escape the threat of Luftwaffe bombing raids (they, quite literally, didn't mention the war . . .)

In wartime, Sinclair served and Beatrice speculated. With a flair for cookery and interior decor she established a small hotel named Greenacres, the success of which underwrote the more expansive fifteen-apartment Gleneagles, opened on a commanding cliff-top site in 1964. Beatrice had named it after the esteemed luxury hotel in Perthshire. A symphony in seaside Corbusier, the boxy Gleneagles was shaped by Beatrice's (then radical) insistence that each room be en-suite. Donald chipped in with an advertising slogan – 'This is New and Beautiful' – only half of which was true. 'Donald ran the bar and was invaluable in keeping the books and accounts, but I was the boss,' his wife recalled years later. Throughout the 1960s the hotel grew in size and reputation. By the start of the following decade the Gleneagles boasted four stars, 41 rooms and an outdoor swimming pool kept at a constant, skin-blistering 86 degrees Fahrenheit.

Just the place, then, for a troupe of up-and-coming television comics, newly arrived in the locale, to film for the second series of their sketch show. The show was *Monty Python's Flying Circus* and its stars were a motley bunch of Oxbridge graduates, five of them – Graham Chapman, John Cleese, Eric Idle, Terry Jones and Michael Palin – plus American animator Terry Gilliam. It is highly unlikely Donald and Beatrice Sinclair would have recognised their guests, whose television careers had largely been in the late-night realms of absurdist and satirical comedy. 'Mr Sinclair, the proprietor, seemed to view us from the start as a colossal inconvenience,' wrote Palin in his diary for 11 May. 'When we arrived back . . . he just stood with a look of self-righteous resentment, of tacit accusation, that I had

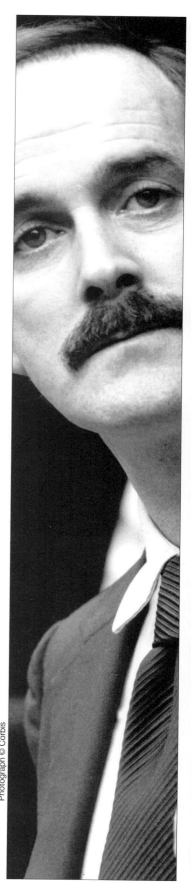

not seen since my father waited up for me fifteen years ago.' Later, when Chapman 'tentatively' requested a brandy, Sinclair refused, though when Chapman ordered a three-egg omelette later he did produce an omelette topped with three fried eggs. The hotel had no porter, night porter, lunch-time bar person or sitting-room assistant; each role was performed, after a fashion, by Sinclair himself. Duly appalled, three of the Python team, plus wives and girlfriends, decided they would leave the following morning: 'Mrs Sinclair made our stay even more memorable,' Palin added 'by threatening us with a bill for two weeks, even tho' we hadn't stayed.'

With greater tolerance for the ridiculous, Idle and Cleese stayed on, and this was when Sinclair's singular approach to hospitality stepped up a gear. When Idle briefly set down his briefcase in the lobby Sinclair repositioned it behind an outdoor wall some distance away, on the grounds that it had provoked a bomb scare. Sinclair displayed conspicuous distaste for foreigners, whether tourist or staff, and for builders working on the hotel. Later, Sinclair's staff remembered him cancelling at short notice a dinner-dance then, when guests complained, depositing a record player on the dance floor, minus records, and stomping off to bed: 'I have never come across anyone quite like Mr Sinclair,' recalled former Gleneagles waitress Rosemary Harrison in 2002. 'He was a square peg in a round hole.'

Such, of course, is virtually the working definition of a comedic subject, and so it would prove. Cleese filed away his memories of Sinclair and retrieved them a year later when writing episodes of London Weekend Television's *Doctor at Large* series. In an episode titled *No Ill Feeling* Sinclair was reincarnated as Mr Clifford, the vexing proprietor of a dismal suburban hotel used as digs by locum

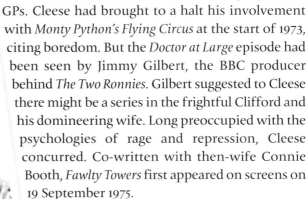

Donald and Beatrice Sinclair, inspiration for *Fawlty Towers*.

GPs. Cleese had brought to a halt his involvement with *Monty Python's Flying Circus* at the start of 1973, citing boredom. But the *Doctor at Large* episode had been seen by Jimmy Gilbert, the BBC producer behind *The Two Ronnies*. Gilbert suggested to Cleese there might be a series in the frightful Clifford and his domineering wife. Long preoccupied with the psychologies of rage and repression, Cleese concurred. Co-written with then-wife Connie Booth, *Fawlty Towers* first appeared on screens on 19 September 1975.

Nearly four decades later *Fawlty Towers* is regarded widely as the glittering peak of television situation comedy; in 2002, the British Film Institute placed it top in a poll of television's 100 greatest programmes. Just as Walter Mitty has come to stand for the fantasist and Alf Garnett for the bigot, so has Basil Fawlty become shorthand for the resentful and incompetent host, the unacceptable face of the service industry. His arrival was well timed, for he appeared just as social mobility was allowing more of the British to be served. Fawlty was the embodiment, yet also the nemesis, of this newly aspirational British lower-middle class, with its golf weekends and gourmet nights, its wedding parties and patio extensions. He was a bitter social climber, trapped in a hamster-wheel of humiliation.

Donald Sinclair died in 1981; Beatrice – the original of Basil's formidable wife Sybil – followed in 2010. She went to her grave maintaining that, while her husband certainly didn't suffer fools, the show had overstated wildly. 'Donald came to me and said they [the Monty Python team] should go,' she recalled in 2002. 'He said they would upset the other guests. But it was off-season and they were filming for about three weeks and I argued that it was good money. The entire cast behaved so badly it defied belief.'

Reading Michael Palin's diary, though, it's difficult to give the account credence; the rump of the team stayed one night only and those who stayed were off filming during the day. The Sinclairs' daughter Helen wouldn't be drawn, though she did make mention in an interview of her mother's 'challenging spirit', while former employees lined up to recall the 'extraordinary experience' of working there. John Cleese, meanwhile, always responds tartly to any accusation of exaggeration: 'My recollection is somewhat different from Mrs Sinclair's,' he told Torquay's *Herald Express*.

The real truth of Donald Sinclair, of course, is drowned out by a laughter that echoes through time, to say nothing of cultural history. What can be said with certainty is that the essence of a very recognisable Glaswegian type – rough, ready and rather reactionary – will live forever at the highest level of comedy legend.

And the hotel itself? Now run by the Best Western chain, the Gleneagles Hotel was renamed . . . the Hotel Gleneagles. The name was reordered following – appositely enough – a complaint from the original Gleneagles Hotel in Perthshire.

CRAIG FERGUSON
(comic, 1962–)

Like a political fixer, Ferguson has, to a quite astonishing extent, fallen upwards, ascending to Parnassian heights in spite of a somewhat oily demeanour few audiences have ever found remotely engaging. The *Mary Celeste* and the assassination of John F. Kennedy present mysteries less baffling than Ferguson's daydream tickertape victory parade through American network television.

As recounted in his (admittedly quite readable) memoir *American on Purpose*, Ferguson grew up in the satellite town of Cumbernauld, location of *Gregory's Girl* and of *Cumbernauld Hit*, then moved to Glasgow in time to pop up, Zelig-like, during the final days of the punk boom. He played drums in the Dreamboys, with Peter Capaldi, then developed dependencies on drink and drugs that it took until the early 1990s to conquer. In the meantime, Ferguson became a comic; first as Bing Hitler, a desperate attempt to board the bad-taste bandwagon set rolling by Jerry Sadowitz and Bill Hicks, then as himself in an instantly forgotten 'alternative comedy' sketch show, *2000 Not Out*, made in Glasgow by the Comedy Unit. Ferguson dallied with acting and writing until he relocated to Los Angeles in 1996 and landed a small but regular role on *The Drew Carey Show*, a sitcom based, *Roseanne*-style, around the life of its titular star. With this show Ferguson parlayed his passage into films, writing and appearing in the hairdressing mockumentary *The Big Tease* (1999) and in the rural farce *Saving Grace* (2000).

The Late Late Show, the chat show he began hosting in 2005, was something of a godsend for Ferguson inasmuch as it asked little of him beyond an ability to whoop his studio audience into orgasmic hysteria and to ask Jennifer Aniston when her new movie was due in theatres. These talents notwithstanding, Ferguson is a rather vexing figure, short of any distinct comic voice or perspective, and sustained principally by an almost messianic, half-admirable, half-creepy, refusal to acknowledge his limitations.

FRANCIE AND JOSIE
(double act, 1962–1970)

In the second half of the century Glasgow watched as its comedy made a circular journey, from the variety theatres then to television then back to the theatres, only this time in nostalgic and sentimental triumph. The trip was undertaken by virtually every major member of Glasgow's comedy old guard, perhaps the sole meaningful absence being (the by now late) Lex McLean. As the 1990s approached, Stanley Baxter, Johnny Beattie, Jimmy Logan, Walter Carr, Chic Murray, Una McLean and Dorothy Paul were treading the boards still, but in a kind of emeritus capacity, as elders of the tribe, as embodiments of a tradition that was vanishing rapidly.

Jack Milroy and Rikki Fulton as the gullible and garrulous street-corner philosophers Francie and Josie.

Francie: See that Mary, Queen of Scots, I meant to ask you – what was that big plaque in the middle of the floor there?

Josie: That was where Rizzio fell.

Francie: Ah'm no' surprised, Ah nearly tripped over it myself. That's dangerous, they should have a wee sign – Watch Plaque. Plaque Must Be Watched.

Josie: No, you see, it's all to do with events that took place in the sixteenth century.

Francie: Sixteenth century – is that AD or BC?

Josie: Awa' and don't be stupid, they didn't have electricity in they days.

Of all these names, none enjoyed affection of the intensity that attached to Francie and Josie, incarnated by Jack Milroy and Rikki Fulton. As lovable layabouts and street-corner philosophers the duo introduced a twist to the classic stage partnership formula, that of a dominant character interacting with a stupider one. With Francie and Josie each was the stupider one; each strove to outdo the other in their ignorance of the world, the fairer sex and the social niceties.

This was the principal conceit of the routine, that the dim and puppyish Francie took as his fount of all knowledge Josie, an individual rather more plausible but equally dim-witted. The joke was intensified by the pair's styling. In their lurid over-tight suits, brothel creepers and bootlace ties Fulton and Milroy were aping the Teddy Boys, the prevailing youth tribe of the era in which Francie and Josie emerged. This lent a layer of topical lampoon to the routine, doubly effective in that the Teddy Boys – then considered rather thuggish – were debating, or were attempting to, matters of high-flown consequence, and Glasgow audiences have always loved watching characters trying, but failing, to better themselves. Possibly they felt the joke echoed their own lives. Later, as the Teddy

Boys passed into memory, Francie and Josie assumed a layer of sentimentality, a remembrance of things past.

The characters were created by writer Stan Mars in 1960, for a routine during a run of the *Five Past Eight Show* at the Alhambra Theatre in Waterloo Street. Stanley Baxter played Francie. The characters were grownup versions of two street urchins Mars had created for an earlier show. When Baxter relocated to London, Mars reworked his scripts and, with Jack Milroy stepping in, produced in 1962 *The Adventures of Francie and Josie*, a six-part series for STV. The shows were hugely popular and turned the duo into household names. Two further series followed, though the recordings were wiped and no episodes survive today.

'We discovered this quite incredible rapport,' Fulton would recall. 'It was a sort of joyous thing. We both seemed to delight in working together. And things that had been only moderately funny before suddenly got great belly-laughs. The roof was coming off.' Glen Michael played character parts on the television shows and, when Milroy was ill, even replaced him briefly, as Francie's cousin. 'One week I would be an Arab chief, the next an American oil tycoon, then the boss of MI5 in a spoof spy story. Every week was a challenge and I loved it. I was always a comedy character the boys could feed off.'

'The queues went right down from the box office to the Mitchell Library,' Jack Milroy said, recalling the duo's heyday at the King's Theatre in Glasgow. 'I'd been on holiday and missed the first three shows going out. I bumped into Rikki in London. He said, "Have you been to Glasgow? You won't believe what's happening. I came back to Glasgow, I went in for petrol and everyone was shouting, 'Oh, hello china, how's it goin'?' I couldn't believe it. Kids coming out of school, they were all doing the Francie and Josie walk. It was ridiculous."'

By the time *The Adventures of Francie and Josie* completed its STV run Mars was heading south to write for Harry Secombe and Dickie Henderson. Fulton secured his permission to take up the writing reins. Francie and Josie persisted in a range of stage shows and pantomimes until their farewell production at the King's Theatre in Glasgow in 1996. Today, Francie and Josie reside in the pantheon of the city's comedy, for the unrelentingly cheerful delight of their material and for the role they played in teaching the city to laugh at itself.

GREGORY'S GIRL

'Did you know, twelve tons of cornflakes pass under this bridge each day?'

THE GIRL IN THE PICTURE
(film, 1986, directed by Cary Parker)

If imitation is the sincerest form of flattery, *The Girl in the Picture* flattered Bill Forsyth as though he moonlighted as a North Korean dictator. Throughout the history of cultural production few works have ever been quite so imitative of another as *The Girl in the Picture*. We could almost see the pencil outline on the sheet of tracing paper. Like much of Forsyth's output to that point, *The Girl in the Picture* was a modest, winsome comedy in which a gentle Scottish male struggled to match his daydreams to his real life. In Forsyth's films, this male was often played by John Gordon Sinclair, just as he was in *The Girl in the Picture*, with an identical degree of affable puzzlement.

Our hero is Alan, a photographer who subsidises his art by churning out family portraiture in the Snappy Snaps studio in Glasgow's West End. Alan lives with Mary, a willowy undergraduate of a calibre few men tend to take issue with. Alan does, of course, and embarks upon a gloomy quest to replace her, before eventually coming to appreciate his folly and engineering a reunion. Along the way he runs across the contents of Bill Forsyth's wastepaper bin; characters who display the same distracted charm as Forsyth's but only a fraction of their originality: Smiley (Paul Young), the studio proprietor, growing tomatoes in his darkroom; Ken the assistant (David McKay), forever thwarted in love; Bill (Gregor Fisher), a half-hearted groom; and Sheila and Fiona, a pair of chirpy lesbians.

None of this is to say *The Girl in the Picture* is without merit. For several reasons it is worth tracking down a VHS (the film did not earn a release on DVD). Aficionados of film location porn will relish its shots of the West End in the 1980s, particularly of Glasgow University, Kelvingrove Park and the corner of Partickhill where the Snappy Snaps studio was sited; Glasgow is rendered as leafy and implausibly scenic. The performances are good Caledonian repertory stuff and, ultimately, it's all quite obliging, soppy and painless. And astonishingly derivative. Its writer and director, Cary Parker, never made another film. These facts may not be unconnected.

THE GLASGOW EMPIRE
(variety theatre, 1931–1963)

Not since the operational heyday of the Tower of London has a venue aroused so much terror in so many breasts. For comedians, and particularly those raised south of Carlisle, the Glasgow Empire could be the worst place in the world – a Room 101 with choc-ices. Legendarily, it was the theatre of cruelty, proverbial graveyard of English comics. Even today, when two or three old stagers gather together out will come the Glasgow Empire anecdotes, burnished with the Brasso of fond memory and a half-century of rehearsal. The day-rooms of many a Surrey showbiz retirement home echo yet with the horrors of first house on a rainy Tuesday.

Common sense tells us the Glasgow Empire could never have been all it was reputed to be. The theatre was in business for over three decades, yet we hear the same handful of war stories repeatedly.

The graveyard of English comics – the Glasgow Empire on West Nile Street.

Remember also that the theatre was staging an average of fifteen shows each week. It's probably more accurate to conclude that the fearsome reputation of the Empire has much to do with the popularity in the 1970s of the television chat show. The veterans of variety theatre – Morecambe & Wise, Ken Dodd, Frankie Howerd, Bob Monkhouse *et al* – became fixtures on these shows, as hosted by Russell Harty, Michael Parkinson and the like. Tales recounting the terrors of the Glasgow Empire were welcome for two reasons: because the stories tended to be lurid and funny in themselves, and because they upheld the view of Glasgow that the southern suburbs

The so-called graveyard of English comics was the location of some of the best-known horror stories in the annals of British show business.

Dame Shirley Bassey

The minute she walked in the joint she could tell it would be a gig of distinction, though perhaps not in the way she'd hoped. As an aspiring eighteen-year-old, Shirley Bassey played the Empire in 1955, hoping to become a fixture on the prestigious Moss Empires circuit. 'As I sat backstage at the Empire,' she recalled, 'I could hear this terrible noise coming from the hall. There was a juggler on stage and the abuse from the audience was incredible. He was so scared he was dropping balls all over the place. I'd never heard anything like it. A comedian went on next and the abuse got even louder. They were constantly shouting out and putting him off. It was dreadful.' The treatment continued when Bassey took the stage, obliging her to perform her livelier numbers earlier to buy time. 'I walked to the edge of the stage and said, "Now listen here – in a broad Welsh accent they probably couldn't understand – I've come tonight to entertain you lot and if you don't want to listen, then I may as well bloody go home." The abuse stopped and they sat quietly through the rest of my act.'

Max Miller

Following his debut engagement at the Empire, the comic was contacted by its booker, Cissie Williams, and asked if he'd like to return. 'I'm a comic,' he replied, 'not a missionary.'

Des O'Connor

The singer and comedian has gone down in legend as having found the Empire so daunting he fainted on stage, though he has argued the collapse was a strategy to curtail his performance. O'Connor's account has it that, only a month into his showbusiness career, he'd been placed on a bill following a Glaswegian husband and wife accordion act, the male half of which had died in a road accident the previous week. Accompanied by her nephew, the wife was on stage when she was overcome suddenly by weeping. Half prepared, O'Connor was rushed out to take over, whereupon he discovered an immovable pall had been cast over the evening. 'Why doesn't anybody laugh in this town?' he asked a stagehand. Having struggled vainly for some minutes, O'Connor opted to vacate the stage by feigning collapse. The head of the bandleader emerged over the lip of the stage, inquiring, 'Is this in the act, son?' For years after, Eric Morecambe described O'Connor as the only comic selling advertising space on the soles of his shoes.

Will Fyffe

Though from Dundee, the singer, actor and comic entered the city's pantheon in 1920 when he penned 'I Belong to Glasgow', soon adopted as an unofficial civic anthem. He was a frequent visitor to the Empire. On discovering that the theatre was staging a Will Fyffe lookalike contest the comic adopted heavy disguise and entered himself. He came second.

Morecambe & Wise

Having already ensured that £10 danger money would supplement their fee, the popular comics arrived at the Empire's stage door in West Nile Street. Morecambe pointed out to Wise some nearby roadworks. 'They're digging our grave already,' he told him. The performance itself was received with silent indifference and the weary duo trudged offstage. In the wings was the theatre's duty fireman, who nodded to the audience. 'They're beginning to like you,' he said.

Harry Houdini

In the too-good-to-check category is the legend that Houdini, the greatest escapologist in history, accidentally locked himself into a Glasgow Empire toilet.

Victor Seaforth

It took until the comic impressionist's fourth visit to the Empire for trouble to start. He was performing in the late 1950s with the American rock'n'roll singer Charlie Gracie but was interrupted constantly by fans screaming for the headliner. So impassioned were the cries that Seaforth had to stop his act thirteen minutes early. 'I felt physically sick knowing I had to go on in the second half, and when it was time for my entrance all I could hear was, "Bring on Charlie Gracie!"' he wrote. 'I broke into a cold sweat, knowing that I had to finish on my impression of Charles Laughton as Quasimodo, the Hunchback of Notre Dame. 'I tried to announce what my final impression was going to be, but that was pointless as all I could hear was the endless "Bring on Charlie Gracie!" I proceeded to get myself into the character, the lights went down to green spots, and there I was all twisted up going into the dialogue. A really loud Scottish voice shouted, "Away hame, you humpy-backed old bastard!" Still as the Hunchback, I worked my way up to the mic and looked up into the Circle. "Don't you recognise your father?" I said in my loudest voice. It was the longest week of my life.'

Ken Dodd

'Freud said that the essence of the comic was the conservation of psychic energy. But then Freud never played second house Friday night at the Glasgow Empire.'

Mike & Bernie Winters

The best-known Empire anecdote probably concerns Mike and Bernie, a slick double act popular in the 1960s. Mike was the suave straight man and Bernie the gurning comedian. On the night in question Mike appeared on stage first, hoping to warm up the crowd. His jokes, however, were being met with stony silence, so brother Bernie decided to join him so the act proper might get underway. He popped his head round the curtain to announce he was on his way when an audience member in the stalls spotted him. 'Oh Christ,' he shouted, 'there's two of them . . .'

already held. The Empire anecdote belonged to a certain genre, in which growling shipyard workers struggled to keep their tempers in check, certain they could smell the blood of an Englishman – a kind of showbusiness fairy in reverse.

The natives, though, had fonder memories altogether. 'I remember walking down from the STV studios one day and bumping into a bloke as he came around the corner,' wrote Glen Michael in his autobiography *Life's a Cavalcade*. 'Stopping in his tracks, his jaw dropped and I thought he was about to have a heart attack.

'Where is it?' he gasped.

'Where's what?'

'The Empire,' he burst out.

'I told him it was no longer there and, nearly in tears, he told me that he'd been abroad for about ten years, and the one thing that had kept him going when he was homesick was the thought that one day he would be back and could go to the second house Saturday at the Glasgow Empire. He had his money ready in his hand, poor soul!'

THE GLASGOW SMILE

Definition: nickname for the form of gangland punishment that involves cutting a victim's face from the edges of the mouth to the ear, the cut, or its scars, forming an 'extension' that resembles a smile.

The Urban Dictionary

GLASGOW INTERNATIONAL COMEDY FESTIVAL
(event, 2002–)

Founded as British stand-up comedy was embarking upon its current arena-capable phase, the Glasgow International Comedy Festival is an attempt to rival those fixtures of the global comedy circuit, Toronto and Melbourne. Under the directorship of Tommy Sheppard, proprietor of The Stand comedy venues in Glasgow, Edinburgh and Newcastle, the festival ranges now from gigs in pubs to huge benefit shows for charity, involving comics, such as Kevin Bridges, whose careers were developed in Sheppard's clubs.

GLASGOW'S MILES BETTER
(tourism slogan, 1983–1989)

Nearly three decades after the fact, the Glasgow's Miles Better interlude still feels like a mild hallucination, something it is difficult to accept really happened. Oh, to have been present when the campaign was mooted; to have witnessed the orgy of ingenuity needed to make the case that Glasgow's PR problem was addressed best by a bulbous, canary-yellow cartoon character named Mr Happy.

Except it didn't quite happen like that. It all began in New York City, a decade earlier. With crime in the city running rampant, New York was in dire need of regeneration. Graphic designer Milton Glaser conceived the I ♥ NY campaign, and it kick-started the resuscitation of the city's self-confidence. By the early 1980s, something similar was needed in Glasgow, or so thought Michael Kelly, Glasgow's energetic Lord Provost, bedevilled as the city was by socio-economic woe. Glasgow was in a Catch-22: without inward investment little could improve, but why, Kelly pondered, would private enterprise wish to invest in 'a dark, dangerous and dismal conglomeration of slum housing, religious bigotry and urban decay'?

One solution was to change perceptions. Kelly consulted John Struthers, an advertising veteran in the city. 'I need a slogan I can die for,' he told him. During a trip to London Struthers conceived the Mr Happy concept, reasoning that a degree of levity had worked for the Big Apple. Kelly loved it. Glasgow City Council, though, felt differently. 'Councillors objected to spending money on "advertising" when so many roofs needed repairing,' Kelly recalled. The council declined to back the campaign financially until funding had been secured from the private sector, which it duly was. Before long the Glasgow's Miles Better campaign had received the greatest tribute possible, when Mr Happy hoardings were banned from the buses of Edinburgh.

Today, traces of Mr Happy are still to found in the strangest places – on gasometers, murals and the like. He can appear when you least expect it, like a mugger in reverse, a cheerful reminder of the least likely saviour any city ever had. He was even brought back, briefly, in 2004, in an echo of one of the most bizarre, brave and flamboyant gambles in civic history.

'THE GLASGOW UNDERGROUND'
(song, 1963)

Written by the novelist, playwright and newspaperman Cliff Hanley, a figure of ubiquity in Glasgow for many decades, this ditty was associated particularly with Francie and Josie, who would interpose their discursive ramblings between choruses. Though Hanley's original was scarcely more than a nursery rhyme, it articulated, as did many songs in the Glasgow folk tradition, the city's comically exaggerated self-image, as a place so inherently splendid that even its bowels were delightful.

> I know a lot of folk go to fancy places at the Fair
> They like to sail on steamers or to hurtle through the air
> But I've a favourite route that goes to many ports of call

Although unless you looked you'd never notice it at all

The Glasgow Underground, 1974.

Chorus
There's Partick Cross and Cessnock,
Hillheid and Merkland Street,
George's Cross and Govan Cross,
Where a' the people meet
West Street, Shields Road
The train goes round and round
Oh it's lovely going your holidays
On the Glasgow Underground

JOHN GLASHAN
(cartoonist, 1927–1999)

The name John Glashan may be unfamiliar, but the style of his cartooning won't be. Glashan, who was born in Glasgow and went to Glasgow School of Art, was a cornerstone of the broadsheet press, and of magazines such as the *Spectator* and *Private Eye*, throughout the 1960s and 1970s – even today, the merest glimpse of his hand stirs a Pavlovian urge to play the *White Album* while opposing the war in Vietnam.

More precisely, classic Glashan came in two styles: the scrawled,

mordant quickies he produced for *Private Eye* (a glum man tells the clerk in a Labour Exchange 'I want some means to live beyond'; another Labour Exchange functionary tells a client 'No jobs for a genius, we could retrain you to drag things across a steel floor') and Glashan's most abiding creation, the Genius series that he drew for the *Observer*, in which were chronicled the absurd and epic adventures of Anode Enzyme and his companion Lord Doberman, often in a style more painterly than illustrative, a fantasia of Gothic psychedelia in which tiny, scribbled punchlines would skulk at the foot of vast, elaborate depictions of cathedrals or art galleries. Anticipating the graphic novel, Glashan's work was a reflection, some say, of his troubled character, engendered by his inability to prosper as a fine artist, as his father, Archibald McGlashan, president of Glasgow Art Club, had done. Once, when giving a speech at the Royal College of Art, Glashan took the stage, shouted at the students, 'You're wasting your time, all of you!' and walked off. A similar spirit pervades his clever, glum and edgy work.

PASTOR JACK GLASS
(preacher, 1936–2004)

Throughout the 1970s, few afforded Glaswegians such a constant supply of evil mirth as Pastor Jack Glass. Only Billy Connolly came close. The pairing was apposite; Connolly and Glass engaged in verbal combat throughout that decade, though Glass was plainly and hilariously oblivious to the reality that he was unlikely to emerge the victor.

Unblinking and intense, Glass was a Protestant fundamentalist and Biblical literalist of singular conviction – even the Reverend Ian Paisley was said to consider him 'a bit of an extremist'. Glass's favoured causes were the maintenance of the Unionist status quo in Northern Ireland and resistance to Papal authority, though Connolly gave him a target that was conveniently local. As Ron

Ferguson of the *Herald* wrote in Glass's obituary: 'He would go anywhere to protest about the Pope, the Church of Scotland, Billy Connolly, the ecumenical movement, religious satires, sexually explicit movies, bad language and tolerance of gays.'

And go anywhere the Pastor did, becoming as much a fixture in the Glaswegian newspapers of the period as the sports reports. Connolly's sketch 'The Crucifixion' was the one to which Glass took particular exception. Its depiction of Jesus as a gallus Glaswegian convening his apostles in the Saracen's Head pub was one Glass considered the very definition of blasphemy, an opinion he was seldom slow to disseminate on the occasions Connolly returned to the city. A typical example came in March 1980 when Connolly was the guest of honour at a Variety Club dinner in the Central Hotel. Glass and his Twentieth Century Reformation Movement held a demonstration outside the hotel, during which a bag containing 30 pieces of 'silver' was thrown at the comic. 'You've got the right initials – W.C.,' shouted Glass. 'You're a walking water closet.'

Connolly somehow withstood this. 'I'm not a blasphemer,' he told reporters. 'I think nothing of these people. They are nothing.' Previously, though, his attitude to Glass, while adverse, at least acknowledged that the pair were locked in some kind of elemental battle, however one-sided. Glass was made to appear frequently in the Big Yin strip in the *Sunday Mail*, co-written often by Connolly; on one occasion it featured Pastor Jack's Fun Page, which included a join-the-dots puzzle and an illustration of the Pastor with a badge reading 'Ra Pope's a Stoatir', with 'Spot the Deliberate Mistake' appended beneath. The pair's antipathy fizzled out in the 1980s as Connolly visited Glasgow less frequently. It ceased for good in 2004 when Glass died from lung cancer.

Yet the Pastor's humorous potential wasn't activated solely by Connolly. In 1969, miscreants attacked the church he ran in Calder Street, Polmadie. Surveying the damage, he was asked by a reporter to whom he attributed the vandalism. Jack Glass mused upon his answer gravely. 'Religious fanatics,' he replied.

JANEY GODLEY
(comic and writer, 1961–)

In many ways, Godley resembles an observational comedy octopus (not physically, that would be horrible). She has dipped a tentacle into every comedic puddle possible – live stand-up, radio presentation, television (as both performer and talking head), newspapers, compering, playwriting, charity fundraising, memoir, blogging, acting, podcasting and tweeting. You name it and she'll do you five minutes, some of which will no doubt touch upon her upbringing (Dickensian), her family (terrifying), her sexual abuse (by an uncle), her mother (murdered) or her first marriage (to a Glasgow gangster). In search of a quieter life, Godley then became a publican in the Calton, which is a bit like becoming a paramedic in Brixton. At the Weavers Inn Godley staged the first performance by Jerry Sadowitz. She recalled this period of her life in her best-selling autobiography, *Handstands in the Dark,* in an anecdote revealing how, in Glasgow, three-year- old children can develop easy intimacy with infamous murderers:

Davey (Bryce) was not the only person involved in running the Calton Athletic Support Group. One other, well-dressed man often came to the pub to collect the keys for their meetings. I knew Old George disliked the man and, one evening, when I was sitting with Ashley (Godley's infant daughter) waiting for Old George to arrive at the Weavers, I looked through a window and the neatly dressed man was standing in the street outside.

'Oh fuck!' I said without thinking. 'All I need is Old George to walk in now!'

'Who is that man?' Ashley asked.

I grabbed our fat bunch of keys and muttered, 'He's someone who was locked up in prison for killing another man and he smeared his own shit up the cell wall.' I ran towards the door and looked out to see if Old George had parked his car yet. It was OK: there was no car yet, but he was due at any time. I did not want to talk to the man.

'Ashley,' I said quickly, 'go and give these keys to him for me.'

She happily trotted off and approached the well-dressed man, who smiled down at her. 'Hello,' she said brightly, 'are you the man who killed someone and spread jobbies up the walls?'

I gasped, but I heard the man laugh. 'Yes, I am. How did you know that? Are you Mij's niece? You sound a lot like the wee girl he told me about. Do you have an uncle called Jim?'

'Yes, I am Ashley Storrie. What is your name?'

'I am Jimmy Boyle.'

He looked over her head at me and smiled through the window. I did not smile back.

ALASDAIR GRAY
(writer and artist, 1934–)

The shortfall in the quantity of Glaswegian comic novels has long been counterbalanced by the work of Alasdair Gray. The novels, plays and short stories Gray writes are seldom in themselves comic; rather, they tend to be quixotic and fanciful, admixtures of science fiction, psychological brutalism, political theory and literary pornography.

If Gray's work has any unifying quality it is that of acute self-awareness – of the social, cultural and historical processes that have shaped contemporary Scotland. That self-awareness extends to Gray's status as writer. He is not an author who retires into the background; he is always somewhere in the vicinity, orchestrating the reader's experience. Usually, Gray has designed and illustrated the book you hold. Sometimes he appears as a character in his own tale, as he does in *Lanark*, explaining to Duncan Thaw why he has created for him such an unhappy fate. Or Gray plays practical jokes, most famously by inserting in the first edition of *Unlikely Stories, Mostly* an erratum slip which declared 'This Slip Has Been Inserted By Mistake'. Other books, particularly *Lanark*, explain in detail from where Gray plagiarised incidents and dialogue in the narrative.

And, sometimes, Gray adopts the role of critic, putting on the covers of his books fictional newspaper reviews by non-existent writers, explaining the deficiencies of the work therein. They are funnier than the proper writing of most authors.

The Fall of Kelvin Walker (1985)
'A slander upon the tribulations besetting the early career of a great and good man.'
Peter Geikie, *The Sunday Post*

Unlikely Stories, Mostly (1983)
'Too clever for its own good in parts, but otherwise a damned good read.'
Col. Sebastian Moran in *The Simla Times*

Something Leather (1990)
'Despite the plot's elaborate Keltic knotwork, despite some crafty baits for the prurient, I doubt this book will be taken seriously south of the border – or north of it either.'
Author's own dust jacket comment

Poor Things (1992)
Erratum slip: 'The etching on page 187 does not portray Professor Jean Martin Charcot, but Count Robert de Montesquiou-Fezensac.'

Novelist and artist Alasdair Gray in Glasgow's Necropolis cemetery.

GREGORY'S GIRL
(film, 1981, directed by Bill Forsyth)

The cinematic equivalent of finding an ex-girlfriend's knickers down the back of the sofa, *Gregory's Girl* floors us with its sentimental force, with the acuity of its evocation of adolescent yearning. Grown men depart screenings insisting they have something gritty in their eye. The movie is as disarming as the sight of a kitten climbing out of a Wellington boot.

There's something supernaturally insightful about the film, something magically redolent of every tortured teenage moment: the sniggery outbreaks of boyish prurience; the shifts spent outside the local chippie; the negotiations required to get the right girl to the right place at the right time; the sexual urban myths that swell in the telling; the ceaseless teenage seesaw between arrogance and uncertainty. What *Gregory's Girl* gets particularly right, though, is its atmospherics. Its climax takes place across one of those unending evenings of early summer, the proper dominion of the young and the carefree.

The film captures beautifully, also, the essence of the Scottish secondary school as half institution and half adventure playground. At Cumbernauld High there are no proms, no pupils who drive themselves to school in new Ferraris; nobody bursts into song in the canteen. There's just the servitude of lessons and the compensatory

Chic Murray as the piano-playing headmaster of Cumbernauld High in *Gregory's Girl*.

rumour-mongering in the corridors and stairwells.

Forsyth set his film in Cumbernauld, the third New Town built in Scotland, because he wanted surroundings the same age as the characters, as square and gawky as the boys and girls themselves. There are parents, too, resentful that their homes are incubating these creatures in metamorphosis. 'Christ, you're worse that my dad,' one schoolgirl tells our hero. 'He's old – at least he's got an excuse for being a prick.'

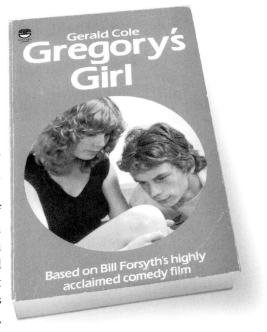

In Cumbernauld, thirteen miles northeast of Glasgow's city centre, Gregory Underwood (John Gordon Sinclair, though credited here under his birth name of Gordon John Sinclair) lives in teenaged limbo. He spends his days practising on his drum kit or at school among a coterie of adolescent eccentrics pursuing their micro-obsessions such as photography, fashion and females. It is with these characters that Forsyth's passion truly lies, as we might expect of a director who cut his teeth at the Glasgow Youth Theatre. Obsessed personally with the dreamy passage of adolescence, Forsyth is *simpatico* with the pair who are hiking to Caracas because the city boasts a favourable ratio of women to men; or with the schoolmaster (Chic Murray) who taps out music-hall standards on his study piano ('Off you go, you small boys!'), with the child who waddles around the school dressed, mysteriously, in a penguin costume, the boy with an abiding interest in the logistics of road freight ('Did you know, twelve tons of cornflakes pass under this bridge each day?').

Gregory is centre-forward in his school football team; a role he fulfils, like so much in his life, with a certain goofy levity. Team coach Phil (Jake D'Arcy) switches him to goalkeeper and replaces him with, horror of horrors, a girl, the bonny but straight talking Dorothy (Dee Hepburn), who swiftly becomes the focus of Gregory's romantic interest while she helps him sharpen his football technique. Gregory finds himself further schooled in feminine wiles when the girls of Cumbernauld High contrive to save Dorothy from his fumblings and pair him with Susan (Clare Grogan), a character every bit as sweet and quixotic as Gregory. After an evening of horizontal dancing in the country park Gregory realises he is in love and ready to emerge from his languid cocoon of awkwardness.

'Hard work being in love, eh?' says Gregory's precociously knowing little sister Madeline. 'Especially when you don't know which girl it is.'

It would be easy to dismiss *Gregory's Girl* as a trifle, as though it were merely a superior offering from, say, the Children's Film Foundation. But this scarcely accounts for its longevity, or for the uniquely tender place it occupies in Glaswegian hearts. The film depicts our yesterdays adroitly but is infinitely more than a cinematic high-school yearbook. It is a tale deftly told, full of reversals and inversions: children, like Madeline, who behave like adults; girls, like Dorothy, who behave like boys; teachers who behave like pupils; pupils who behave like get-rich-quick entrepreneurs; small boys who behave like penguins. Like *Tutti Frutti*, the film persists because its message is timeless: there will forever be a need to be reminded of the merciful agency of women and their civilising effect upon menfolk of each and every age.

ANNIE GRIFFIN
(writer and director, 1960–present)

Proof that Glasgow's self-obsession can survive outwith the host entity is furnished by Annie Griffin, the New York emigré whose work presents an obtusely hilarious view of the city's middle classes. In Griffin's world, neurosis and self-interest infest anyone who dares declare possession of finer feelings. In *The Book Group* (2002–2003), which ran to two series on Channel Four, sexual jealousy runs rife through a group of misfits meeting regularly in the west end to discuss literature. In *Coming Soon* (1999), a three-part drama and Griffin's masterpiece, a troupe of avant-garde thespians are forced for funding reasons on a tour of God-forsaken Clyde-estuary holiday resorts: the reaction the citizens of Saltcoats give *Blood and Oatmeal*, the troupe's improvised tour de force, lingers long in the memory.

Having moved, both physically and creatively, to Edinburgh, Griffin lavished similar attention upon the city's annual arts jamboree in the film *Festival*, and in the architectural comedy series *New Town*. Displaying a preternatural grasp of local idioms and concerns, Griffin's work is in a Glasgow tradition that endorses egalitarianism and plain-dealing, though with a comedic sophistication few have equalled, fusing the city's rough wit the finesse of a *New Yorker* back issue. Her latest work is *Bob Servant Independent*, a television adaptation of the popular Bob Servant books.

GROUNDSKEEPER WILLIE
(animated character voiced by Dan Castellaneta, *The Simpsons*, 1989–)

He is one of the most fondly regarded characters in the world's favourite animated comedy, but is Groundskeeper Willie a Glaswegian? The debate is ongoing. It has been stated in the show more than once that Willie, janitor of Springfield Elementary School and the living embodiment of every unhappy school functionary we encountered during our childhoods, does indeed hail from Glasgow, though alternative locations have been identified in the show, too, among them Orkney and Aberdeen. It all underlines the old claim that anyone aiming to confuse an American should show them a map.

Groundskeeper Willie, ferocious school janitor in *The Simpsons*.

The Teachings of Groundskeeper Willie

'Now, the kilt was only for day-to-day wear. In battle, we donned a full-length ball gown covered in sequins. The idea was to blind your opponent with luxury.'

'Brothers and sisters are natural enemies. Like Englishmen and Scots! Or Welshmen and Scots! Or Japanese and Scots! Or Scots and other Scots! Damn Scots! They ruined Scotland!'

'I warned ya. Didn't I warn ya? That coloured chalk was forged by Lucifer himsel'.'

'If elected mayor my first act will be to kill the whole lot of ya, and burn your town to cinders!'

'Get your haggis, right here! Chopped heart and lungs boiled in a wee sheep's stomach! Tastes as good as it sounds.'

Certainly, so far as the cartoon's Californian creators might define them, the growling, aggressive Willie possesses all the proper Glasgow credentials: he's hairy, bellicose and quasi-feral. In one episode he defines the English as 'bath-taking, poodlewalking, noodle-armed underpant-wearers' and, famously, he considers the French to be 'cheese-eating surrender monkeys'. Spiritual native Willie may be, but it can't be claimed Glasgow was where Willie was born. In the episode 'Monty Can't Buy Me Love' Willie, Homer and Monty Burns visit the Scottish Highlands with a plan to kidnap the Loch Ness Monster. Willie revisits the pub featuring the very pool table upon which he claims he was 'conceived, born and educated'. Yet clearly he relocated early, for in an episode spoofing *Mary Poppins* we hear of Willie's relationship with nanny Shary Bobbins. This relationship went well enough while Shary was experiencing a bout of blindness. On regaining her sight, though, Shary reconsiders her position and, 'Suddenly, the ugliest man in Glasgow wasn't good enough for her,' Willie rages. Case, as they say, closed.

'The Glaswegian knows life is meant to be hell, but by God he can take it, especially under an anaesthetic'

CLIFF HANLEY
Glasgow Herald, 2 January 1990

Parochial heresy apart, we are the people

If we spend our life in one place, it is tempting and natural to assume that that place is the world. The language, the customs, the habits, are common to everybody. Any variation, if we happen to look briefly at other places, is some kind of mistake. We are the norm. We were handed down on tablets on Mount Sinai. (We can't quite recall where that is – probably the Southside.)

My own name for this delusion is the parochial heresy. I once met a Glasgow woman, a bit after the last war, who had finally managed to visit relatives in New York, and she was absolutely enraptured to report that that far-flung city had acquired a branch of Glasgow's own shop, Woolworth's. She was serious.

So I approach the nature of the Glaswegian with a lot of caution. My father worked for the Anchor Line, he was crazy about New

York and probably knew Manhattan better than he knew Maryhill. So did he represent the Glasgow character, or did that daft woman?

My money tends to go on him. But in analysing the Glasgow character – and sometimes I feel I have been doing nothing else since I left school – I am apprehensive. I have travelled a lot, and I know where Woolworth's came from; but I am still observing Glasgow from inside, my marrow is infused with the place, and I could be a parochial heretic without knowing it.

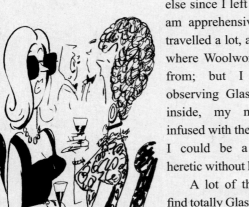

"Don't you agree that the quality of life in Giffnock is vastly superior to that of Newton Mearns, Fiona?"

A lot of the things I find totally Glaswegian can no doubt be found in Newcastle and Liverpool and quite possibly Rostov. The analysts try to hoist themselves and view the place from above, so that we can see the blotto, undersized citizens, speaking a dense aboriginal patois as they crawl along the gutters, mumbling Will Fyffe's immortal words, 'Well, a man's got to get home, hasn't he?'

He is the archetypal Glaswegian. He is a slightly skilled worker in a heavy industry, he quite fancies the birds but in practice prefers the boozer and his masculine mates, he knows life is meant to be hell, but by God he can take it, especially under an anaesthetic.

Let's call him Hughie. I once met a successful professional chap (one does tend to meet people in Glasgow) who had risen from his slum background to make good. He then had a sore time trying to reconcile his

social life among well-spoken executives with his encounters with his scruffy Uncle Hughie. He wasn't sure whether he was being a tolerant snob to Hughie or a hypocritical sook among his exalted colleagues.

Maturity struck him one afternoon, possibly after a good lunch in town or a lot of noggins with the relatives. He realised that he belonged on both levels – and that probably a lot of his high-class chums did, too.

All Jock Tamson's bairns sort of thing, what? (Jock Tamson was a primordial Pict with a prodigious libido and a 10-speed bike.) And yes, there's truth in it. It would be silly to say that there's no snobbery in Glasgow. Snobbery is part of the fun. I myself was born on the wrong side of the tracks, in Gallowgate, and was therefore quite properly despised by folk in Dennistoun. Dennistoun, in the name of the wee man! I suppose we all have to feel superior to somebody, especially if we live in Dennistoun.

But the snobbery is harmless, and in Glasgow we try to disguise it in case somebody meets our Uncle Hughie. In Edinburgh, a city I very much like, the snobbery has more reality to it. Edinburgh folk have told me that their town is a cold, aloof place compared with mine, so I have to believe it. The Glasgow character is a friendly specimen. I generalise, but the generalisation is legitimate. He makes strangers feel at home because he's interested (she's interested, too, but the Glasgow character is still very much a masculine thing, I don't care who calls me sexist).

The keelie has a history of travel, he feels at one with faraway places, and many of us have gone to them, sometimes without the option. He is egalitarian, whether he happens to be Hughie or Hughie's nephew. He is a racial mixture, of course, but richly Celtic, if I may say that without infuriating Rangers fans. He is a citizen of the world, less in-turned than the average citizen of San Francisco. The Glaswegian, in history, has fled to this city from oppression or starvation in other places, and been glad to arrive. There was work here – the big industrial beehive, the second city of the empire, all that nonsense.

In quite rapid sequence, the great industries went down the drain. And that bred a tough acceptance of life as hard and dangerous and even disastrous. To cope with that, you have to be able to laugh. The natural comics of the world are Jews and Glaswegians because for both the joke is the survival mechanism.

We're getting near a calm analysis of the Glasgow character. It is tough, it is warm and it is funny. And those among us who pause from laughter often get right to the top, here or in London or anywhere in the world. Why? We have more resilience and more intelligence than the average bozo, and we shall survive anything. Have I lapsed into the parochial heresy? Well, it's my parish, isn't it? And isn't it the greatest parish in the world?

NAVID HARRID
(sitcom character, *Still Game*, 2002–2007)

If, as argued elsewhere here, the comedy of Glasgow is historically and inherently mongrel, if it drew its vitality and its distinctiveness from the range of voices it incorporated, whether Irish, Jewish, Italian or Highland Scots, it might be worth asking if this assimilatory process continues into the modern day. The answer is elusive. At around 65,000, the Asian population in Glasgow is its largest minority, but, whether through reticence, prejudice or cultural difference, its contribution to comedy has yet to bloom.

A recent exception has been Sanjeev Kohli, who plays Navid Harrid in the BBC sitcom *Still Game* and who co-wrote the Radio 4 series *Fags, Mags and Bags*. Kohli was involved also in *Meet the Magoons*, a Channel 4 series from 2005 set in an Indian restaurant and directed by his brother Hardeep Singh Kohli. Harrid, meanwhile, is something of a sacred monster, a fearsome, foul-mouthed sentinel of confectionery counter and biscuit aisle, fending off the schemes and scams of his wily customers. Here, Kohli, the man who plays him, considers the meaning and appeal of Navid.

'I am surprised constantly, on a daily basis even, by the popularity of Navid. Why has this bearded, sixty-something Indian Muslim shopkeeper caught fire? Possibly it has something to do with the high polyester content of his tank tops.

All I know is this: that everyone from pensioners in flat caps to freckly eight-year-olds to a rock star at T in the Park wearing a hair hat *love* him, and I am not in the habit of examining gift-horse tonsils. What it means further is guys running after me in IKEA brandishing their mobiles, asking me to call their wives '*a lazy baaastaaard*'. If that will help save their marriage, of course I oblige them.

The key to Navid – apart from the killer lines – is the authenticity. Ford Kiernan and Greg Hemphill, who wrote *every single word of Still Game*, identified a character at least one hundred people have told me is based on their own local shop owner. Each, apparently, has a line in brutal sarcastic patter. Why? Well, most successful convenience stores are successful because they are located in neighbourhoods where there is little else that is convenient; places other retailers don't bother with, or flee with their tails between their legs. And a half-brick on their parcel shelf. In other words, places that Jack and Victor (and geography lecturers) term 'shiteholes'. Often, Asian shopkeepers in these areas are the only brown faces to be seen, so they're in for stick, anyway. And, given that they have a degree of power – such as the ability to withhold Aftershocks from four-year-old purchasers – they are also in for some envy. This is intensified by the fact that they may well drive home in a tan Mercedes with a private number plate. The law, however, decrees that you cannot defuse such tension with a baseball bat, so shopkeepers have to get creative. Put simply, Navid's brutal wit is his shield against any lanky ned asking for a single fag.

The fact is that Navid, fictional though he is, may be the only 'ethnic' with whom many will have any meaningful contact. And he's sarcastic. He's funny. And he's popular. He doesn't come with the baggage other ethnic characters in television drama and comedy seem to be lumbered with. He does not get racist abuse. He is not immolating his daughter for having a white boyfriend. Hell, we wait till the end of series one before a wedding is even mentioned. He has managed to prove that we can concentrate on the 95 per cent we have in common rather than the 5 per cent that might make us different. And people can learn through comedy; mainly because it doesn't feel like they're being taught. He has, also, I think, reminded Glaswegians, and Scots, how funny their own vernacular can be. Because they take it for granted. Maybe if they are to appreciate it fully they need Navid, with his Govanhill accent, to re-present their own words back to them, on a silver salver. I cannot tell you how many times I've been asked to say 'foosty pish'. And, for the record, I'm happy to do it. *Foosty pish*.

LORD HAW-HAW
(Second World War propagandist)

Named for his braying enunciation and his fondness for mocking British military misfortune, Lord Haw-Haw was a broadcaster on *Germany Calling*, the English-language shortwave station established by the Nazis at the outset of the Second World War. Understandably unaware of how the whole affair would turn out, Haw-Haw attempted to sap morale and encourage negotiations with Germany by goading the Western Allies.

The epithet Haw-Haw was applied at various times to a variety of German English-speaking broadcasters, most famously William Joyce, but it is believed the role was filled for a spell by a Glaswegian. Eduard Dietze was a broadcaster of mixed German–British parentage. Known as a moderate, Dietze ran the German news propaganda service during the phony war of 1939–40 then adopted the Haw-Haw persona. Legendarily, the Barrowland Ballroom in Glasgow removed its distinctive rooftop sign, featuring a man pushing a barrow, after Haw-Haw described it in sufficient detail to render it identifiable to German bombers.

I

'*We're told to try and take stock of our lives but that leads to people realising that somewhere in their life they took a wrong turning. Probably about eight years ago*'

ARMANDO IANNUCCI
(writer and producer, 1963–)

With the exception of Billy Connolly, no figure reigns over modern British comedy quite so magisterially as Armando Iannucci. To discuss the topic without citing either man is like discussing Morecambe & Wise without mentioning Morecambe. Or Wise. The two Glaswegians – both of whom, curiously, attended the same primary school, St Peter's in Partick, though two decades apart – are the twin pillars upon which so much has been constructed. Connolly was to make his mark with stand-up, Iannucci in print, on radio and television. Their styles were markedly different: Connolly stayed on the street corner while Iannucci favoured a po-mo, university-wit assault on the media's treatment of politics and celebrity. Yet each man had an impact that was seismic and, particularly in the case of Iannucci, torrentially, tumultuously influential.

As a comedy producer, Iannucci had one great insight: that what we say was becoming of less importance than the manner in which we say it. In a media-saturated age, the delivery of the message was coming to outrank the message itself. Style had triumphed over substance. Iannucci had found his subject – the media, and how it paints its pictures with its palette of hysteria, speculation, insinuation and guesswork.

Iannucci's background was that of the buff, the bedroom aficionado, his teenage years spent dissecting the routines he was hearing on Monty Python records. His coming of age was concurrent with the advent of alternative comedy, with the added local gloss of the Connolly connection. 'When I grew up, Billy was a local hero, as opposed to a national and international superstar,' Iannucci told Radio Scotland. 'I was there when he was given a sort of hero's welcome back to St Peter's, except the teachers weren't too sure what to make of him. He'd done that notorious sketch about the Crucifixion, which we all recited in the playground. But this being a Catholic school I remember the teachers feeling a little bit awkward about the fact that, yes, they found it funny but must never admit that to the pupils.'

Innately studious, Iannucci undertook a degree in English literature at University College, Oxford, then began a PhD in seventeenth-century religious language with particular reference to John Milton. He couldn't help notice that the metre of the opening line of 'Paradise Lost' – 'Of Man's first/Disobedience/and the fruit/Of the Forbidden Tree' – scanned to the theme tune of *The Flintstones*, setting the tone for a comic style that later would harness high intelligence to low farce. At this point destiny inter-

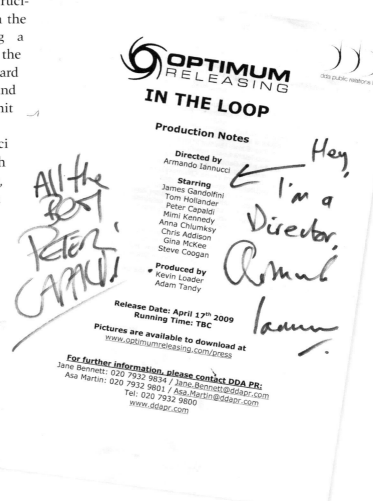

Armando Iannucci, the puppet-master of modern British comedy.

vened and Iannucci appeared at a Union debate on whether Scots were funnier than the English. On Iannucci's team were Arnold Brown, Radio 4 presenter James Naughtie and comic Andy Cameron, who was so impressed by Iannucci's wit he commended the student to controllers at Radio Scotland. Iannucci spent a year at the station, there devising *No' the Archie Macpherson Show* and co-presenting with Siobhan Synnot an impish youth programme, *Bite the Wax*.

Relocation to London followed as Iannucci grew accustomed to the up escalator of Corporation preferment. *On the Hour* proved his big break, debuting as rolling news coverage and satellite broadcasting were transforming the climate of broadcast media. Iannucci was only too happy to further muddy the water. It helped also that he had fallen among a gilded generation of performers, including Steve Coogan, Rebecca Front, Doon Mackichan, Kevin Eldon, Peter Baynham and Patrick Marber, many of whom appear in his productions still.

On The Hour and its television spin-off *The Day Today* were deadpan and pokerfaced, deploying familiar presentational formats to deliver bulletins of spiralling absurdity, such as a report on an infestation of horses in the tunnels of the London Underground. The shows spawned Alan Partridge, a self-aggrandising sports commentator so bewitchingly monstrous that Iannucci would go on to give him his own radio show, a television chat show, two further series charting his steep career decline and, ultimately, his own feature film, *Alpha Papa*, in which Partridge is taken hostage at his new workplace, an online radio station in north Norfolk. Another highlight was *The Armando Iannucci Shows*, a set of ambitious television essays that combined philosophical enquiry with surreal wit. Four years later came *The Thick of It*, in many ways the main event of Iannucci's career. Visceral and naturalistic, this was also cannibalistic comedy, as Iannucci went behind the scenes and feasted on those who'd long provided the raw material of his satire: the bungling footsoldiers of British party politics. What he revealed was an aneurysm world of perpetual crisis management, casual duplicity, second-guesswork and verbal brutality, embodied in spin doctor Malcolm Tucker, played by Peter Capaldi, a character who when chided that he couldn't organise a gang rape in a barracks smiles and replies: 'Au contraire.'

Eventually, it became obvious Iannucci was less a producer than a force of nature, such was his prodigy, industry and versatility. He became the Swiss Army knife of British comedy; tirelessly ingenious and adaptable, an Orson Welles of Television Centre. He wrote and he performed, he devised and invented. He worked across media: on television, film and radio, in books and in newspapers. He has won two Sony Radio Awards and three British Comedy Awards. In 2006 he was the subject of a South Bank Show profile and is the Visiting Professor of Broadcast Media at his alma mater. In 2011 Iannucci became an honorary Doctor of Letters of the University of Glasgow and received the Writers' Guild of Britain award. Eventually, all that prevented his omni-competence from bordering upon the nauseating was his own diffidence and likability. There is much for which comedy owes to Andy Cameron a debt of gratitude.

Magic moments from the work of Armando Iannucci

No' the Archie Macpherson Show (1988)

With a title lampooning the channel's profusion of sports programmes, this Radio Scotland sketch show was a (better-natured) precursor of *On the Hour*.

'And you join us now in High Street, Paisley, for this historic occasion, marking the first ever collection of the Poll Tax. The crowds and local dignitaries make their way to 45 Sunderland Avenue, where Scotland's first Poll Tax payment is to be collected. And as the procession swings round now into the avenue itself the streets are filled with men and women, all hoping to be out when the collectors come round to their houses later.'

On the Hour (1991)

Chris Morris rounds up the evening's news in this revered parody of radio current affairs.

'Just got time to look at tomorrow's headlines. *The Times* has "More Oxygen Still Needed, Say the French". There's a picture of Mr Mitterrand there. The *Telegraph* opts for "Meat Man in Commando-Style Soap Attack". The *Mail* leads with "Dead Rhino Blows Through Glasgow". The *Star* sticks with "Slow-Motion Stunt Man In Leg Fury" – that's for the second day running. "Hallelujah Warden in Song-Fest Barge Torment", that's in the *Express*.'

Armando Iannucci (1993)

Made for Radio 1, this was a poker-faced satire of indie-rock, zoo-format music shows with a clearly bemused Iannucci introducing music and news, aided by Suzy with her updates on the heights of buildings.

'Right, well, Glasgow to start off with. The Holiday Inn at the corner of Sauchiehall Street and Renfield Street is 210 foot high this morning and the Exhibition Centre is going to be 74 foot high all day.'

The Day Today (1994)

Chris Morris takes a jaundiced view of Janet Breen and her London Jam Festival in this TV upgrade of *On the Hour*.

'I think the only reason you've done it is to make yourself look important! How dare you come on this programme and say, Hey, look at me, I'm raising £1500 for the homeless. You could raise more money sitting outside a tube station with a hat on the ground – even if you were twice as ugly as you are, which is very ugly indeed! (Breen sobs) Has this been very upsetting for you?'

Knowing Me, Knowing You with Alan Partridge (1994–1995)

Alan welcomes to his breezy chat show Wanda Harvey and Bridie McMahon, presenters of the lesbian magazine show *Off the Straight And Narrow*.

'You're both lesbians, we know that, I don't mind, it's no problem. But does it bother you when you hear people use these slang expressions – you know, lesbos, lezzers, lesbefriends, dykes, bulldykes, Dick Van Dykes. Spare Rib-ticklers. Baggage handlers. Left luggage. Do those names hurt?'

The Saturday Night Armistice (1995)

Late-night, studio-based topical sketch show for BBC 2, co-hosted with Peter Baynham and David Schneider.

'And it was a bad whore of a week for the Conservatives, defeated in the Saddleworth by-election. However, they revealed plans to avoid further election failure by the setting up of a Rapid Reaction Majority, a permanently airborne fleet of 75,000 Tory voters ready to land on a marginal constituency within days of the calling of a by-election.'

The Friday Night Armistice (1996)

'Now it's time to examine the tall, thin regurgitating body of Diana, Princess of Wales. Following her caring example of turning up at scenes of distress with a two-man camera crew and a van full of electric cabling we decided to go further by filling a bus with twelve Dianas, to see how good they were at comforting the miserable. First stop for the Diana-bus was a traffic jam on a road full of road rage.'

I'm Alan Partridge (1997/2002)

Alan fields calls from listeners during his phone-in show *Norfolk Nights*.

'Now, I have someone on the line who fears he may be a gay. He's married, he wishes to remain anonymous, so I shall only be using his Christian name. I'm talking to . . . Domingo in Little Oakley . . . Nope, he's gone. That's a pity, marvellous little tapas bar there.'

The Armando Iannucci Shows (2001)

In this lavish eight-part series for Channel 4, Iannucci turned roving philosopher to consider in sketches and monologues subjects such as aging, work, communication, imagination, neighbours, morality, reality and twats.

'This man is waking up today realising he is a maths teacher (*distant scream*). It's dawned on this woman that she designs baking packaging (*shouts of No! No! No!*). These two people are in charge of Bedford's water (*cry of Aaargh, sweet Jesus!*). We're told to try and take stock of our lives – but all that leads to is people waking up screaming at four o'clock in the morning, as they realise that somewhere in their life they took a wrong turning. Probably about eight years ago.'

The Thick of It (2005–)

Malcolm Tucker discusses strategy with Civil Service press officer Terri Coverley.

'Terri, I thought we had a deal, right? When I need your help I'll give you the special signal – which is me being sectioned under the fucking Mental Health Act.'

Armando Iannucci's Charm Offensive (2005–2008)

Lasting four series, this was a Friday night Radio 4 panel discussion show in which Iannucci and guests considered the subjects of the hour,

leading to a Sony award for the show in 2007.

'As you know, the public have been losing trust in the BBC, ever since the corporation was revealed to be mostly liars. All sorts of scandals have emerged in the past few weeks; for instance, that the BBC's weather reports bear no relation to actual meteorological events.'

Time Trumpet (2006)

A series of retro-engineered mockumentaries for BBC 2 recounting British life in the early years of the twenty-first century, as recalled by pundits and 'celebrities' 30 years later.

'By 2012 Tesco's had a superstore in every square mile of Britain. Tesco's were brokering world heavyweight bouts, representing entertainment stars, they were making most of the films that were being made. Tesco's slogan changed from "Every Little Helps" to "We Control Every Aspect Of Your Lives". Soon, Tesco's got planning permission to build anywhere in the country, even on the side of a cliff.'

In the Loop (2009)

Iannucci's first full-length film, this Oscar-nominated black comedy saw a slightly altered version of the *The Thick of It* crew take on the power elites of Washington DC.

'Just fucking do it! Otherwise you'll find yourself in some medieval war zone in the Caucasus with your arse in the air, trying to persuade a group of men in balaclavas that sustained sexual violence is not the fucking way forward!'

Veep (2012)

Heralding Iannucci's entry into American television, Veep stars Julia Louis-Dreyfus, of *Seinfeld* fame, and resembles a turbocharged version of *The Thick of It*, charting tribulations in the office of Selena Myer, the ambitious but crisis-plagued Vice-President of the United States.

'I need you all to have . . . make me . . . not said that. I need you to . . . have make me . . . unsaid . . . it.'

Alpha Papa (2013)

Iannucci served as a writer and executive producer as the maladroit disc jockey Alan Partridge, host of *Mid-morning Matters* on North Norfolk Digital, transferred to the big screen.

'I BELONG TO GLASGOW'
(Will Fyffe, 1920)

I belong to Glasgow,
Dear old Glasgow town;
But what's the matter wi' Glasgow,
For it's goin' roun' and roun'!
I'm only a common old working chap,
As anyone here can see,
But when I get a couple o' drinks on a Saturday,
Glasgow belongs to me!

I've been wi' a couple o' cronies,
One or two pals o' my ain;
We went in a hotel, and we did very well,
And then we came out once again;
Then we went into anither,
And that is the reason I'm fu';
We had six deoch-an-doruses, then sang a chorus,
Just listen, I'll sing it to you:

I belong to Glasgow,
Dear old Glasgow town;
But what's the matter wi' Glasgow,
For it's goin' roun' and roun'!
I'm only a common old working chap,
As anyone here can see,
But when I get a couple o' drinks on a Saturday,
Glasgow belongs to me!

There's nothing in keeping your money,
And saving a shilling or two;
If you've nothing to spend, then you've nothing to lend,
Why that's all the better for you;
There's no harm in taking a drappie,
It ends all your trouble and strife;
It gives ye the feeling that when you get home,
You don't give a hang for the wife!

DR SAMUEL JOHNSON

'Pray, sir, have you ever seen Brentford?'

THE REVEREND I.M. JOLLY
(character, 1978–1999)

Those doubting the existence of a higher power might think again on discovering the Reverend I.M. Jolly – perhaps the most abiding of the many characters incarnated by Rikki Fulton – was the brainchild of John Byrne, the polymathic creator of *Tutti Frutti* and *The Slab Boys*.

Byrne was a humble writer on the sketch show *Scotch & Wry* when he was struck by the comic potential of *Late Call*, a nightly five-minute interlude on STV on which sundry Church of Scotland ministers dispensed spiritual food for thought. Made by STV's underemployed Religious Department, *Late Call* went to meet its maker two decades back, but Byrne's sketch was such a hit that ministers became a *Scotch & Wry* fixture. 'I decided we should do what they call a "God Spot" to finish off every episode,' wrote Fulton in his autobiography *Is It That Time Already?* 'Mr Jolly was created when I saw a pathetic, mournful creature who was taking his turn on *Late Call*, and I realised this guy was suffering from deep depres-

sion and unable to help anyone, not even himself.' Variants on the Reverend included the Very Reverend A. King Bones, the Reverend David Goodchild and Father Kevin Dulally. The lugubrious churchman droning on about his daily trials took on a life of his own, with his sermons repackaged into compilation shows and three books of mock-biography published, written by Fulton's friend and collaborator Tony Roper, creator of *The Steamie*. Today the Reverend's name is a Glaswegian byword for anyone of an excessively gloomy disposition.

DR SAMUEL JOHNSON
(author and lexicographer, 1709–1784)

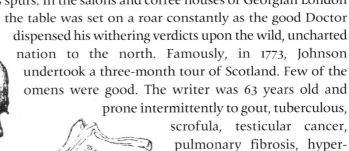

Les Dawson had mothers-in-law; Bernard Manning had ethnic minorities; Dr Samuel Johnson had the Scots, and Scotland. For the celebrated wit, author of the first English dictionary, the Scots were favoured targets, hobby-horses he seldom missed a chance to prick with his spurs. In the salons and coffee houses of Georgian London the table was set on a roar constantly as the good Doctor dispensed his withering verdicts upon the wild, uncharted nation to the north. Famously, in 1773, Johnson undertook a three-month tour of Scotland. Few of the omens were good. The writer was 63 years old and prone intermittently to gout, tuberculous, scrofula, testicular cancer, pulmonary fibrosis, hypertension, depression, obsessive compulsion and Tourette's syndrome. Rarely do any of those conditions enhance a trip to the Gallowgate.

'On our arrival at the Saracen's Head Inn, at Glasgow,' Boswell wrote, 'I was made happy by good accounts from home; and Dr Johnson, who had not received a single letter since we left Aberdeen, found here a great many, the perusal of which entertained him much. He enjoyed in imagination the comforts which we could now command, and seemed to be in high glee. I remember, he put a leg up on each side of the grate, and said, with a mock solemnity, by way of soliloquy, but loud enough for me to hear it: "Here am I, an Englishman, sitting by a coal fire."

'On Friday, October 29, the professors of the University being informed of our arrival, Dr Stevenson, Dr Reid, and Mr Anderson breakfasted with us. Mr Anderson accompanied us while Dr Johnson viewed this beautiful city.

'He told me, that one day in London, when Dr Adam Smith was boasting of it, he turned to him and said: "Pray, sir, have you ever seen Brentford?"

'This was surely a strong instance of his impatience and spirit of contradiction.'

The Journal of a Tour to the Hebrides with Samuel Johnson, James Boswell (1785)

K

'Nothing on God's green Earth is as odd, bizarre or perturbing as the Krankies. Nothing. Nothing.'

HARVEY KEITEL
(actor, 1939–)

Known these days, principally, as an actor whose movies go straight to Betamax, Harvey Keitel was at one time a really big deal and, also, curiously, an habitué of Glasgow. He appeared (with Robbie Coltrane) in the chilly, Glasgow-filmed sci-fi picture *Death Watch* (1980), then starred in *Down Where the Buffalo Go*, as a US Marine based on the Holy Loch. Keitel was back in Glasgow in 2005 and found himself loitering outside a bar as closing time approached. On a nearby wall was a poster advertising a theatrical production of *King Lear*, beneath which a crowd was gathering. 'Queuing to see *Lear* at midnight,' a newspaper reported Keitel as noting to his companion, 'I love this city.' Correspondence to the newspaper was quick to point out that a) the poster advertised a production being staged at a conventional time at another venue, and b) the queue was in fact awaiting entry to the bar's basement nightclub.

'KELVINSIDE MAN'
(Cumming/Masson)

We're from a place known as Kelvinside,
We're well-known faces in Kelvinside,
We're known as the trendy thespians,
Some of our friends are . . .
less well-known than us,
I don't take a good tan but I'm a Kelvinside Man.
My loaf is a pan, I'm a Kelvin-bred man.
We're from out west in old Kelvinside,
The things we like best about old Kelvinside
(silence)
There's yuppies and nouveau-riche out there,
Who eat croissants and broccoli quiche out there,
My fruit is a yam,
I'm a Kelvinside Man,

I get fish from a van,
I'm a Kelvinside Man.
We're just two guys who try to do our best,
We're so surprised at our success,
Two boys made big and that's the size of it.
Some people would move away if they had to pay,
The kind of poll tax we don't pay,
But Utopia is on our doorstep,
Kelvinside is it.
What you're needing is Kelvinside,
A Garden of Eden is Kelvinside,
Even Eve and Adam would feel at home,
With all the big plants and garden gnomes.
No more rainbows to chase,
It's an oasis of taste,
It's one heck of a place,
That's why we're Kelvinside Men.

THE KRANKIES
(comedy duo, 1969–)

Nothing on God's green Earth is as curious, bizarre or perturbing as the Krankies. Nothing. *Nothing.*

It isn't just one thing that makes the Krankies so exceptionally weird; it's everything, really. A man in his sixties, Ian Krankie, plays the father of a schoolboy, who is played by a woman, who is also a pensioner, and who in real life is married to Ian. This stew of (implied) transvestitism, deviance and pederasty has given the act an awkward layer of awkward comedy that is really quite awkward. But there's more: Ian and Janette Krankie admitted in 2011 that they are enthusiastic swingers: 'Dancers, magicians and musicians were among their conquests,' wrote the *Daily Mail.* 'Janette had an affair with a circus leopard-tamer while Ian carried on with the act's glamorous assistant.' Put this way, it begins to feel like the Krankies are some teatime Day-Glo rewrite of Sophocles.

All of which makes their career all the more remarkable. Throughout the 1980s and 1990s the pair were fixtures on children's television, starring in a succession of series such as *The Krankies' Klub* (1982) and *The Krankies' Elektronik Komik* (1985–87). They had a hit single, 'Fan'dabi'dozi', that reached number 46 in 1981. Round about now began the second act of their career. Their 1970s audience had grown up and grown sentimental, allowing the pair a second suck at the lollipop. For the delectation of student unions and the corporate after-dinner circuit the pair developed a more suggestive version of their act. They nurtured a second career in Australia. They were adopted by the comedienne Jennifer Saunders and appeared in such shows as *Absolutely Fabulous, Murder Most Horrid, French & Saunders* and *Dinnerladies.*

They continued also to appear in pantomime, trading on a schtick direct from the variety theatres of the 1930s, with Ian struggling to keep in line the mischievous Jimmy. Essentially,

The Krankies regret booking a king-size room.

the Krankies were really just a ventriloquist act, and their oddity had many antecedents, like Old Mother Riley, a septuagenarian washer-woman, played by Arthur Lucan, whose real-life wife played Riley's daughter; or Little Tich, a six-fingered midget in clown shoes. To these ancient showbiz templates, however, the Krankies added detailing that, in its way, was distinctively . . . *modern*.

KRAZY HOUSE
(shop, 1970s)

Like a hybrid of *The Beano* and a Soho strip joint, Krazy House brought a particularly Glaswegian levity to the business of flogging togs to teenagers. Spread over two floors at Glasgow Cross, at the literal and figurative heart of the city, Krazy House was a clothes shop with a difference, the difference being that the clothes were quite well hidden. Instead, toys held sway. All around, pinball machines rattled, automata clanked and whirred, a toy train set chugged away at head height alongside a Scalextric circuit, puppet theatres and stuffed bears looked on, and in strategically placed cages young ladies frugged to the strains of T-Rex and David Bowie. Altogether, it resembled some mad, low-lit junk shop for the libidinous.

All roads led to Krazy House, a uniquely Glaswegian take on retail.

Unsurprisingly, the youth of Glasgow were so bedazzled by the distractions Krazy House presented that they seldom purchased anything. In 1984, Krazy House downsized to a unit around the corner then closed forever.

GILLIAN KYLE
(designer, 1978–)

By identifying the middle ground between Andy Warhol and a pensioner's larder, Gillian Kyle turned a few tongue-in-cheek screenprints into classics of modern design, certainly if their ubiquity in Scottish gift shops is anything to go by.

A graduate of the Glasgow School of Art, Kyle hit upon the idea of producing giftware – tea-towels, mugs, coasters etc. – emblazoned with renderings of the packagings of various Scottish staple foodstuffs, principally plain bread by Scottish Pride, the soft drink Irn-Bru and sundry confectionery products made by Tunnock's. The idea had an accidental genius to it. Tunnock's, Scottish Pride and Barr's, being independent concerns, had left their packagings much as they always had been. On the shelves of Scotland's grocers and supermarkets their products were fixtures of the landscape, hiding in plain sight, seen but not seen, and requiring only a discerning eye to appreciate their evocative power. This was particularly true of the Tunnock's items, whose wrappings were nostalgic to an almost parodic degree. Along came Kyle to reclaim these couthy classics, and reveal in the process a beauty few had ever bothered to see.

In highlighting these totems of the dairy and the biscuit tin, Kyle did several things: she acknowledged some continuities in Scottish life; applauded the continued vitality of a few well-kent contributors – but most crucially she coined a coy and charming in-joke now shared by every soul in the city, and thousands beyond it.

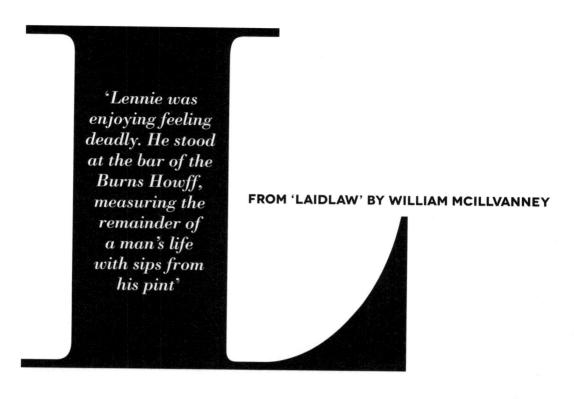

'*Lennie was enjoying feeling deadly. He stood at the bar of the Burns Howff, measuring the remainder of a man's life with sips from his pint*'

FROM 'LAIDLAW' BY WILLIAM MCILLVANNEY

LAIDLAW
(novel, William McIlvanney, 1977)

Laidlaw was not intended to be comic; in fact, in its combative way, it is anything but, and it'll *break your face* if you suggest otherwise. But *Laidlaw* is hilarious inadvertently. On publication the novel – in which D.I. Laidlaw hunts a sex killer through the city's interzones of violence and squalor – was highly acclaimed, and it has assumed the status of a classic. With hindsight, however, we see the novel also coined the entire lexicon of cliché pertaining to the roughness, toughness, grimness, grittiness and grumpiness of the Glaswegian soul.

Alongside *No Mean City* and *The Dear Green Place*, *Laidlaw* stands in a triumvirate of Glasgow ultra-texts, a holy trinity of two-fisted, hard-faced fiction. Oscar Wilde wrote of *The Old Curiosity Shop* that 'One would have to have a heart of stone to read the death of Little Nell without dissolving into tears of laughter'. Contemporary readers might act similarly when confronted with prose like this: 'Lennie was enjoying feeling deadly. He stood at the bar of the Burns

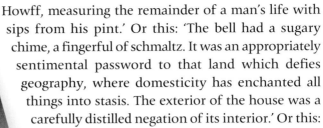

Howff, measuring the remainder of a man's life with sips from his pint.' Or this: 'The bell had a sugary chime, a fingerful of schmaltz. It was an appropriately sentimental password to that land which defies geography, where domesticity has enchanted all things into stasis. The exterior of the house was a carefully distilled negation of its interior.' Or this: 'The man with the scar drove past the Seven Ways and the Square Ring. They weren't just pubs to him. They were part of his strange, personal horoscope. Six nights a week they went on manufacturing aggro and hangovers, sustaining the confused climate that was his natural habitat.'

It isn't that *Laidlaw* is a poor novel *per se*; indeed its descriptions and phrase-making can flare like Molotov cocktails. But it does take itself incredibly seriously (which is always funny) and its narrative voice is the low-throated growl of a philosophy lecturer discovering his creative writing workshop has been cancelled. Really, once the vomit is hosed off the prose, it is charity-shop fiction masquerading as literature, or hip ethnology. *Laidlaw* does, though, offer an intriguing historical footnote. Fans of *Taggart* might be gratified to know that the show's famous – though never actually used – catchphrase, 'There's been a murder', appeared first on page 27: '"There's been a murder," he said. Ena paused over the vegetables she was chopping for Monday's soup.'

R.D. LAING
(psychiatrist, 1927–1989)

Psychiatrists in film and television tend to come in two varieties: the pensive, white-bearded Mittel-European, who is modelled on Freud, or the eccentric, excitable Glaswegian, modelled on R.D. Laing. The latter was the controversial, and let us not put too fine a point on the matter, barkingly tonto creator of anti-psychiatry, a discipline that throughout the 1960s kept newspaper colour supplements packed with portraits of the picturesquely deranged.

The finer points of Laing's psychiatric method we are not

qualified to critique, beyond pointing out their howling nuttiness – but, happily, Laing's method is not what concerns us here. Rather, it is his poetry, the hilarious hobbyist pretentiousness of which Laing himself was, quite uniquely, unable to diagnose. In 1979, several years prior to being struck off, though, amazingly enough, not for his poetry, Laing published *Sonnets,* a volume that could squeeze peals of laughter from the catatonic. For example:

> Is it our proper destiny to spurn
> The mortal vessel of our frail desire?
> To drench our flame in flame and so expire
> In pure, white, cold, dead ash, and then to burn
> To naught the final dross until all's lost?
> We moths may be mistaken. Not thus
> May we awaken from the evil curse
> Of spirit blighted in a fiery frost.
>
> Amor and caritas, as one surpass
> The impasse of their severed discontent.
> No fragrant token of their immanent
> Atonement wafts from transcendental ash.
>
> We learn to reconcile the high and low
> In consummation's warm and gentle glow.

Nurse, the screens!

STAN LAUREL
(film comic, 1890–1965)

It's 1932 and Glasgow's Central Station is heaving. The train has been eagerly anticipated and the crowd has been swelled by several thousand, causing mayhem for the police. Stepping into this maelstrom is a heavy-set American with the air of a Southern gentleman. He bows politely to the crowd and twiddles his tie in an exaggerated comic gesture of shyness. Behind him a thin, redheaded figure emerges from the train and blinks in awe at the assembled throng. Tears begin to brim in his eyes. 'Are you OK, Stan?' Oliver Hardy whispers to his companion. 'Of course I'm OK, Babe,' he replies, his voice choked with emotion. 'It's just . . . this is like coming home.'

from *Stan Laurel's Glasgow*, BBC Radio Scotland, December 2011, written by David Flynn

Towns and cities often overstate their importance in the creation myths of the notable. For Glasgow, one such example might be that of Stan Laurel, the blinking, head-scratching half of Laurel and Hardy, perhaps the most adored comedy duo of the early Hollywood era. To be factual, Laurel was born in the Lancashire town of Ulverston in 1890, and he died 75 years later in the suite of the Oceana Hotel, Santa Monica, where he resided. In the Glaswegian mind, however, Laurel is practically a native, even if few could tell you the precise reason why.

Laurel, birth name Stanley Jefferson, lived in Glasgow from 1905 until approximately 1910, completing his education at Rutherglen Academy before going on to make his stage debut in Glasgow in 1906, at the Britannia Panopticon music hall on Argyle Street (oddly, it was on a street of the same name in Ulverston that Laurel was born). The family business was showbusiness: Laurel's father Arthur managed the Metropole Theatre on Stockwell Street. Stan sold tickets.

When he finally made it onto the stage, he had a turbulent apprenticeship inasmuch as the Panopticon was notoriously rambunctious. Male customers were known to bring shipbuilding rivets to performances; with greater gentility the women threw fish heads. Laurel started as a 'patter' comedian, billed as 'Stan Jefferson

– He of the Funny Ways'. In 1910, he went to work for Fred Karno, the British music-hall impresario, in whose troupe he understudied Charlie Chaplin. Stan changed his name in 1917, though erroneous reports claim he appeared as Stan Laurel while at the Britannia. He'd long been unhappy that Stan Jefferson contained thirteen letters. More prosaically, he was perhaps also aware, as he was forging a career in the film comedies of Hal Roach, that 'Laurel' possessed more marquee appeal than 'Jefferson'. The name came from a book on Roman history. He paired up with Oliver Hardy in 1927, and by 1932 had made 65 films. Laurel was their principal creative engine, Hardy being a less ambitious character concerned more with the golf course.

Unaccustomed As We Are in 1929 was the pair's first sound film. Laurel was heard to use the phrase 'Any nuts?', which was to become a catchphrase. The Laurel and Hardy template was perfected, with Hardy as the prissily bumptious, tie-twiddling anchor and Laurel as his blithe, bemused foil.

Global renown and Academy Awards followed. And then things began going rather awry. After the duo's most profitable film, *Bonnie Scotland* (1935), they split with Hal Roach in a disagreement over salaries; Laurel's disproportionate input meant he received greater remuneration. Hardy made an unsuccessful film without his partner. The pair failed in their attempts to produce their own films, a decline that the Second World War compounded. To eke out their rather parlous finances the pair became a theatre act, performing in the variety theatres of Britain and the United States in the late 1940s. For their appearance at the Glasgow Empire Stan insisted the pair don kilts. Further ill-advised projects and formulaic movies followed before the alliance was brought to an end with Hardy's death in 1957. Laurel followed eight years later.*

It was the summer of 1933. I read in the *Evening Times* that Laurel and Hardy were coming to play at the Empire. The day they arrived at Central Station, the whole place was packed with fans waiting to welcome them. I happened to know a ticket collector called Billy Moir and he let me stand inside the barrier. The Royal Scot finally arrived at platform five. Photographers' bulbs flashed everywhere. The crowd surged forward and pandemonium broke out. Suddenly a short man in a dark suit and a homburg emerged from the mêlée. For some reason he approached me and said in broken English, 'My name is Albert Einstein. Can you direct me to the Central Hotel? I'm here to receive an honorary doctorate from Glasgow University, and I must say, in all my years as a scientist, no other city in the world has turned out in their thousands to pay homage to me. I am deeply touched.'

Of course, I got Einstein to sign my autograph book, but I didn't have the heart to tell him they'd all come to see Laurel and Hardy.

from *Are You Looking At Me, Jimmy?*,
Arnold Brown, Methuen, 1994

* One of the duo's final screen appearances was on a 1954 edition of *This Is Your Life*. The arrangements were made by impresario Bernard Delfont, who at the time was managing the affairs of Chic Murray.

LIMMY
(Brian Limond, comic, 1974–)

Until the end of recorded time, Bob Dylan will be linked to the protest song. Christopher Lee will always be Dracula. The mark an artist makes on first acquaintance can prove indelible, even if they change as soon as we've registered their existence. Similarly, Limmy may be trapped in aspic forever, known decades hence as the internet comic, despite the fact that the Glasgow absurdist moved on some while back to live performance and to television. The internet was Limond's portal, as certainly and definingly as newspaper strips were for Lobey Dosser. Not for nothing did Limond become known as the Dot Comic.

Limond's back story is a decidedly modern one, that of an educational misfit who stumbled through an early life of alcoholism and self-harm in some charm-free zone of outer Glasgow, on his way towards a series of McJobs. But it fostered in its turn a particularly modern style of comedy, in which technology and weapons-grade provocation are fused. For the likes of Rikki Fulton, an apprenticeship in comedy comprised twenty years in Gang Shows and musichall. For Limmy, it consisted of popping out to purchase the appropriate software.

Comedically, Limmy's closest analogue is perhaps Chic Murray. They share the same delight in jokes that fall on their sides and routines that discover they can't get the door open. It's a disconnected, ruminative sort of humour. A certain constituency will feel it was made expressly for them. The remaining 99 per cent will stare as though at a policeman delivering bad news.

For initiates, there is what might be termed the Limmy litmus test; if you do not find the sketch known as 'Requiem' amusing, move on, there's nothing for you here. Shot on video and uploaded to YouTube, a man telephones a series of children ('Is your wee sister there?'). On being put through he screams 'Requiem!' in a variety of threatening voices, then slumps in his chair as if having sated some vile addiction. The clip is sinister, unspeakably odd, yet, to those of a certain bent, insanely funny.

'I think it's something that's hard-wired into me,' Limond says of his capacity to shock. 'I don't get the joy out of life that other people do, so I need quite extreme feelings to keep me going. My thrill comes from putting something horrible online, sitting back

and waiting to see what the reaction will be. Your heart palpitates, you're hyperventilating. Nice things like going to a concert just don't do it for me.'

His peak, perhaps, remains a series of podcasts entitled 'Limmy's World of Glasgow', in which a gallery of characters send dispatches from their daily lives. Among them was Jacqueline McCafferty, a sort of Hyacinth Bucket of recovering heroin addicts, and Tom, a priest with homicidal fantasies: 'I whispered quietly, Christ! Christ! Why have you put her in the lift with me? She will surely die.' The series was the stepping stone between Limond's online comedy and greater recognition on television, via *Limmy's Show*, made for BBC Scotland by the Comedy Unit as it began to move away from sitcoms in which drunks squabbled over fish suppers. 'It'll be another 50 years, I think, until television and the internet are as appealing as each other to young kids,' Limond states. 'The telly is still the thing. Being on the internet is fine, but it's not the telly, because the telly is what we had when I was a boy. It's the real thing, you can almost get your teeth into it. The internet's fine; you can make something up and it's round the world in seconds, it doesn't involve money. But the telly is a friend in the room – it's a different thing completely from the internet.'

Limond was raised in Carnwadric, an area on the south side of Glasgow rough enough to supply him with his superbly observed cast of gimlet-eyed Glasgow chancers and nasal neds. 'I didn't really know it at the time, but now that I've moved to Partick, I can see that Carnwadric's atmosphere was one of fights and trouble. I'm scared of saying that it was a tough place because I don't want anyone who was there accusing me of pretending that I had a hard upbringing. But I don't want to say it was fine because I don't want to argue that it's fine for people to get stabbed.'

By his own account, he was a dislocated child, unable to mesh with the typical teenage mindsets: 'I was always the last person in class to get the hang of something. The last to learn how to write my name, the last to learn how to tie my shoelaces.' He was, though, proficient in self-harming, most notably slashing his wrists on the beach during a family holiday to Millport when fifteen. 'It was an attention-seeking cry for help; my way of saying to the world, "I'm all weird, me, please everybody come and help me."'

Limond was of the appropriate age, though, to find solace in the rudimentary, though burgeoning, computer industry. 'Always had a Commodore or a ZX-81 kicking around. Or I'd try to create my own sort of pre-internet, phoning up helplines and customer service lines. I ran up a phone bill of £1,000 from making prank calls. I'd dial an American number and when someone answered I'd say, "Hi, is this the Bronx?

After school, Limond drifted through a chain of further education courses connected with information technology. He established several website design businesses, and created one which soon featured some small Limmy whimsies, such as a digital Xylophone which emitted swear words. Eventually the site featured his self-filmed sketches. He expanded into 'World of Glasgow', in 2006 sat next to Ricky Gervais in the iTunes download chart. Live shows at the Edinburgh Fringe followed, then a BBC Scotland pilot and finally a full six-part series. During it all, there was a drink problem for him to beat. 'I'd binge here and there, usually I'd end up a complete fucking mess, then it culminated in 2004. I was meant to go to a party with my girlfriend Lynn. I didn't. I took the bottle of wine we had and went to the office, stayed up all night chatting on the internet and drinking. Then I headed for home and had a couple of pints in every pub along the way. Lynn found me slumped at Bridgeton Cross, eating a curry, using the carton lid as a spoon. I walked right past her, didn't recognise her.

'And that wasn't the lowest point. The problem was that I just liked the feeling of being drunk too much – all that matters is the here and now. Your worries about the past and future vanish, and I loved that. I ended up on Glasgow Green, planning to jump from the suspension bridge. I wanted to punish myself for being so fucking worthless. I wanted no way back.

'Then, when I began to realise I was seriously thinking about it, I thought about giving up the drink and, honestly, in that moment I suddenly felt alive again. It was like a spiritual awakening. I felt reborn, like a Christian almost.'

Ultimately, says Limond, his problem is that he 'falls between the cracks of various mental disorders'. He harbours, he says, a touch of attention deficit hyperactivity disorder; he's somewhere unspecified along the autistic spectrum, borderline dyslexic and functionally hypochondriac.

'I'm a bit of all of them, enough to be a pain in the arse but not enough for a doctor to say, "Fine, we've found out why you do these terrible things."'

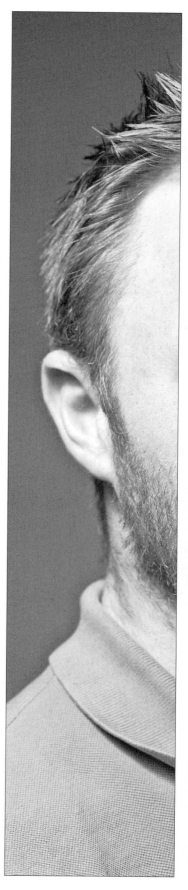

Benjamin: finger-clicking advertising executive, turning everything he encounters into a marketing pitch.

'We at BAMN Concepts recently secured a contract to promote D-Day, a brand new ground-breaking first-person shoot-'em-up game. We sent them back a sheet of A4 paper with BAMN in 128 point with our email address below.'

Tom: diffident churchman struggling with his urge to kill.

'Lord, it is Tom, I am fearful. I do not want to speak in front of these people for, although my own congregation lack the wisdom to see the evil that lies within me at times, this lot won't.'

John Paul: deeply malignant ned.

'He's like, please, please I have to meet my mother. I was like, fucking walk, don't fucking tempt us, I'll fucking stab you tae death on the track right now.'

Phil: ebullient middle-aged man from Blackpool with a fondness for Glasgow's female population.

'So the copper dragged the little guy back to his police van, dragged him by the hair. Absolutely unbelievable, just typical Glasgow! I have got to move up there, just sensational!'

Xander: well-intentioned, but relentlessly predatory, young gay man guides us through Glasgow's hidden sexual underbelly.

'I saw this old alcoholic on a bench. He was very downbeat, so I thought, "Let's just give him a wee private dance to cheer him up."'

Derek 'Dee Dee' Dury: committed stoner permits a glimpse into the small-hours landscape of his TV-addled imagination.

'I was watching *Jeremy Kyle* and a fly lands on the telly. So I chucks a cushion at the telly. Fucking thing doesnae budge.'

Vijay: cheerful Asian youth who refuses to let the cruelty of the natives sour his outlook.

'I tried to come up with a good idea to help people, I got completely let down and now that half of my dad's customers have gone elsewhere he's not speaking to me, I'm in the doghouse and the laughing stock of my whole family.'

Wee Gary: playground powerbroker, obsessed with boiled sweets and vengeful violence.

'Well, Vinnie, you did go and admit you're a virgin, be fair. He says, Gary, that's coz Ah am a virgin. You're a virgin. Everybody in my class is a virgin. We're all about eight years old, Gary. Ah don't give a fuck what they say, I know they're virgins.'

Jaqueline McCafferty: recovering heroin addict who detects insult in most encounters.

'So Ah head intae the dance hall. Every guy in there's goat a fucking kilt on. But none of the lassies huv – except me. Ah'm standing there looking like a fucking guy. And they're thinking – she must be a fucking junkie.'

LIP SERVICE
(television show, 2010–)

Like the novel *Laidlaw* or the New Town film *Cumbernauld Hit, Lip Service* wasn't, we're sure, *intended* to be funny. No one, though, be they man, woman or gender-transitional, could take the BBC 3 series entirely seriously, positing as it does a Glasgow stalked by gangs of gorgeous predatory lesbians, freshly liberated from drama schools in the Thames Valley.

Lip Service is the very definition of a guilty pleasure. It is, undeniably, rubbish; a sexy, six-hour Flake commercial set in a branch of All Bar Men. It is, however, *moreish* rubbish, replete with stock types and familiar scenarios that have been ripped from the diary of a teenage *Guardian* reader. Why, it asks, is Frankie such a two-faced *bitch*? Internet dating – is it *really* for losers? Can Cat find happiness with police inspector Samantha, or will the urge to make truncheon gags prove overwhelming?

Even though the series shows Glasgow in a seductive light, as a city of colour-supplement interiors, moody river views and alleyways designed expressly, it would appear, for wildly gymnastic sexual congress, the series is an innately colonial affair, commissioned in London and shipped to Glasgow purely to tick a checklist of boxes pertaining to diversity and regional production targets. At no point is any character pursued by a train of small boys shouting 'Hey, missus, where's yer man?' For this, and for many other reasons, we can doubt the show's authenticity and sincerity, even while finding it a hilariously lurid fantasia of Glasgow and its sisterhood of the flatter shoe.

JIMMY LOGAN
(entertainer, 1928–2001)

Logan was the P.T. Barnum of Glasgow comedy, the genre's soft-shoe-shuffling, crowd-pulling, song-and-dance impresario king: a singer; a comic, a writer, director, pantomime dame and theatre owner. When occasion demanded he probably sold the choc-ices too.

It was in his blood. Logan's parents comprised the music-hall act Short and Dalziel, and his sister became the jazz legend Annie Ross, who acted too, appearing as the moll in *Charles Endell Esquire*, a series in which Logan also featured. He belonged more to a classic Scottish showbiz tradition than to anything that was distinctly Glaswegian. Logan's guiding light was Sir Harry Lauder, about whom he produced the one-man musical *Lauder* in 1976. Holder of the record for the greatest number of performances in the *Five Past Eight Show* at the Alhambra Theatre, Logan spent some of the later years of his career transforming the derelict Empress Theatre into the New Metropole, a project he funded by appearing in two of the better *Carry On* films, *Carry On Abroad* (1972) and *Carry On Girls* (1973).

Kenneth Williams and Jimmy Logan in *Carry On Abroad*, 1972.

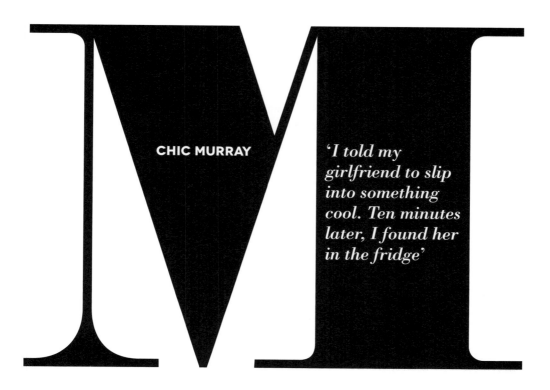

CHIC MURRAY

'I told my girlfriend to slip into something cool. Ten minutes later, I found her in the fridge'

THE MCFLANNELS
(RADIO/TELEVISION SERIES, 1939, 1958)

Remembered now only by those who struggle to remember much else, *The McFlannels* was a Glasgow phenomenon in its day, the city's answer to the Broons strip featured in the *Sunday Post*, wherein a clan of couthy Scottish archetypes chuntered on about their missing doormat and the like.

Initially a set of books by Helen W. Pryde, the stories became a serial on the Scottish Home Service, then transferred to television on the BBC TV Service Scotland, providing early mainstream exposure for that multitalented dynamo of Glesga pathos Molly Weir.

Weir appeared as 'Poison' Ivy McTweed – each character in the show, as a way of establishing their social status, having been named after a type of fabric. There were also the McSilks and the McVelvets (posh), the Corduroys and Mr and Mrs Canvas (lower middle-class) and, further down the scale, Mr and Mrs McGauze and their friends the McPoplins. Rikki Fulton joined the show in 1952, as the Reverend David McCrepe.

The McFlannels detailed the exploits of a working-class Glasgow family. Willie and Sarah McFlannel were augmented by their children Peter and Maisie and by the impecunious Uncle Mattha. Like Weir, Pryde had been raised in Springburn in the north of the city. Although not explicitly comedic, the series took a fond and cheerful view of the McFlannels and the people around them. 'I was that wee Glasgow keelie, Ivy McTweed,' Weir recalled in *A Toe on the Ladder* (1973), sister volume to the amusingly titled *Shoes Were for Sunday*. 'I felt I knew everything about Ivy, from the top of her frizzy perm to the peerie heels of her dance shoes, and I devised a sort of basic gallus laugh for her, which apparently was so true to life that I was unable to convince a man met on a train journey from London to Glasgow that I hadn't based it on the neighbour round the corner from his house in Rutherglen.'

Great days . . .

MATT MCGINN
(songwriter, 1928–1977)

Putting to one side merchandise offered by Tam Shepherd's Trick Shop, the earliest occasion on which a Glaswegian sense of the comic is inculcated in the city's young is through exposure to the songs of Matt McGinn, taught in the schools of Glasgow to this day.

In numbers like 'Skinny Malinky Long Legs', 'The Red Yo-Yo' and 'The Wee Kirkcudbright Centipede', McGinn caught beautifully the sly wisdom of the childish mind as it battled the iniquities of the grown-ups.

An Eastender by birth, nature and inclination, McGinn was active for many years in left-wing politics, joining and resigning from the Communist Party so frequently he received a perforated membership card to aid in the process of its ceremonial destruction. He worked in Glasgow's shipyards, became a teacher and was central to the city's folk revival in the 1960s. His unique perspectives on the issues of the day, not to mention the eternal struggles of young and old, were detailed in many much-loved songs, such as 'Ban The Beatles', 'Big Orange Whale', 'The Sugary Cake And Candy Man' and 'I Was Born 10,000 Years Ago'. With their colloquial language and nippy wit, McGinn's songs demonstrated with lasting genius that the Glasgow worldview can be induced from any age. A line in

'Skinny Malinky Long Legs' was borrowed as a title by Billy Connolly for his documentary *Big Banana Feet*. McGinn has a pub christened in his honour, too, the Two-Heided Man in Hope Street, named after his 1972 album. It is criminal that today McGinn is not better known; though he does have devotion where it really counts, with the children.

JOE MCGRATH
(writer/director, 1930–)

Joe McGrath was one of the pillars of the 1960s British satire boom, producing the BBC's *Not Only But Also* for Peter Cook and Dudley Moore; taking the Goons to television; directing (or being one of the six directors) of the ill-starred Bond adaptation *Casino Royale;* and, generally, since the late 1950s, ducking and diving at the classier end of British light entertainment. Through his connection to Cook and Moore he landed a gig making promotional films for the Beatles. Also, he directed *Digby: The Biggest Dog in the World*, which we shan't mention again.

Raised near the docks in Govan, the son of variety performers, McGrath made it to Glasgow School of Art and then deployed a flair for set design to transfer to television, which at the time was handing out jobs with abandon. Soon, he was directing arts programmes, producing on Michael Bentine's sketch show *It's a Square World* and directing the television drama *Justin Thyme*, starring Leonard Rossiter. 'I did lots of commercials as well as working at the BBC. I wasn't BBC staff – I was BBC contract. Frank Muir and Dennis Norden

Dudley Moore, Peter Cook and Joe McGrath on the set of *Not Only But Also*, 1964.

advised me when I arrived, "Don't join the staff – be freelance", and I still get repeat fees to this day!' McGrath produced also *Candid Camera* and a sitcom, *The Big Noise*, with Bob Monkhouse, then was assigned to the Corporation's newest darlings, Cook and Moore, cresting at the time on the success of the theatrical revue *Beyond the Fringe*. When the show featured a sketch in which a public lavatory doubled as a swinging nightspot, with John Lennon as its doorman, McGrath fell into the circle of the Beatles: 'Brian Epstein, the band's manager, phoned me,' recalls McGrath, 'and said, "I see you went over my head and you've got John Lennon as a guest. Now, you're going to have to pay him something." I said, "Well, how much?" He said, "Five pounds." And that was it. We got John Lennon for five pounds.'

His strongest alliance, though, was with Peter Sellers, who played one of several James Bonds in the calamity that was *Casino Royale*. Beset by script and performer chaos, the production, co-starring Orson Welles and Woody Allen, was described by the critic Roger Ebert as 'possibly the most indulgent film ever made', though the circumstances in which the film originated live forever in cinema lore. 'We started shooting at Shepperton, and on the first day Sellers didn't turn up and I thought, this is what this film is going to be. It was the biggest-budget movie being shot in the world at that time. I had a script by Wolf Mankowitz and it was about 400 pages long. It was ludicrous.' With Sellers, McGrath went on to conduct a protracted and tumultuous friendship, along the way directing the highly-strung actor in the TV adaptation of *The Goons*, and in two films, *The Magic Christian* (1969, with Ringo Starr) and *The Great McGonagall* (1974), a spoof biography of the incompetent Dundee poet.

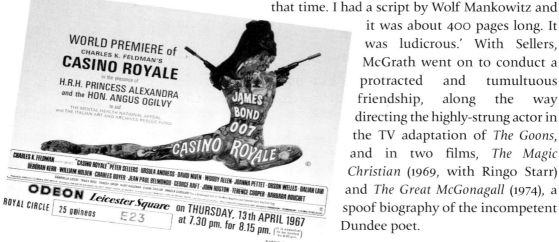

In later years, McGrath pursued a mixed portfolio in television and film, drama and comedy. He directed the cinema adaptation of *Rising Damp* (1980) and *Night Train to Murder* (1983), the cinematic swan song of Morecambe & Wise. There were highs, like his Sherlock Holmes spoof *The Strange Case of the End of Civilisation as We Know It* (1977), with John Cleese and Connie Booth – and there were lows, such as the sex comedies McGrath directed as British cinema was calling for the last rites, namely, *Girls Come First* (1975) and *I'm Not Feeling Myself Tonight* (1976), featuring, bizarrely, Chic Murray.

Currently working on *Short-Term Memoir*, his account of the *Casino Royale* debacle, McGrath is, to some extent, the forgotten man of British comedy, in equal parts nursemaid to and collaborator with a galaxy of stellar talent . . . and the director of *Digby: The Biggest Dog in the World*, which, regrettably, we appear to have mentioned again.

A Woody Allen self-portrait done for Joe McGrath during production of *Casino Royale*.

FULTON MACKAY
(actor, 1922–1987)

With Charlie Endell departing the scene upon the cancellation of *Budgie* in 1972 it seemed a gap existed for the type of character Endell represented: the fearsomely humourless and unsentimental Glaswegian disciplinarian, part Calvinist, part psychopath. Into the vacuum stepped Fulton Mackay in the hugely popular BBC sitcom *Porridge*. As his own namesake Prison Officer Mackay, Fulton Mackay gave the part a callous ferocity as he strove to neutralise his least favourite prisoner, Fletcher (played by Ronnie Barker), with whom his relationship sat on a seesaw of contempt and grudging respect. On returning from a training course, Mackay warns the inmates of HMP Slade change is imminent: 'There's going to be a new regime here, based not on lenience and laxity but on hard work and blind, unquestioning obedience. Feet will not touch the floor. Lives will be made a misery. I am back, and I am in charge here.' In a confrontation with Fletcher, Mackay asks if the inmate considers himself working class: 'I did,' Fletcher responds, 'until I visited Glasgow. Now I think I'm middle class.'

Born in Paisley, Mackay was a familiar face on British television throughout the 1960s and 1970s, appearing in, among other things,

Z-Cars, The Avengers, Dad's Army and *Doctor Who*. He had two (curiously contradictory) specialities: the unyielding officer type, as seen on *Porridge*, and gentle rural eccentrics, seen to best effect during his appearance in the Bill Forsyth film *Local Hero*. He had been in serious contention to play the Doctor Who that would succeed Jon Pertwee, though the role would go eventually to Tom Baker. A member for many years of the company at the Citizens Theatre, and a playwright for the BBC, Mackay died of stomach cancer at his home in Surrey.

KENNETH MCKELLAR
(singer, 1927–2010)

Born and raised in Paisley, McKellar would become a tenor of world renown and the very personification of braw, upstanding Caledonian propriety, a kind of singing caber, appearing frequently on stage and on television Hogmanay spectacular to praise in song the bonniness of the Scottish landscape and the constancy of its woman folk. As such, McKellar's connection to the world of comedy is not apparent immediately. In the 1960s he'd appeared in the fondly-remembered pantomime *A Wish for Jamie* with Rikki Fulton but otherwise, to the naked eye, McKellar's career was little more than one long, warbling obsession with the winsomeness of Loch Lomond.

Upon McKellar's death, however, something curious would occur. Each of his obituaries made a point of mentioning a most counterintuitive fact about the man, that once he had written a sketch for the comedy troupe Monty Python's Flying Circus. This was like hearing that Molly Weir had been a founder member of the Bonzo Dog Doo Dah Band. Certainly it was difficult to square the clever-clever university wits of Python, begetters of the Dead Parrot sketch and the Summarise Proust contest, with McKellar, who'd been as plain and wholesome as a box of porridge oats. Yet there it was in every eulogy, this claim that McKellar had been a bit of a dark horse whose Burnsian egalitarianism had seen him accepted by the kinds of people we'd least expect.

Details were scant; all we knew from the tributes was that McKellar's sketch had featured in *The Secret Policeman's Ball*, a charity benefit show in 1979 in which the Monty Python team had appeared.

This was when the scent of rat first became apparent. For not only was the Python team famously protective of its creative process but at the show in question they had unveiled no new work, only sketches they had performed previously on television. Pressed on the matter, McKellar's daughter Jane averred the connection had been mentioned by Python mainstay John Cleese 'in his autobiography', despite the fact that Cleese has yet to write an autobiography. Something closer to the truth was found in an interview the team gave to the *Sun* in 1971. During it, Cleese claimed he'd received a sketch idea from McKellar: 'But we want him to do it himself in the show,' he said. 'It's the only outside idea we've ever been interested in.' Even at this, little was established beyond doubt. There is every likelihood Cleese was joking. Kilted Highland culture of the kind embodied by McKellar was frequently a Python target, from the miser poet Ewan McTeagle ("Lend us a couple of bob until Thursday/I'm absolutely skint/But I'm expecting a postal order/And I can pay you back as soon as it comes.") to their satires of the novels of Sir Walter Scott. In its Oxbridge way, the team showed repeatedly that it found the sentimental and couthy ways of far-flung Caledonia intensely amusing. Its most renowned embodiment, of course, was Kenneth McKellar. Thus was entrained an odd but stubborn little misunderstanding. In the mists of time, a quip became a rumour that was barnacled by exaggeration until it ended up a strange-but-true Wikifact, trotted out by the credulous in a hundred obituaries. Suffice to say, no supporting evidence for the claim can be found. But a measure of its persistence was found at the Scottish National Portrait Gallery in February 2013 in *Stop Your Tickling Jock*, an exhibition of works depicting comedic Scots. McKellar was among those honoured, for his work on . . . *Monty Python's Flying Circus*.

ALEXANDER MACKENDRICK
(film director, 1912–1993)

As director of *The Ladykillers* (Ealing Films, 1955), Mackendrick made what is arguably the most deeply loved film comedy in the history of British cinema. That he made *The Maggie*, *Whisky Galore!* and *The Man in the White Suit*, too, then departed for America where he directed the vicious media satire *The Sweet Smell of Success*, is

testament to a talent of no small majesty, even if that talent is still little acknowledged by a wider public.

When Mackendrick's father died in the influenza pandemic of 1918, the boy was given over to his grandfather, who raised him in the West End of Glasgow. A lonely and downbeat character by his own admission, Mackendrick attended Hillhead High School, then Glasgow School of Art, and landed a job as an art director for the advertising firm J. Walter Thompson. Making commercials furnished a bridge to film, leading to a post making propaganda films at the Ministry of Information during the Second World War.

Mackendrick went then to Ealing Studios, a small concern known for cheerful wartime personality pictures starring the likes of Gracie Fields and George Formby. A takeover by the Rank Organisation saw Ealing forge a new identity, through comedies that took a skewed and quixotic look at the British national character. A laconic and thoughtful character, with a deep understanding of film craft, Mackendrick possessed precisely the right credentials for Ealing.

At the heart of his films was a fascination with innocence and its corruption, a theme redolent of a childhood derailed by loneliness. In *Whisky Galore!*, on the island of Todday, relationships are rent asunder when a cargo of contraband whisky turns up on its shores; in *The Sweet Smell of Success*, showbusiness reporter Sidney Falco (Tony Curtis) has his assumptions reassembled by the demonic PR man J.J. Hunsecker (Burt Lancaster); and in *The Ladykillers* the blitheness of Mrs Louisa Wilberforce is dismantled heartlessly by the spivs and gangsters who take over her home.

Subtle and persuasive, and never less than striking visually, the films of Alexander Mackendrick smoulder on in our imaginations with a true comic classicism. Finding the film industry increasingly difficult to navigate, Mackendrick moved on, and in 1969 became dean of the film course at the California Institute of the Arts, where he remained an influential instructor and administrator until the end of his life.

JACK MCLEAN
(columnist, 1946–)

In the old days, it was said of the *Glasgow Herald* that the newspaper featured 'more columns than the Parthenon'. In Glasgow, an opinionated editorial slant is always welcome. Until his departure in the nineties, Jack McLean had for decades dispensed precisely that and became in the process the doyen of Glasgow journalism, with a view on the passing scene which blended erudition, arrogance and a certain refined aggression. Each quality is evident in this (rather foresighted) despatch concerning Scottishness in television, from March 1982.

'Jings' cried the craggy-faced, lantern-jawed, sidelocked, granite-brained, mealy-mouthed whisky magnate, 'Ah see the noo, och aye, that yon TV prrrogrrramme is gettin' a rrright hammering.'

He lay back in his whisky magnate's big fake leather chair which had come from The Onedin Line and lit a rrrruminative pipe. 'Och Ferrrgus,' remonstrated his pale dreary daughter from Godalming, Surrey. 'Dinna fash yersel', ken,' she said. The craggy-faced, lantern-jawed etc person started in surprise.

'Ferrrgus, the name's Ferrrgus,' he said in a stage whisper, ther's no Ken in this!'

The daughter tried to explain. 'Nae Fatherrr, ye've got to sye ... er, 'ken' all the taime. It's how they talk in Glasgie', she added.

'Ock, I mean ochhhhhhh' said Fergus, nearly being sick. 'Ah ken ye need to get the right accent, but it's nae easy bein frae Glasgie all the wheel an' ...'

A voice could be heard coming from the BBC canteen. 'I say, you chaps!' the voice could be heard clearly enunciating.

'This must be Rrrrobert,' said Ferrrgus. 'Is that you, Rrrrobert?' asked Rrrrrita.

'I say,' said Rrrrobert, springing on to the set. 'I've just heard the most super news ... what's wrong with you fellows?' He stopped and stared at the glares of disapproval being directed towards him.

'Oh God, yes,' the youth wailed, 'that bloody accent!'

'How about this then ...' Rrrrobert cleared his throat and began: 'Ah've just heared a spot of unco guid news. Dae ye ken that we are off tae Lunnon toon,' he announced, 'tae feenish off this drivel this six month' nicht ye ken!' Sudden wild cheers permeated the studio.

'Hurrah! Hurrah!' the Thespians shrieked, and so did the camera crew and the director, and everybody else who didn't want to be in Glasgow in the first bloody place even if it did mean taking the bread out of a few Scottish mouths and having to live in the slums of Great Western Road with only a few local carpet-baggers to talk to at any time.

Actually, for what it's worth, and a lovely phrase that is itself, my view of King's Royal

The Herald

over which there is, predictably, what some Scottish idjits might call a 'stushie', is that the presence of the foreign actors and actresses was the only good thing in this malt opera. It was a series of such lobotomising dreadfulness that the only only entertainment which could be gleaned lay in the tortuous attempts by posh RADA-trained mountebanks to utter like any kind of Scot.

Obviously their lecturers had once told them that a Scottish accent could be obtained by speaking most of the time as if you were a long-term mental patient whose teeth had just been extracted with a monkey wrench.

Also that all sentences should rise in both tone and volume towards the end. This latter advice resulted in 50 minutes' worth of what appeared to be strangely splenetic questions.

I know what Phil McCall, fine wee man that is and a decent man too, says. He says that Scottish actors should have got the parts and you more than see his point. What other nation of our size can boast so many wonderful actors? And not only the famous ones like Iain Cuthbertson, Andrew Keir, Fulton Mackay.

There's Billy Paterson, Sean Scanlan, Eileen Nicholas to mention just three favourites of mine. (Another favourite, Jimmy Cosmo, is already in the series, and he's the living exemplar of exactly the correct Glasgow accent of the period portrayed.) Aye, I know what Phil McCall says is right at that.

I myself, yer Urban Voltaire, was once rejected by an English STV producer because, he said, I spoke 'like a yob'. (A charge I strenuously deny. I have in fact a perfectly respectable Glasgow accent. A rough voice, yes, but respectable enough. BBC and STV please note.)

But is it not the fact that all radio and TV announcers have got anglified, if not outright anglo, accents? is it not a fact that every time some captain of Scottish industry, or some head of social work, or lecturer in Scottish Studies, or some damned boss anywhere gets up to speak, we all sit back and expect the sod to enunciate in a posh English voice, and we are rarely disappointed? If the truth be known anyway, very few Scottish actors and actresses can speak in Glasgwegian themselves. If it's no the genuine plum-in-the-mooth elocution, it's one of those prissy wee Hutchie Grammar accents you'll hear from them.

Not that very much is ever said in the approved English/ Englified accent anyway, for such tones are not designed for content but for such bromides as political speeches and Nationwide news and talking down to the lower orders. It is no coincidence that the only people in the media, mass or otherwise, who can speak our magnificent language with any feeling at all are regional comedians, from Les Dawson to our own Andy Cameron.

Nor is it a coincidence that the only 20th-century English writer of real worth was D.H. Lawrence, who wrote and thought in his native Nottingham idiom. And no coincidence at all that the Irish, who maintain their own Limerick and Kerry and Cork and Dublin accents, are the most literate people in the world. Or that so many of our 'Scots' litterateurs earn a decent wee living writing about the Scots when the lot of them would pass muster at High Table or in an expatriates' club in Simla.

And we worry about a bunch of play-actors? Am I right? I mean, am I right? 'Rrrrright!' says Ferrrrgus. And Rrrrrobert and Rrrrrita too, as they practise their accents all the way to the bank.

LEX MCLEAN
(comic, 1907–1975)

McLean poses a conundrum. Wildly popular in his day – to the extent that mounted police kept order outside the Pavilion Theatre as McLean's matinee audience filed out and his evening audience filed in – he represented the last hurrah of the old patter comic, the teller of quickfire gags, based typically around marital disharmony. Never again would the Scottish mainstream accord such popularity to a performer whose style had been honed in such far-off days. Additionally, McLean was the last in a line, a sequence of three Glasgow comics that reached back to the days of variety theatre and music hall: namely, Tommy Lorne, who worked the city in the early years of the twentieth century; Tommy Morgan, who handled the wartime period; and McLean, who brought the comic inheritance into the modern day.

Known colloquially as Sexy Lexy, McLean's material, particularly later in his career, could display a blue edge, a smear of the *risqué*, though McLean persistently feigned ignorance of it. 'One o'clock in the morning, Arbroath, there's a fella walking about in his shirt-tails. A polisman comes and says, "Ye canna walk about in your shirt-tails like that, Ah'm gonna huv tae take ye in. Huv ye any family?" Fella says, "Aye, Ah've goat fourteen." The polisman says, "Away ye go. Ah don't want to lift you in yer workin' clathes."' He adapted smartly to what the Northern club comics of the time were bringing to television. His own television shows, meanwhile – *Lex* and *Lex Again* – were notable as among the few Scottish sitcoms to be shot before a live studio audience. Set in its hero's local pub, *Lex* and *Lex Again* do seem striking. Lex and his circle of chums (played by Walter Carr, Irene Sunters and Larry Marshall) read the papers, squabble and do battle with the daily vexations of Glasgow life. Football loomed large, particularly McLean's passion for Rangers F.C. In one of the few episodes surviving, Lex and co. are erroneously awarded a pools win, but at a

lavish ceremony in the Central Hotel are thwarted persistently in collecting it.

What was remarkable about the show was that the principals were recognisable, standard-issue Glaswegians, rather than the grotesques and stage proletarians who populate the works of the Comedy Unit. In *Lex* and *Lex Again*, characters were familiar comic archetypes: Mrs Murphy was scatter-brained, Carr as Hughie was the affable foil, and Larry Marshall was the cynic on the sidelines. McLean, meanwhile, was outraged and crafty in equal measure, a Glaswegian take on the American sitcom stars of the time, such as Jackie Gleason or Phil Silvers. It was innocent and amiable stuff but, with its focus on duplicity and complaint, also oddly modern. A keen sailor, McLean semi-retired to Helensburgh, where he died following a long illness.

ADAM MCNAUGHTAN
(songwriter)

A product, like Matt McGinn and Billy Connolly, of the 1960s folk revival in Glasgow, McNaughtan has an ineradicable place on the syllabus of Glasgow, courtesy of 'The Jeely Piece Song', a work of quite unparalleled popularity among the city's schoolchildren. Social history you can hum to, the song captures beautifully Glasgow's trepidation as skyscraper housing estates began supplanting the tenement communities of old.

> I'm a skyscraper wean, I live on the nineteenth flerr
> But I'm no goin' oot tae play any mair.
> 'Cause since we moved to oor new house
> I'm wastin' away
> For I'm getting one meal less every day.
>
> Oh ye canna fling pieces oot a twentystorey flat,
> Seven hundred hungry weans will testify to that.
> If it's butter, cheese or jeely, if the bread is plain or pan,
> The odds against it reaching us is ninetynine tae wan.
>
> On the first day my Maw flung oot a daud o' Hovis broon,
> It came skitin' oot the windae and went up instead o' doon.

Noo ev'ry twenty-seven hours it comes back into sight,
'Cause my piece went intae orbit and became a satellite.

On the next day my Maw flung me oot a piece again,
It went up and hit a pilot in a fast, lowflying plane.
He scraped it off his goggles, shouting through the intercom
'The Clydeside Reds have got me wi' a breid 'n jelly bomb'.

On the third day my Maw tho't she would try another throw,
The Salvation Army band was standin' doon below,
'Onward Christian Soldiers' was the tune they should've played,
But the Oompah man was playing piece 'n marmalade.

We've wrote awa' to Oxfam to try an' get some aid,
We all joined together and have formed the Piece Brigade,
We're gonna march to London tae demand our civil rights,
Like nae more hooses over piece-flinging height.

MICHAEL MARTIN
Baron Martin of Springburn (peer, aka Gorbals Mick, 1945–)

The bulk – the noun is apposite for any entry on Michael Martin – of characters in these pages have one thing in common: they are entertainers, or creators of interesting things. They are of limited consequence socially. The comedically inclined seldom get to involve themselves in anything that's truly important; like government.

The same cannot be said of Michael Martin, former Labour Member of Parliament for Springburn, in the north-east of Glasgow. No parliamentarian since Jeremy Thorpe – acquitted of fronting a murder plot that succeeded only in assassinating a Great Dane – has enriched the gaiety of nations like Michael Martin. Flailing his way like a wheezing, red-faced Toby Jug through the expenses scandal of 2009, Martin fulfilled every tabloid cliché extant about Glaswegians: that they are unlettered, inarticulate, combustible and seldom averse to a few freebies. Never had Martin's newspaper nickname of Gorbals Mick seemed so apposite. For nine years he'd been Speaker of the House of Commons, though never a particularly cherished one for a number of reasons, including his bias in the

House in favour of Scottish male Labour MPs, and for the fact that he was, as sketch writer Quentin Letts put it, 'as thick as cold custard'.

But one thing really did for Martin and created a media circus in which he himself became Coco the Clown. The expenses scandal was startling enough, yet Martin pushed the envelope of fiduciary ingenuity to a new extent. He spent lavishly on himself, his wife and on his apartment in the Palace of Westminster. When threatened with exposure Martin engaged eminent law firm Carter-Ruck to counter the accusations, and paid the bill from public funds. One newspaper drew attention to the fact that Martin had 'plundered the public purse for an almost grotesque array of personal perks and foreign junkets'. And yet, the nation was treated to the hilarious, rib-tickling, lip-chewing sight of Martin claiming something to the effect that a big boy had done it and run away. He became the first Speaker since 1696 to be forced out of office by a motion of no confidence, resigning before it could be voted upon. His resignation coincided neatly with news that he had claimed £1,400 for chauffeur-driven cars to the Jobcentre and to the ground of his beloved Celtic FC.

GLEN MICHAEL
(television presenter; 1926–)

For a generation of Glaswegians, specifically those born after 1960, early exposure to the city's humour came in all likelihood from an avuncular figure in pastel knitwear, accompanied by a dog and a talking paraffin lamp. From 1966 until 1992 *Glen Michael's Cartoon Cavalcade* was a much-loved fixture of STV's Sunday afternoon schedule, thereby introducing children to the exploits of Bugs Bunny and Road Runner, and also to the punning, harmless humour of a native and long-lost style of variety theatre.

Such was the realm from which Glen Michael hailed prior to hosting his cartoon compilations in the company of a sentient lantern. Born in Paignton, Michael served his comedy apprenticeship in the Entertainments National Service Association and in the *Gang Show,* then came to Glasgow in 1952 to fulfill an engagement as feed to the then-unknown comic Jack Milroy. He never left, going on to feature regularly in the *Half Past Seven* and *Five Past Eight* shows at the Alhambra Theatre, and in the ongoing theatre and television shows of Milroy and Rikki Fulton as Francie and Josie. From there he served a spell as foil to comedienne Una McLean in the STV comedy series *Over to Una* and its spin-off film *Did You See Una?* and in the television productions of Stanley Baxter. He appeared in dramatic roles, too, most notably in *The Blue Lamp*, the Ealing Films *policier* from which *Dixon of Dock Green* was spun.

Glen Michael, avuncular purveyor of Sunday-afternoon animation.

The story is told in *Life's a Cavalcade* (2008), an autobiography that does sterling work outlining how an entertainer passes his fifties and sixties in the company of Daffy Duck more often than he might relish. Michael's is the tale of an entertainer with a nose pressed against the plate glass of showbusiness; he seldom finds himself in the right place at the right time. His career in variety theatre takes off just as burly men are turning up to throw the fixtures and fittings into the skip of history. Virtually every moment of his golden era with Francie and Josie is erased by the bean-counters of STV. His progress in the dramatic arts is stalled also when his father applies for the post of butler to Sir Laurence Olivier, and uses the job interview to inquire if his offspring's prospects might benefit in the process ('This was a question that Sir Laurence evidently thought should never have been asked and he said so quite forcibly,' Michael admits glumly). He gets close to the greats, albeit only in the lobbies of various hotels and airports. Courtesy of a

childhood fan, comics writer Mark Millar, he gets a cameo in the superhero movie *Kick-Ass*, though his part is cut from the finished film.

The story is told not ironically or self-mockingly, but with the grim jollity of a man who refuses to let his luck defeat him, and who judges himself by his own best intentions; precisely the kind of man to whom Scotland was wise to entrust its children. In its groaning, Christmas-cracker way, *Glen Michael's Cartoon Cavalcade* furnished a charmingly rickety and gallus alternative to the dispatches then being received from Television Centre, shows like *Blue Peter* and *Multi-Coloured Swap Shop*. As Mark Millar recognised, Michael's show played its part in a Glaswegian comedy tradition that encompassed everyone from Charlie Endell to Eddie Clockerty. 'It was the one time on television,' Millar remembered, 'where you heard a Scottish accent and an American accent on the same show every week. Glen Michael taught us to broaden our horizons.'

MONTY PYTHON 'S FLYING CIRCUS
(comedy troupe, 1969–83)

It is difficult, immediately, to discern any comic significance held by the modest range of hills that encircle Glasgow. They don't really have any, save for their appearance in a 1983 film by the team behind *Monty Python's Flying Circus*. In *The Meaning of Life*, Strathblane and surrounding acreages doubled as the South African province of Natal in a sketch that satirised the First Zulu War. Legend has it that on one occasion the Glaswegian extras refused to don their Zulu costumes because it was too cold, causing the cancellation of a day's shooting. The story is probably apocryphal.

STEPHEN MULRINE
(poet, 1937–)

A well-renowned figure, Mulrine has toiled many a season in the vineyard of the written word as dramatist, editor and translator. For two decades he was tutor in creative writing at the University of Glasgow, and is perhaps the only man to have translated Ibsen *and* written for Scottish soap opera *Take the High Road*. His poetry is quoted, too, particularly 'The Coming of the Wee Malkies' from 1967, a work which predated Tom Leonard's pioneering advocacy of Glaswegian dialect poetry. Taught in schools still, 'The Coming . . .' paints a mock-Gothic portrait of the threat posed by school-age Glasgow tearaways, a kind of male Glaswegian analogue to Ronald Searle's St Trinian's girls.

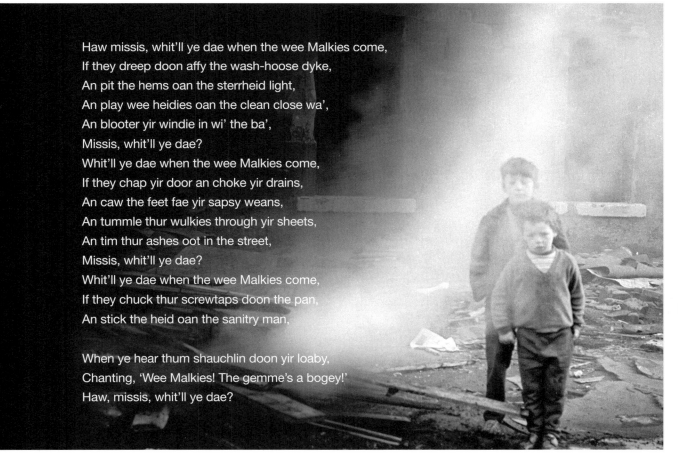

Haw missis, whit'll ye dae when the wee Malkies come,
If they dreep doon affy the wash-hoose dyke,
An pit the hems oan the sterrheid light,
An play wee heidies oan the clean close wa',
An blooter yir windie in wi' the ba',
Missis, whit'll ye dae?
Whit'll ye dae when the wee Malkies come,
If they chap yir door an choke yir drains,
An caw the feet fae yir sapsy weans,
An tummle thur wulkies through yir sheets,
An tim thur ashes oot in the street,
Missis, whit'll ye dae?
Whit'll ye dae when the wee Malkies come,
If they chuck thur screwtaps doon the pan,
An stick the heid oan the sanitry man,

When ye hear thum shauchlin doon yir loaby,
Chanting, 'Wee Malkies! The gemme's a bogey!'
Haw, missis, whit'll ye dae?

CHIC MURRAY
(comic, 1919–1985)

The interesting thing about Chic Murray was that he achieved such popularity – such mainstream, Saturday-night telly, *Radio Times*, guest-on-Parky popularity – with an act that was so wilfully oblique. Not only did Murray patent a brand of twisted Christmas-cracker humour several years before Tommy Cooper, he also did it during one of British comedy's most conformist periods, an era of oily men in ruffled shirts discussing the touchiness and physical dimensions of their wives. Yet Chic prospered. His material, in the main, was comprised of semantic practical jokes, straightforward statements that turned out to conceal a stranger level entirely, such as 'I told my girlfriend to slip into something cool. Ten minutes later, I found her in the fridge.' Or 'My mother christened me Louis. I was the youngest of fourteen.' Or 'Will you join me in a bowl of soup? I know it's cramped but it's great fun.' It was wholly self-penned, which was unheard of for a British comic of the period.

At heart, of course, it was old-fashioned, variety-hall stuff but with an odder, more abstract head. And it was delivered with such poker-faced conviction. A measure of Murray was eventually to be found in E.L. Wisty, Peter Cook's dislocated advocate of trifles and trivialities. A critic in the 1950s saw another parallel: 'The solemn wonderment with which Chic describes the business of minute-by-minute living is as unearthly as a Goon Show.' Such was Murray's charm that audiences were happy to be gulled repeatedly by his linguistic sleight-of-hand. They couldn't help but like him enormously, though often with no small measure of bafflement. He had the bearing of a man tortured happily by whimsy, able to intuit an alternate reality behind the one we know, all described in the drawling, faux-genteel tones of a Bearsden Rotarian indulging an irritating child.

Like his friend and disciple Billy Connolly, Murray was a product of the shipyards, though the claim requires qualification. These weren't the sulphurous infernos found in Connolly's routines but a more refined milieu altogether: the yards of Kincaid and Co., a marine engineering firm manufacturing motorboats.

His family background forged his comedic outlook, too. The young Murray was coddled by parents who stood apart from the norm in 1930s Greenock. His mother, Isabella, was a gentle matriarch and voracious reader. His father, William, was kindly and impaired by injuries sustained in the First World War. He turned to evangelism and founded in Greenock the Burning Bush Society, a Christian fellowship at whose meetings the seven-year-old Murray made some kind of showbusiness debut providing accompaniment on the organ. The society took a bizarrely literal approach to Scripture and concluded its gatherings with members going outdoors and setting light to actual bushes. The line between this and Murray's comedy later scarcely needs elaborating.

In due course, Murray by now having formed a stage partnership with wife Maidie, the standard apprenticeship followed around the theatres and music halls of provincial Britain, with Maidie providing musical interludes and straight feeds. The Marx Brothers were making their mark in cinema and their influence on Murray was obvious, particularly in Groucho's way with the wordy hoodwink. 'Outside of a dog, a book is a man's best friend. Inside of a dog it's too dark to read' went one Groucho line we can almost hear Murray deliver. The Murrays' agent Billy Marsh followed a policy of keeping Chic and Maidie out of London until their act had been perfected, and in 1956 they made a huge impact at the Royal Command Variety Performance. The ensuing prosperity was ploughed into establishing a hotel in the Bruntsfield area of Edinburgh,

where for his public Chic would hold court. 'Ordinary persons are ten a penny, but characters, real people are my main hobby,' he said. Maidie tired of the relentless touring and retired herself from the act.

Her timing proved propitious. Created by performers such as Tony Hancock and Kenneth Williams, Bob Monkhouse and Frankie Howerd, the call at the dawn of the 1960s was for nightclub comics whose personal foibles were advertised clearly. In an era defined by *Beyond the Fringe*, a man–wife double act with musical instrumentation ran a risk of being considered hopelessly anachronistic. Alone, Chic was able to align himself more with the tenor of the times; as a strolling observer of the passing scene, a correspondent from the nearer reaches of strange. He even appeared in that monolith of Swinging London whimsy, *Casino Royale,* (1967), starring Peter Sellers and Orson Welles and directed by, along with others, Glaswegian Joe McGrath. He was divorced from Maidie in 1972 and spent his later years loitering amiably between stage performance, panel show, television special and film cameo (in *Saigon: Year of the Cat* and *Gregory's Girl*). He also turned up in more than his share of suburban sex comedies, virtually the only work British cinema offered at the time. Even if the roles he played in the films were just variants on his wry misfit persona, the titles – including *The Ups and Downs of a Handyman, Secrets of a Door to Door Salesman* and *I'm Not Feeling Myself Tonight* – remain curious additions to the canon of a comic whose background and bearing evoked so precisely the Scottish lower middle classes of the interwar years.

Chic Murray died in Edinburgh, in January 1985, mere weeks after his final television appearance on a calamitous Hogmanay broadcast for BBC Scotland. 'I'm over here!' he was heard to shout to a cameraman unable to locate him. 'In the long grass!' Which was pretty much where he'd been all along.

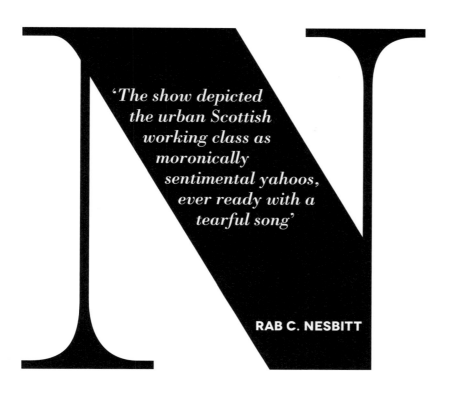

'The show depicted the urban Scottish working class as moronically sentimental yahoos, ever ready with a tearful song'

RAB C. NESBITT

BUD NEILL
(cartoonist, 1911–1970)

Neill was the cartoonist laureate of Glasgow from the late 1940s until the end of the 1960s, first as writer of pocket dailies for the *Evening Times* ('Drink yir milk or ye'll no grow up tae be a lazy, shiftless auld layaboot like yir Daddy!'), then, most famously, in the *Evening Times* as the creator of Lobey Dosser, sheriff of Calton Creek, an American frontier town with a curious similarity to a certain city in the west of Scotland. Neill's work, particularly Lobey Dosser, is held in high nostalgic regard, though for contemporary readers it is often impenetrable, relying on events, personalities and fads now long forgotten.

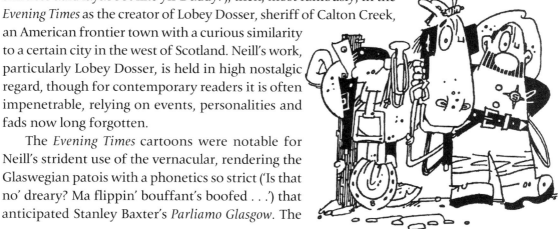

The *Evening Times* cartoons were notable for Neill's strident use of the vernacular, rendering the Glaswegian patois with a phonetics so strict ('Is that no' dreary? Ma flippin' bouffant's boofed . . .') that anticipated Stanley Baxter's *Parliamo Glasgow*. The

deep fondness Glasgow reserves for Neill was demonstrated in 1992 when, by public subscription, a statue was unveiled on Woodlands Road depicting Dosser and Dosser's horse El Fideldo. It is the only two-legged equestrian statue in the world. Its designer and tireless Neill advocate Ranald MacColl here considers the cartoonist's genius.

Mention Lobey Dosser to most inhabitants of the West of Scotland and a flicker of recognition will register in their eyes: 'Yes, the wee Glasgow cowboy sheriff with the two-legged horse and the baddie – what's-his-name – Rank Bajin.' Most will be aware of the bronze statue dedicated to these cartoon characters, erected with funds from a popular public subscription. But those younger than thirty will probably draw a blank at the mention of the creator of the famously quirky Keelie Western cartoon tales.

Bud Neill's little eponymous hero was first published in 1949, to immediate popular acclaim. This was, however, no overnight success story for the cartoonist. Bud had already established a large following of *Evening Times* readers since his first pocket cartoon appeared five years previously in 1944. He began his career in newspaper cartooning relatively late in life. At 33 he wrote a succinct and barbed reply to a series of complaints by passengers of the wartime buses in the *Letters to the Editor* section of a Glasgow newspaper. The editor was intrigued and not a little suspicious that a bus driver could compose such an eloquent letter. A consequent investigation of the writer's credentials found him to be a legitimate transport worker. There followed a meeting at the editor's office, where Bud mentioned that he could 'draw a wee bit', and he was offered a job as a pocket cartoonist for the *Evening Times* on a piecework basis.

Although much of his early work inevitably targeted wartime issues, it was underpinned by the basics of that mischievous brand of Glasgow humour which he made his trademark. Classic nuggets of Neill's style of Glaswegian humour began to punctuate the *Evening Times's* pages.

The readers recognised themselves in Bud's wee drawings and pithy one-liners, and they laughed. Bud's cartoon heroes and heroines, the wee Hughies and Mrs Ts of his world, had three-dimensional earthiness. The not-so-wee wimmen looked all of their '3 oz, 12 lb and 18 stane' and the smell of stale nappies was almost palpable. You felt you had met them before, based as they were on the ordinary city people whose spirit and feistiness gave (and still give) Glasgow its unique identity. Bud caught them in his frame and, with the unique voice he had developed, allowed us to eavesdrop on his Neillian gems.

In what were to be his last five years, Bud, ever the creative artist, experimented with 'cameraless photography', as he dubbed it, using an assortment of nuts, bolts and screws et cetera as his cartoon characters, sculptural pieces and his own versions of the Rorschach ink blot test. These inventive and innovative artworks were an indication of Bud's intention to explore new forms and approaches to his cartoon art, and had he lived his three score and ten, who knows what delights would have awaited us in our daily paper?

RAB C. NESBITT
(television series, 1988–)

If ever a television show exposed a certain callousness in the system that spawned it, that show was *Rab C Nesbitt*, the BBC Scotland sitcom concerning a garrulous Govan drunk, played by Gregor Fisher, and his family of benefit scroungers. With blithe viciousness, Nesbitt encouraged us to cackle at the most deprived and degraded members of our own society. The show depicted the urban Scottish working class as moronically sentimental yahoos, ever ready with a tearful song or a catty quip if confronted with words involving more than two syllables. Nesbitt not only depicted idiocy but endorsed it, implying that the working class deserved little more than their heinous diets and their limited vocabularies. All attempts authority figures made to improve the lot of Nesbitt and his family were dismissed with derision, thus contriving a view of working-class life where betterment was considered to be betrayal. Community was merely a closed circle of wilful ignorance and bestial pride.

In 30 years' time it will be difficult to believe that such vile and pernicious cack ever got broadcast, just as we are scandalised by the racist sitcoms of four decades ago. Injury was added to the insult when, throughout Britain, Nesbitt was adopted as the archetypal Glaswegian.

In 2010, after a break of eleven years (with the exception of a Christmas special in 2008), the show was reanimated for a ninth series, an occasion that let its creators scale even greater heights of double-speak, 'Rab is a commentator on life,' said producer/director Colin Gilbert. 'Enough has happened to give him a whole lot of new things to talk about.' Quite. Towards the end of the previous series, Rab's life had blossomed gloriously, taking in such wholly unstereo-typical topics as his battle with cancer, his wife Mary Doll's rape and her affair with Rab's best friend. All of which was perfectly feasible in a proper comedy, written by skilled professionals. Nesbitt, however, was written by a man wearing boxing gloves while scratching the backs of his paymasters. The sooner this shaming proletarian Uncle Tom were to die the better.

'Here's
a penny for
your thoughts/
Incidentally you
may keep the
change'

ORANGE JUICE

THE ONE O'CLOCK GANG
(television show, 1957–67)

This was a midweek lunchtime magazine show screened by STV, in which Charlie Sim, Dorothy Paul, Jimmy Nairn and Larry Marshall sang numbers, did skits and commented upon events of the moment. Though remembered fondly, the show was essentially an early attempt by STV to pad out the space between commercials with the cheapest programming it could get away with. This it did quite successfully until 1965, when Charles Hill, chairman of the Independent Television Authority, visited the station and watched an edition being produced. 'My God,' he exclaimed, 'how long have you been getting away with this?' The show was axed soon after.

But not before the following incident, recounted by Dorothy Paul in her autobiography *Revelations of a Rejected Soprano*:

There was a famous morning when one of the cameramen came in with a horrific hangover. As the morning progressed, he looked worse and worse. He made the mistake of ordering a bacon sandwich at tea break. By the time we got to transmission he was positively green. He managed to keep going through the show until the last song, which was mine; some light and airy musical ditty. When I got to my obbligato the cameraman could contain himself no longer and, during a big close-up, he vomited in a projectile fashion all over his camera. Bits of his bacon sandwich landed on my frock. Of course I carried on, under great stress, and at the end of the show I said to Charlie (the producer), 'Wasn't that just awful? He's a disgrace, that fellow.'

Charlie said, 'Well, Dorothy, everyone's entitled to their opinion.'

ONLY AN EXCUSE?
(television comedy, 1993–)

Stepping into the breach on the demise of *Scotch & Wry, Only an Excuse?* was built upon a baffling premise: that New Year's Eve would only be enhanced if it included a sketch show comprised of punning skits lampooning the workings of Scottish professional football. Every Hogmanay, then, for the show's duration, the half of the population that wears a bra is required to depart the room and find something else to do. When you think on it, this is quite scandalous. Imagine if the Christmas movie after the Queen's speech were replaced by documentaries on handbag design and the existence of angels. Effectively, this is what *Only An Excuse?* does – it is a closed shop.

The show began on Radio Scotland in 1987 as a vehicle for the comic impressionist Jonathan Watson. Its format was that of a sports report covering items of the moment, with Watson playing the real-life personalities. Transferring to television in 1993, the show required a wider pool of performing talent, which has included stalwarts of the Glasgow comedy scene such as Tony Roper and Greg Hemphill. On television the show incorporates parodies of films and commercials, and with a certain winning silliness makes the point that Scottish football is little but a realm for the finger-sniffing aficionados of sporting dismay.

ALAN ROUGH

Edwyn Collins, mischievous lyricist of Orange Juice.

ORANGE JUICE
(pop group, 1979–1984)

The lyrics of rock and pop songs can be many things, and seldom are those things ennobling or amusing. Most commonly their focus is romantic love, a preference reaching its apotheosis with the Beatles. As for rock lyrics, these have tended to concern themselves with amatory pluralism or the (self-perceived) outlaw status of their authors. A further variation is the fourth-form lyric, full of cryptic allusion and oblique declaration, such as was pioneered by Bob Dylan. It took until the early 1980s for a humorous flair to appear in the British pop lyric, in the work of, among others, Scritti Politti, ABC, The Human League – and, most gloriously, Orange Juice.

Written in the main by vocalist Edwyn Collins (1959–), Orange Juice lyrics were by turns sardonic and camp, waspish and loquacious. They rendered a world where precocious Glasgow hipsters measured their sensitivity against their articulacy, in a syntax that was defiantly fey and mock-ironic. And, most, crucially, non-American. Orange Juice used their humour to become the mildest of insurrectionists. For many years Glasgow had been dominated by a particular school of rock music, derived from the blues and amplified to the point of pain. Against it, Orange Juice took their own manner of civic stand, forging an approach that was bitchy and confounding, with words that delighted in their own eloquence.

The effect wasn't limited to musical output. The clothes the band wore were amusing too, a mixture of plastic Jesus sandals, Harris tweeds and American thrift-shop vintage. Their personal bearing was funny, catty and unstintingly dismissive. Everything about Orange Juice, in fact, articulated puckish delight in the rejection of so much that had gone before in Glasgow. It was a delight that made Orange Juice perhaps the funniest, certainly the most delightful, band in the history of British popular music.

Combining Dorothy Parker's waspishness with, well, the waspishness of Warholian camp, Orange Juice brough a new comic articlacy to the lyric, as represented in this range of examples:

I wore my fringe like Roger McGuinn's,
I was hoping to impress,
So frightfully camp, it made you laugh,
Tomorrow I'll buy myself a dress
How ludicrous.
'*Consolation Prize*'

I'm so transparent you can guess without question,
I need something or other to cover my expression,
Buy me some sunspecs like the ones you wore,
From the local hipsters store.
'*Untitled Melody*'

You and I could frolic in the dew, only
I've something better to do,
And with that I bid you fond farewell.
'*Breakfast Time*'

Here's a penny for your thoughts,
Incidentally you may keep the change,
And here's a book of etiquette,
I bought to keep you sane.
'*Flesh Of My Flesh*'

I used to do my utmost to suspend belief,
Until the day it hit me like a kick in the teeth,
In the sensitivity stakes you're less than a non-starter,
You don't need a lover you need a sparring partner.
'*I Guess I'm Just A Little Too Sensitive*'

It may be my imagination and of course
I'm prone to exaggeration,
But in the moth-eaten gloom of my shabby room,
I saw the strangest manifestation,
One possible explanation is that it was
merely a trick of the light,
But that's little consolation 'cause it's
gotten so that I can't sleep at night.
'*What Presence?!*'

P

RAPERORUM
TUMMUL-TINTY
BED

*The romantically
minded twosome
fell together into
bed*

**PARLIAMO
GLASGOW**

PARLIAMO GLASGOW
(television series, 1960–1967)

Parliamo Glasgow was a series of spoof language tutorials operating on the principle that non-native ears found the Glaswegian accent so impenetrable it was effectively a foreign language.

Stanley Baxter, the face of *Parliamo Glasgow*, described its genesis in *The Bedside Book of Glasgow Humour*: 'Alex [Bell, co-creator] and I were watching with great interest one instalment of a television series giving instruction on the Italian language. It showed a man and a girl speaking Italian and buying stamps, postal orders and other articles. The sketch was then recreated, the players speaking the lines in carefully enunciated English. It then occurred to us that a similar method could be used to teach the Glasgow language. And so we evolved the *Parliamo Glasgow* series.'

The series had its roots also in a character Baxter created in 1959 for the BBC sketch show *On the Bright Side*. Named the Professor, he gave mock-lectures on the accents and characters of Glaswegians 'as if they were creatures he'd found in Western Samoa', Baxter recalled.

The joke was such a good one we hear it still: in, among others, *Chewin' the Fat*'s camp devotees of the 'Glesga banter', or in the *Burnistoun* sketch where two Glaswegians battle in a lift with an American automated voice recognition system. When Baxter and Bell expanded their idea for a BBC series, the two hosts would watch a typical Glasgow domestic scene and note the natives' perplexing dialogue. 'The mother suddenly reproaches her husband "Oh God, she says, look at you, sittin errinyur simmit." In the carefully spoken and reasonable tones of sociologists they would go on to decode the dialogue: 'Thus, she intimates to him that she disapproves of his informal attire. The word *errinyur* is frequently used by ladies who are critical of their husbands' sartorial deficiencies. And so we have "Staunin errinyur shurt."'

As parochial as it was, *Parliamo Glasgow* appeared at a critical juncture in the history of British comedy, when the comic potential of the everyday was beginning to reveal itself. In 1960, the final episode of *The Goons* went out. With the show went the last vestige of a comic style that had been in place for two decades, a clubby kind of slapstick devised in the entertainment divisions of the armed services, as heard on, among others, *The Navy Lark* and *It's That Man Again* (featuring Colonel Chinstrap). Its most popular outlet, however, was *The Goons*.

And then it wasn't. In 1959, *Hancock's Half Hour* transferred to television, introducing viewers to a new comic style, one that was naturalistic and downbeat, concerned more with the travails of daily life than with funny voices or eccentric brigadiers. And so Tony Hancock would struggle to pass a rainy Sunday in his grim bedsit; in *The Strange World of Gurney Slade*, Anthony Newley would daydream that the figures in advertising hoardings had come to life. *Beyond the Fringe* provoked a vogue for satire and with it came renewed interest in the daily news, as well as *That Was the Week That Was*. The *Carry On* franchise strove to find the seamier side of familiar institutions, and the increasing accessibility of television intensified this interest in the prosaic and the proximate. *Parliamo Glasgow* played its part, too, feeding into the prevailing school of comedy vérité, as was occurring on the Glasgow stage with Francie and Josie. Baxter's show demonstrated several things: the Glaswegian love of linguistic flexibility and the perverse pride Glasgow reposed in speaking a dialect few could decipher. Simultaneously, the locals adored the back-handed compliment in Baxter's attempt.

Zarra marra oanra barra Clarra?
Is that a pollinated squash on that handled cart, Clara? (Is that a marrow on that barrow, Clara?)

Goaramferrburstin
I discover I am in need of an urgent visit to the gentlemen's convenience. (God, I'm fair bursting.)

Hazzebrungabo'al?
Inquiry made upon an acquaintance's arrival at a Hogmanay party. (Has he brought a bottle?)

Pirrasoaknit
Please be so kind as to curtail the repetition of your complaints. (Put a sock in it.)

Erzagerskelpedratimzagin
I see Rangers have beaten their Old Firm rivals convincingly once more. (There, we see that the Gers have beaten the Tims for the umpteenth time.)

Seezoweragless
Could you pass me a drinking vessel? (Hand me a glass.)

Whissamarramurra?
What ails you, Mother? (What's the matter, Mother?)

Whenra-helza party startin?
When might the festivities begin? (When the hell is the party starting?)

Raperorum tummul-tinty bed
The romantically minded twosome fell together into bed. (The pair of them tumbled into bed.)

Glasgow has long been a city that bore out Wilde's dictum that the only thing worse than being talked about is not being talked about. *Parliamo Glasgow* not only talked about the city, it told us how the city talked about everything else.

DOROTHY PAUL
(comedienne, 1937–)

Like some warrior queen of old Dalriada, Dorothy Paul has been on the battlefield of Glasgow light entertainment since Adam was selling the choc-ices. She has been the city's chippy, lippy auntie for an almost geological span of time. After any future holocaust, chances are survivors will be limited to cockroaches and Dorothy Paul, holding forth, in the time-honoured fashion of the Glasgow banter, on the purchase of gammon from that wee butcher wi' the squint.

Known best these days for the succession of one-woman shows she has fronted since 1991 – including *Now That's Her, Now That's Her Again* and *Retiring from Retirement* – Paul began on *The One O'Clock Gang*, a lunchtime chat-and-variety show that ran on STV from 1957 to 1965. Paul (birth name Pollock) lent some blonde to a cast that otherwise brought to mind a bank manager's funeral: 'The show was a nervous breakdown that lasted six years,' she recalled in her autobiography *Revelations of a Rejected Soprano*.

The Gang was disbanded in 1967, after the controller of the Independent Television Authority described the show as unwatchable. She was cleaned out in an ill-advised business venture and, being associated so closely with an STV show, found the doors of BBC Scotland closed. She was widowed young. To make ends meet, Paul worked as a market researcher and converted her home into a drama studio where she taught stagecraft to children. She succumbed to a huge drink problem and grew so desperate for performing work she found herself petitioning the producers of

Doctor Who. 'I wrote to suggest I could be an assistant,' Paul recalled. 'They wrote back and said, "We're not really looking for Scottish aliens at the moment."'

Very occasional parts aside – in the STV soap *Garnock Way* and in *Taggart*, plus a spell as a seamstress at STV – Paul remained a civilian until the late 1980s, when she played Magrit in *The Steamie* on stage and then on television. The show reminded Glasgow audiences that Paul embodied a type central in the city's psychopathology – the fading, tough-but-tender survivor. 'I had done a couple of jobs for Michael Boyd at the Tron Theatre and Michael had always been really supportive, so I asked him if he had any work coming up,' she recalled. 'Nothing. I tried again. Nothing. I tried again. And he was fed-up and got a wee bit shirty with me. He said, "Dorothy, I'm looking at my diary and the week of June 12 is free. Go away and write a one-woman show and I'll give you that week."'

With such shows, Paul wrote for herself some kind of second act and so commenced a two-decade trawl through the bottom drawer of the female Glaswegian psyche, or at least that psyche as it stood circa 1958, an era when husbands idled and housework was a daily Sisyphean battle: 'He's gettin' oan ma nerves, you know, that ornament ah keep in the hoose. Ah'm no' kiddin', it wid take a stick of dynamite to separate that man's arse from that chair in front of the telly . . .' Defiantly sentimental, yet bracingly plainspoken, Paul's reminiscences gave voice to the eternal woes of the city's homemakers. Her shows became a fraying thread connected to Glasgow's days of variety theatre and the homely, self-reflecting routines of Lex McLean, *Parliamo Glasgow* and Francie and Josie. Her routines are founded almost entirely on a bittersweet nostalgia; those unfamiliar with ticket collectors on Corporation buses, stairhead toilets or wally closes will exhibit naught but glum incomprehension. For the remainder, Paul represents the very last of a dying breed.

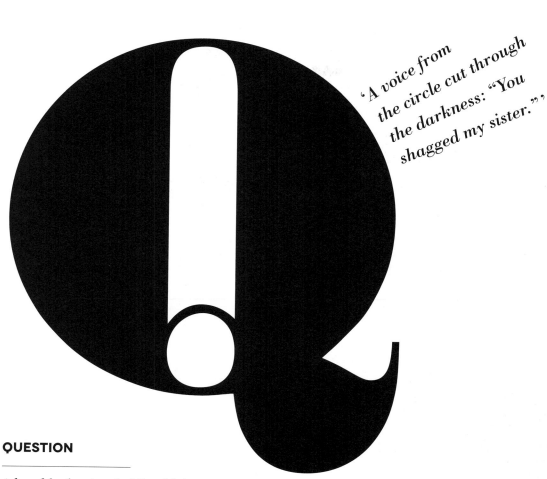

QUESTION

Adored by bovine, balding blokes now approaching their seventh decade, the Sensational Alex Harvey Band (SAHB) enjoyed a brief heyday during perhaps the darkest hour yet endured by British popular music, from roughly 1974 to 1976 (see the Wombles). SAHB and its growly brand of pub metal was appreciated especially by engineering students and the like, who for reasons known to themselves (translation: unacknowledged homosexuality) enjoyed seeing the turgid music augmented by hammy stage dramatics. One night at the Glasgow Apollo the band was performing its song 'Framed'. This required of the vocalist that at the song's conclusion he drop to one knee, a broken man, and gaze up beseechingly towards the spotlight. 'Ah didn't do nothin',' Harvey informed his unseen persecutor, by way of enquiring why fate had chosen to bring him so low.

A voice from the circle cut through the darkness. 'Aye, you did,' it said. 'You shagged my sister.'

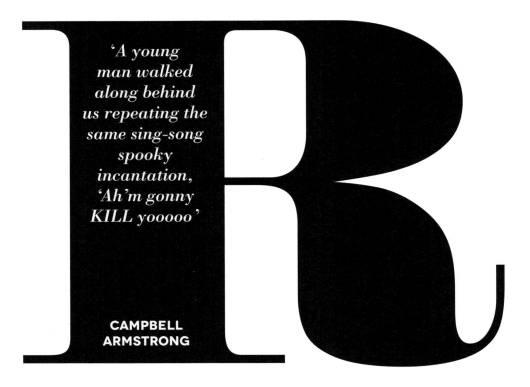

'A young man walked along behind us repeating the same sing-song spooky incantation, 'Ah'm gonny KILL yooooo'

CAMPBELL ARMSTRONG

REVOLUTION
Campbell Armstrong, novelist, on Glasgow in the 1990s:

In 1990 I made a visit. It was the year of the City of Culture – for me the year of culture shock. Where was everything I'd expected to see? I suspected some kind of sorcery had altered the city, and I was strolling through a holograph of a Glasgow that bore no relation to the one I remembered.

Where were the trams and the green and yellow corporation buses? And where in the telephone directory were the names of old schoolfriends? Missing in action, uprooted, emigrated, perhaps dead – who could tell? They were lost to me. And the black tenements I remembered, how had these staunch, grim fortresses been transformed into pink and ginger and honey-coloured sandstone extravaganzas? And where were those tantalising closes with tiled walls that almost invited you into the lives of complete strangers – why were so many of these closes concealed behind security doors? And the subway, why didn't it throw up that characteristic smell of burnt oil and damp and decay? And what was this roaring monstrosity slicing the city at St George's Cross, this motorway that ripped through the heart of Glasgow?

Pubs had developed airs and graces – ferns instead of spittoons. Restaurants were serving something called Scottish cuisine, which invariably seemed to include oatmeal ice cream and a fish soup by the unappetising name of Cullen Skink, and stovies. Stovies? Wasn't that something Maw and Paw Broon ate in the comic strip in the *Sunday Post*? I never had them at my house.

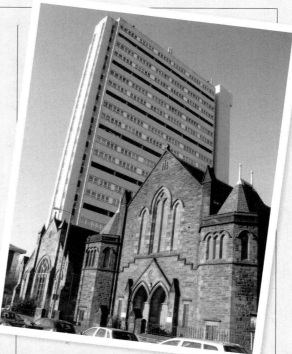

Commercial buildings had been facelifted, and delicate architraves and statuary revealed detailed architectural features formerly hidden under black grime. Old warehouses had been transformed into desirable residences. Lofts.

Something serious had happened here. Glasgow was respectable, attention-seeking, fashionable. The mutton-pie culture, if it hadn't disappeared entirely, disappeared into the shadows.

I visited the street in Linthouse where I'd been born and grown up. The tenements had been airbrushed, my old primary school restructured, the local church converted into a community of sheltered houses. My secondary school, a solid Victorian edifice in the east end of the city, had been demolished entirely, the site a field of grass. It wasn't right, something vital had been plundered, it was too damn clean, too . . . douce. It wasn't the city I'd carried

inside my mind for twenty years. How could it have changed this much? I felt vaguely estranged in the place of my birth, and a little uneasy.

In 1991, I left the United States to live in Ireland. I made three or four trips a year to Glasgow in the years that followed. I realised after a few visits that many of the changes that had so startled me in 1990 were cosmetic – an underlying Glasgowness hadn't been touched at all.

There was the same merciless banter, that barbed dry humour I'd never found in any other city. The give and take between vendors and customers at the Barras had never been so sharp, and the quick-witted criticism of highly-paid but hapless players at football matches was as caustic as it had always been.

Unhappily, there were still many areas of the city where the express train of Glasgow's reformation had simply whistled past. Bleak housing schemes where the despair of unemployment was overwhelmingly evident, the graveyard silence of the yards in Clydeside that had cast a pall of depression over the south bank of the Clyde for years – deprivations like these couldn't be disguised by any amount of cosmetic sparkle.

As people took up residence in modish places like the Merchant City or headed further west down Dumbarton Road, the other Glasgow stumbled along as it had always done – an impecunious cousin on the edge of a ritzy wedding party.

Something else hadn't changed in Glasgow. One night a couple of years ago my wife and I were attacked in the High Street – it wasn't quite a mugging, since no fiscal demands were made – by a young man who'd walked along

behind us repeating the same sing-song spooky incantation, 'Ah'm gonny KILL yooooo.' I sensed it then, and it was unsettlingly familiar – an encounter with the city's darker edge, where violence suddenly looms out of shadowy doorways.

I remembered Glasgow's old reputation as a brutal city, and realised some of that attitude still prevailed, and probably always would. And I remembered how, as a boy, strange kids would stop you and ask you that scary, inevitable question: 'You a Catholic or a Prod?' And while you tried to guess the response that would spare you a hammering, you lived on the edge of tension.

The confrontation with the attacker was brief and injury-free, because a passing taxi driver stopped to rescue us, then called the police, who seized the assailant and whisked him away. I was tense and distressed, as if I'd been whisked back into those bad moments of childhood.

The taxi driver took the matter personally, and said, 'That kind of thing is just not on in Glasgow. No way.'

So there it was. Good and bad, beautiful and shabby, warm-hearted and chilling – the incident contained the distilled essence of the city I loved and would always love. Like the character in the novel about Glasgow I eventually wrote, *The Bad Fire*, I'd come home.

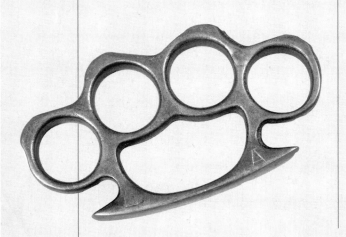

The late Campbell Armstrong (1944–2013) was a best-selling novelist and memoirist.

'It's your luck and, luckily, my luck was in'

JOHN SMEATON

JERRY SADOWITZ
(magician and comedian, 1961–)

It could be argued the truly funny thing about Jerry Sadowitz is the idea that he ever had any real comic talent whatsoever. Few performers have built such lengthy careers upon such meagre foundations. At times, in fact, Sadowitz has seemed less a stand-up comic than a performance artist, an assignment put together by some sociology faculty to establish how truly dismal a comic can be and still draw a crowd. Sadowitz has been a stand-up comedian for more than 25 years, saying unpleasant things about racial minorities, cancer and Aids sufferers, incest and paedophilia. The world's continuing refusal to oblige him with a career has been met with a considerable ratcheting-up of his indelicacy.

It was easy to predict things would end this way. When Sadowitz first appeared, in the late 1980s, British comedy had ground to a halt. Modelling himself upon more combustible American comics such as Sam Kinison and Bill Hicks, Sadowitz enjoyed a brief ascendancy, confined mainly to student unions and late-night arts festival slots, selling himself as a Glaswegian savage prepared to say the unsayable. Then in 1991 he greeted the Montreal Comedy Festival with the salutation, 'Good evening, moosefuckers!' and was assaulted by an audience member. Things have been pretty quiet since. 'My name's quite famous still,' he says, 'but I'm not.'

At this remove it is difficult to recall any Sadowitz routines. Largely they consisted of his citing a well-known personality such as Paul Daniels or Jeffrey Archer, then attaching a gynaecologically derived insult to their name. His most famous quip is perhaps the one about Nelson Mandela: 'I don't know, you lend some people a fiver and you never see them again.'

A problem with Sadowitz's act was that, ultimately, he derived greater pleasure from the unease of his audience than he was prepared to deliver as a performer. It was one-way traffic: if you felt shortchanged, you shouldn't have been so stupid as to be there. These days Sadowitz performs only a handful of shows a year; the business simply won't touch him. 'The way I see it, absolutely nothing is sacred, nothing is worth taking seriously. As long as you accept that I'm just a guy on stage who makes jokes for a living, there's no reason why I should offend anyone. What's really offensive are the things I point out. Like a kid in the Gorbals who wants to put a brick through a window because he can't get a job and who sees the Pakistanis working and thriving in the same area. Making jokes about that isn't racist, it's honest, and I, as a comedian, shouldn't be asked to compromise those observations.

'People come up to me and say, "Would you make those jokes if it was your family who were involved?" and I say, "No I wouldn't, but they weren't, so that's that!" People know what I'm about, so if they get offended easily they stay away. But it's always the same – people will laugh up until you make a joke about them. That's when it's not funny any more. When I made jokes about Lockerbie, the jokes I made concerned the Americans, who deserve to die anyway. America deals out death everywhere it goes, so it's nice to see them on the receiving end for a change.'

As Sadowitz has found to his cost, though, shock-and-awe has a shelf-life. Comics like him can pull the trick only once, after which their imitators get the knack and seize the advantage. Broadly, this is Sadowitz's story. Once out of the bottle, the genie can find himself at a loose end. His personal woes are legion. He believes his material has been stolen and sanitised by many mainstream comedians. His two television series, *The Pall Bearer's Revue* on the BBC and *The People versus Jerry Sadowitz* on Five, were both cancelled. He is the victim, he says, of whispering campaigns that have rendered him unemployable. 'They say I'm difficult,' he rages. 'If it's difficult to want a microphone that works and to get paid then, yes, I'm difficult.' He has no manager and no agent, and organises his own (infrequent) stage appearances. Like Peter Finch in *Network*, he's mad as hell and he ain't gonna take it any more, not unless we start being nice to him.

'I've never been allowed to have anything I've wanted,' he says grimly. 'I wanted to perform because that's the only time life makes sense to me. Can't do that. I wanted a nice flat where I could put my books and props. Can't have that. I have to live in some tiny bedsit in Camden, with all my stuff lying around in bin bags. Maybe a girlfriend? Nope. I'd like some relief from depression and illness [Sadowitz suffers from ulcerative colitis, a condition requiring twice daily steroid enemas.] No chance whatsoever. God hates me; it's just that fucking simple. I accepted that fact a long time ago. God looked at Frank Skinner and said, "Give him millions of pounds, a television series and a mansion." He looked at me and said, "Give him some horrible disease and a life of misery." I really wish he hadn't, but what can I do about it?'

Relief is scant. The comic Stewart Lee has long been a Sadowitz

The magic anti-Christ – Jerry Sadowitz combines conjuring and intense offence.

advocate, writing that 'Sadowitz remains that last word in supposedly offensive comedy, having contrived, by ill-luck, poor genes, or cunning design, to be one of society's eternal outsiders, thus given comic licence to denigrate everyone, from the bottom up'.

Although aggressive on stage, off-stage Sadowitz is thoughtful and courteous (that is, when he's not offering loud and lascivious comments about the group of young girls at the next table). He even has time for the notion that his misfortunes are karmic, some manner of punishment for cultivating a worldview overrun by the weeds of fear and loathing. Like all extremists, he has a tendency to mysticism, one example of which is a belief in the 'third mind': 'There's your conscious mind, right, and your unconscious mind, where you store all the stuff you can't be bothered thinking about. I believe that when the unconscious gets overloaded there's a channel into the body where the thoughts go. I think that's where mine go anyway, explaining why I'm in this state.'

This brings us to a discussion on close-up card magic, of which Sadowitz is an acknowledged master. In the past few years his shows have tended towards 80 per cent magic, 20 per cent comedy, the former being a more marketable commodity than jokes concerning television personalities and their taste for necrophilia. Sadowitz is obsessed with magic. He never leaves the house without a pack of cards and spends every idle moment studying tricks or devising new ones, though he refuses to perform them on request because it deprives magic of 'the dignity it deserves'. His only regular income now is from his job in a magic shop in Clerkenwell, London.

The obsession is understandable, though not necessarily healthy. Isn't the magician consumed by a hatred of his victims, by their inability to see the trick being played on them? Doesn't he come to see them, and by extension the world, as gullible, clueless fools? This has Sadowitz quite worried. 'I don't think so,' he says eventually. 'The magician only cares about the beauty of the trick. Everybody involved knows they're being fooled, that's the beauty of it, the willing suspension of disbelief. You only hate the victims when they start trying to work out how it was done. You want to say to them, "Don't bother, a genius spent ten years creating this trick."'

He foresees the day when he abandons comedy completely. 'It's just too painful,' he says. 'I'm an all-or-nothing person. If I can't do it all the time, why do it at all? Occasionally someone will recognise me in the street and it reminds me that to some people I'm still showbusiness Jerry, not everyday in pain, working-in-a-shop Jerry. It's too much to bear. I don't know what I did to annoy God. But it must have been something pretty serious.'

JERRY SADOWITZ LIVE

'WE HAVE THIS EXPRESSION IN GLASGOW – GLASGOW'S MILES BETTER. BETTER THAN FUCKING WHAT? EDINBURGH? THE FUCKING SNOT IN MY NOSE IS BETTER THAN GLASGOW. IF GLASGOW'S MILES BETTER, HOW COME DAVID ATTENBOROUGH HAS NEVER FILMED 'LIFE ON EARTH' THERE, EH?'

'I USED TO SUPPORT THE ANIMAL LIBERATION FRONT BUT AFTER LOSING 2-0 TO DUNDEE UNITED . . . NEVER AGAIN.'

'I COME FROM GLASGOW, WHICH IS SO DULL AND BORING AND TEDIOUS AND FUCKING DREADFULLY AWFUL THAT WHAT GLASGOW NEEDS IS A NUCLEAR HOLOCAUST . . . JUST TO BRIGHTEN IT UP, MAKE IT A BIT CHEERIER.'

'I HATE EVERYTHING, BY THE WAY. I USED TO LIKE JAFFA CAKES – UNTIL I DISCOVERED THE ORANGEY BIT IN THE MIDDLE WAS ACTUALLY THE COLLECTED EARWAX OF THE MCVITIE FAMILY.'

'I WANT TO MAKE A CONTROVERSIAL STATEMENT ABOUT THE WAR IN THE GULF – I COULDN'T GIVE A FUCK! THE SOLDIERS FUCKING DESERVE TO DIE. THEY DIDN'T LEARN THEIR LESSON FROM THE FALKLANDS. I'VE GOT NO SYMPATHY FOR THESE PEOPLE.'

'I FEEL SORRY FOR NAZIS – I MEAN, IMAGINE INVADING POLAND, ONLY TO DISCOVER THAT IT'S SHITE.'

'SAUSAGES IS THE BOYS'
(catchphrase, 1950–)

Glaswegians of a certain vintage get misty-eyed on hearing the less than grammatical claim that 'sausages is the boys'. This was the catchphrase of the character played by Jimmy Logan in *It's All Yours*, a BBC Scotland radio comedy of the early 1950s. Urban legend still has it that the phrase was the invention of Glasgow comic Tommy Lorne (1890–1935) but this seems a mischievous corruption of the fact that a type of Scottish sausage happens, coincidentally, to be known as Lorne. Only in the confused realms of garbled folk memory was anyone other than Logan first to assert that the plural entities of sausages and boys could be bracketed by a verb in the singular.

Nearer to the truth is that Logan's character in *It's All Yours* had been given a weak line and Logan, playing Sammy Dreep, extemporised to cover it. 'I suddenly said, "You can like eggs, you can like ham, but sausages is the boys,"' wrote Logan in his 1998 autobiography *It's a Funny Life*. 'The response was phenomenal, and before we knew where we were it had really taken on . . . You can build your skyscrapers, you can build your palaces, you can take vast areas of the desert and give us oil and water. But never forget . . . sausages is the boys.

'There's no intelligent explanation,' Logan added, 'but people everywhere were saying "Sausages is the boys". A guy would be telling his pal about a great holiday down the coast, and his pal would say, "Aye, but sausages is the boys". It was amazing.'

For such a footling piece of whimsy, the phrase provoked two oddly consequential ripples. Logan claimed in his autobiography that it was the adolescent fondness of Billy Connolly for *It's All Yours* and, specifically, for the askew nonsense of 'sausages is the boys', that kick-started the young man's affinity for comedy and for performing.

The catchphrase was also cited in parliament by the Right Honourable Arthur Woodburn, the Labour member for Clackmannan. 'During a debate on education in the House of Commons,' wrote Logan, 'Woodburn claimed the BBC was encouraging slovenly and ungrammatical speech – and that I was the chief perpetrator.'

SCOTCH & WRY
(sketch show, 1978–1992)

The literal definition of appointment television, *Scotch & Wry* was for twelve years the must-see event of the closing year, the closest approximation to an electronic fireside the city ever produced. Broadcast each year as the Hogmanay celebrations reached their height and skippered by the redoubtable Rikki Fulton, *Scotch & Wry* was a high-water mark, the peak of a writing and performing pyramid (incorporating Tony Roper, Mark McManus and John Byrne) whose construction had been under way since the 1950s.

Recalling the sharp but amiable comedy of *The Two Ronnies*, *Scotch & Wry* lampooned social and professional stereotypes with a

Scotch & Wry Characters:

Reverend I.M. Jolly: militantly dolorous man of the cloth who, with his catchphrase 'Ah've had a helluva year', proved to be the most popular of several ministers played by Fulton in *Last Call*, a parody of STV's late-night 'God slot' programme *Late Call*. The Jolly monologues usually contained reference to the antics of church organist Mr Bampot and his own mysterious wife, Ephesia: 'This morning started like any other. I awoke to the sound of my dear wife Ephesia's gentle, barely audible snoring – it's barely audible because she sleeps downstairs in a bedroom with double-glazed doors and windows.'

Supercop: an incompetent traffic policeman who uses the catch-phrase 'OK, *Stirling*, oot the car!' only to find himself faced with Batman, an extraterrestial, DCI Jim Taggart, Dr Crippen or other unlikely traffic offenders.

Dirty Dickie Dandruff, the Gallowgate Gourmet: horribly unhygienic TV chef who welcomed viewers with the phrase 'Hullo and welcome to Dirty Dick's.'

Aloysius McGlinchey: a colourful Rab C Nesbitt prototype.

Ticket Clerk: an unnamed ticket clerk, poking fun at British Rail. He would pull down the shutter down before an unfortunate passenger with the line, 'The last train left five minutes ago.'

humour that was adult yet family-friendly, as befitted the show's first-foot status. Appearing initially in 1978 and 1979 as a series, *Scotch & Wry* assumed its Hogmanay berth the following year, aimed particularly, as its references made plain, at a Glasgow-speaking audience. Gradually, though, the show came to take as its basis the major news events of the year that had just passed. Famously, the show birthed the Reverend I.M. Jolly, possibly the defining exemplar of its Scotchness *and* its wryness.

THE REVEREND BILL SHACKLETON
(minister, 1927–)

In his 1994 memoir *Keeping It Cheery* (remember this title, for soon it will assume significance), Bill Shackleton, a minister of the Church of Scotland, recalled his years of soulsaving at St Francis's Church in Bridgeton, in the east end of the city. The job, as you might imagine, had its trials, but the Reverend opts always to turn the frown upside down, to the extent that not even mass murder can rain on his parade. The ability of Glasgow to turn horror into humour, or at least a reason to be cheerful, extends even unto its clergy, it would seem.

> When Fred and Rosemary West were arrested for their appalling crimes, I read that he had lived at one time in Bridgeton (Soho Street), and operated an ice-cream van called 'Mr Whippy'. The name of the van struck a chord with me, and I realised that, on my way home on Friday nights, after the vestry hour, I may well have bought cones for my three children from Fred West! I can picture summer nights – a crowd of weans round the van – a friendly vendor giving priority to my order and bidding me, in an English voice, 'Good evening, vicar!'

CHARLIE SHEEN
(actor, 1965–)

In one of those moves explained by financial considerations of no small complexity, Charlie Sheen, the wayward Hollywood leading man, star of *Wall Street* and *Platoon*, once came to Glasgow to shoot a movie. Its title was *Postmortem* (1998) and it was the tale of an American cop, on holiday, or vacation, in Glasgow (wait, it gets worse) who is sent obituaries of people who, several days later, turn up dead. At the time, Sheen was in the grip of various substance addictions. Yielding to temptation, he went out one night in Glasgow city centre and soon found himself hooked up with a willing supplier in the far east of the city. Sheen, though, was obliged to complete the transaction in the gentleman's home, leading Tom Shields's Diary in the *Herald* to observe that this was the first time in ages an Easterhouse council flat had had the benefit of Mr Sheen.

The movie itself turned out to be farcical, of course. So tight was the grip upon the pursestrings that almost all of *Postmortem*'s location shooting was confined to two streets. The exterior of Central Station was used heavily, no doubt to denote that Glasgow was a thrumming *Bladerunner*-style metropolis, an effect diminished somewhat by copious shots of the old newspaper sellers outside. To this day, cineastes talk admiringly of the R.S. McColl's-to-Boots car chase and the thrilling climactic gun battle outside the Alliance & Leicester. The other location used was York Street, a thoroughfare running between Argyle Street and the river. This street was used in order to suggest that Glasgow harboured pockets of urban squalor to match the hellish *barrios* of Los Angeles, an effect that could have been achieved even if the pleasant bits of Glasgow had been depicted.

TAM SHEPHERD'S TRICK SHOP
(1886–)

It is strangely nice to know that Tam Shepherd's Trick Shop has been serving the public of Glasgow for so lengthy a time, and that what it serves them are items of such profound frivolity. Happily, the small, single-storied concern in the city centre has yet to be dignified by age.

Established in 1886, Tam Shepherd's remains the living definition of an old curiosity shop, and has schooled generation upon generation of the practitioners of slapstick. Had William Gladstone, for example, while on a flying visit to Glasgow,

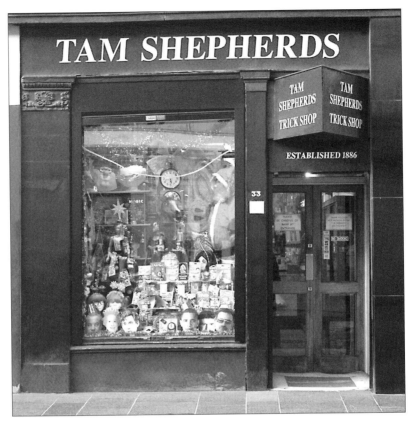

developed the notion for a packet of sweets that turned the mouth blue, Tam Shepherd's was there to oblige him. Likewise, Charles Rennie Mackintosh, Alexander Graham Bell, Sir William Burrell, Red Clydeside or Alex Harvey – any time any of them felt the need of an inflatable sheep or a pair of vampire fangs, they knew where to go. Of course, Tam himself was gathered to the great props cupboard in the sky many years ago. Since the 1930s his shop has been in the ownership of the Walton family, who produced in time Roy Walton, now among the most highly regarded card magicians in the world. Walton mentored the comic Jerry Sadowitz in his studies of sleight-of-hand and was acknowledged in 'The Roy Walton Moment', a recurring close-magic feature of Sadowitz's BBC 2 show *The Pall Bearer's Revue* (1992).

TOMMY SHERIDAN
(politician, 1964–)

Has anything in the past, say, half-century provoked in the saloon-bar humorists of Glasgow a level of hilarity equivalent to the humbling of Tommy Sheridan? It is doubtful. In comedic terms, the downfall of the former socialist MSP had it all. It was a perfect storm of *Carry On* smut, Ray Cooney farce and of a kind of grandstanding that would have given even Rumpole of the Bailey pause for thought.

Each of the two Sheridan trials – the first in 2006, in which he alleged defamation against the *News of the World*, the second in 2010 where he stood accused of perjury – felt as though all the city's comedy Christmases had come at once. With their allegations of four-in-a-bed orgies, visits to dingy sex clubs, the alleged involvement of a Premier League football manager and a titanic challenge to Sheridan's standing as a home-loving, teetotal paragon of socialist rectitude, both trials kept the city in scabrous and gleeful ammunition for the best part of five years.

It could have been argued that Sheridan, co-founder of the Scottish Socialist Party, had effectively sabotaged forever the hard left in Scotland, but he was shrewd in one respect at least. He elected to play along with the joke. There was no way he could remain in the city and do otherwise, such was the extent to which he'd been rebranded in Glasgow's imagination. Whether guilty or otherwise, Sheridan would be associated forever with amatory hobbyism of an impressively strenuous kind, and he'd just better get accustomed to the fact.

So he did. A year after the initial trial, in which Sheridan was awarded £200,000 for defamation, he returned to Edinburgh for the Fringe, in *The Tommy Sheridan Chat Show*. In this, some tepid stand-up routines were bulked out with appearances by any sympathetic celebrities who were appearing elsewhere at the festival. It was disastrously bad. Arriving on stage to the strains of 'King of The Swingers' and surrounded by newspaper hoardings that exclaimed his torrid backstory, Sheridan stayed unbowed and delivered lines of the lowest quality conceivable: 'Edinburgh is so posh,' he said, 'its women don't get crabs, they get lobsters'; neither did they 'get the clap, they get applause'.

Muscular socialism – Tommy Sheridan.

In the red corner

Did you hear Tommy Sheridan is going back into politics? He's forming an Ann Summers Party.

Tommy Sheridan leaves the High Court and arrives home to discover he's left his papers behind. He returns to the court where a cleaning lady is dusting the judge's chair. 'I'm here for my holdall,' he tells her. 'Tommy, do ye not think you're in enough trouble already?'

What's the difference between Tommy Sheridan and a new attitude to gender politics?
Time. Just time.

A new tennis facility in Glasgow will follow the French tradition of naming its courts after renowned figures. The Tommy Sheridan court will be reserved for mixed doubles, trebles and foursomes.

Those listening to BBC news coverage of the Glasgow North-east by-election thought that, given his various legal difficulties, Tommy Sheridan must have had something on his mind to describe his opponents as 'untried candidates'.
The Herald Diary, 23 October 2009

A Premier Inn maid changed a king-sized bed in a world record time of 95 seconds. This beats the previous record held by Tommy Sheridan when Gail got home early from work.

In the years to come Sheridan would continue his collaborations with the media and the expertly calibrated self-lampooning that came with it. He hosted a weekly show on Talk 107 radio. In 2009 he appeared in the celebrity version of the reality show *Big Brother*. He was convicted of perjury in December 2010 and sentenced to three years' imprisonment. In March 2012 it was announced that a play based on Sheridan's story would open in the autumn of that year, written by Ian Pattison, creator of the noxious *Rab C Nesbitt*. The news was kind of an acknowledgement that Sheridan was now among the city's pantheon of comic heroes, alongside Lobey Dosser and the Big Yin, Francie and Josie, and the Krankies. And that is no more than Tommy Sheridan deserves.

TOM SHIELDS' DIARY
(newspaper column, 1978–2002)

Like the newspaper wanderings of Flann O'Brien, written under the pen name Myles na gCopaleen, or the 'Beachcomber' columns of J.B. Morton in the *Daily Express*, Tom Shields' Diary in the *Glasgow Herald* became cult reading, in the city and its environs at least. Derived in the main from anecdotes submitted by readers, the Diary was adored for its pithy and affectionate depiction of Glaswegian foibles, as expressed in tales from the worlds of law, academe, business, sport *et al*, drawing a picture of the city with which the natives concurred heartily – as a plainspeaking and egalitarian city, ever ready to cut pretension off at the knees. Although the diary column – sited customarily on the newspaper's op-ed page – was established by editor Samuel Hunter in the nineteenth century, and has been written in modern times by journalists such as Colm Brogan, Murray Ritchie and William Hunter, it remains associated most definingly with Shields, born in 1948, whose laconic prose style tended to underplay the jokes most winningly; as in . . .

One of Scotland's great characters was the late James 'Solly' Sanderson, sports journalist and doyen of the Radio Clyde phone-in. His highly idiosyncratic style of prediction and controversy attracted a large following, so much so that an advertising agency decided to use his character in a series of radio adverts. They approached the comedian Allan Stewart, who did a very accurate impersonation of Solly. Stewart said it would be no bother and quoted a price of £200. At this point the agency had second thoughts. They approached Solly and hired him to be himself at only £50.

As a young Rangers player, Alex Ferguson, now manager of Manchester United, was unhappy at being left out of the first team. He stormed into the office of legendary manager Scot Symon. 'Why have I been in the second team for three weeks?' he asked. The magisterial Mr Symon replied, 'Because we don't have a third team.'

A Texan complete with boots and Stetson was not prepared to wait his turn in the cocktail bar along with other customers who had not booked a table in a busy hotel restaurant. When a table became vacant he jumped the queue and sat down. The waiters, in a scene reminiscent of a Scotch & Wry sketch, ignored his constant shouts to be given a menu. Eventually the head waiter simply walked up and took away the table leaving the Texan sitting in a chair in the middle of the restaurant. He got the message and returned to the bar.

———————

One of the proud banners of the Scottish Constitutional Convention is the commitment to fair representation for women. Imagine, therefore, the shaking of heads which accompanied these remarks by Mr Harry Ewing, the Labour MP and joint chairman of the convention, at the close of a meeting. Mr Ewing thanked the convention administrator Bruce Black for his sterling work and also 'the lassies in the office who did the typing'.

———————

In a greengrocers' in Byres Road, a university lecturer is causing a small scene. In accordance with his anti-apartheid principles, he refuses to buy the South African oranges he has been offered. The West End lady behind him in the queue chimes in: 'I do so agree, all those black fingers . . .'

———————

Sign in an Ayrshire pub: Welcome – A Pint, A Pie, and A Kind Word. A visitor duly followed the suggestion on the sign. The barmaid slammed his pint in front of him without a word. She was equally taciturn when she dumped an extremely greasy and aged pie on the bar. 'What about the kind word?' he asked. 'Don't eat the pie,' she retorted.

———————

There is an old and oft-repeated joke about a young man in a Glasgow restaurant who is asked by the waiter if he would like ginger with his melon. He replies that he will stick to the red wine, the same as the rest of the company.

DAVID SHRIGLEY
(artist, 1968–)

Not strictly Glaswegian (he was raised in Macclesfield), but resident in the city for more than a quarter of a century, Shrigley is of a lineage that stretches back to Chic Murray and moves towards the modern day via Ivor Cutler and the odder moments in the movies of Bill Forsyth. And some visual artists, too, no doubt; the influence most conspicuous is the cartoons of Gary Larson. By now mainstream and culty simultaneously, Shrigley's work is anthologised and exhibited around the globe, featured on greetings cards, T-shirts, screenprints, playing cards, plectrums and skateboards purchased by the beetroot-eating, *Guardian*-reading classes.

Deliberately and provocatively amateurish, resembling the work of a damaged but precocious child, Shrigley's style was born, he

claims, of his lack of any real technical ability, despite his years at Glasgow School of Art. Whether in photography or illustration, in aphorism or object-making, the tone is one of poker-faced morbidity as it points at the strange and the senseless things filling the world around us. A stuffed Jack Russell holds aloft a placard reading I'M DEAD; a cruet set features two shakers, one containing Cocaine, the other Heroin; a glum stickman waves a flag that reads Ants Have Sex In Your Beer; a sign on a lawn instructs us to Imagine The Green Is Red; and, most frequently, there are crude didactic injunctions: Drugs Make Us Stronger, Please Do Not Show This To Anyone and If I Find Out Who You Are I Will Kill You.

There are also photographs of the works that Shrigley places around Glasgow: scrawled signs reading: Lost Grey And White Pigeon With Black Bits, Normal Size, A Bit Mangy-Looking, Does Not Have A Name; River For Sale; a bottle of yellow liquid in a back court bearing the label Drink Me. Shrigley's own status, meanwhile, and his scepticism for the rules and regulations of the art process is satirised in one of his best-known drawings (see above).

SIGNS

Signs and notices are, by nature, formal; they exist to draw the attention, and for maximum impact should impart their messages as soberly as possible. None of this applies in Glasgow, though, where all formality is ripe for subversion. What else is to be expected in a city where even the most ubiquitous piece of signage, the civic coat of arms, is itself an in-joke, with its tree that never grew, bird that never flew, fish that never swam and bell that never rang? The theme was taken up by artist Ronnie Heeps, who in 2010 adorned the Merchant City with a range of absurdist Blue Plaques. They joined an array of quixotic communiqués.

PRESS BUTTON TO CALL LIFT
OPEN GATE – RELEASE CHAIN
ENTER LIFT
CLOSE GATE – REPLACE CHAIN
PRESS BUTTON TO OPERATE LIFT

DUE TO DELIVERY
ERROR I
REGRET TO
INFORM THAT
THIS SHOP HAS
NO BUCKFAST
AT ALL PLEASE
DO NOT ABUSE
THE STAFF AS
IT IS NOT THEIR
FAULT THANKS

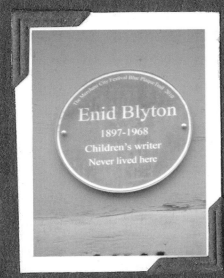

Enid Blyton
1897-1968
Children's writer
Never lived here

THE SLAB BOYS
(dramatic trilogy, 1978–1982)

Striving, perhaps, to compensate for the city's dearth of dramatic comedy, *The Slab Boys* unfurls its tale in lengths of Glaswegian blank verse, in yards of scintillating slang, insult and provocation. John Byrne's sequence of plays is like an anthology of the local lingo at its zenith of drollery, a primer in the patter. It seems fitting that in his semiautobiographical troika Byrne was recalling the late 1950s, also the era of *Parliamo Glasgow* and Francie and Josie, when Glasgow was beginning to hear itself and to like what it heard.

So, the plays are living museums of everything the city kept, and keeps still, in its verbal armoury: the hipster sarcasm of Phil – 'Now, here is what we call a sink. I don't expect you to pick up these terms immediately but you'll soon get the hang of them'; the comebacks of the vengeful Hector – 'I'm sorry to hear you lost your job, Phil, but not to worry, I don't think you'll notice much difference now that you're officially out of work'; sketcher Lucille Bentley – 'Which one of you clatty gannets has been at Miss Walkinshaw's lunch pail? Her sardine and chutney sandwich is covered in raw sienna and her orange has went missing. You're greedy pigs. You know she's got a caliper'; and the gaffer Willie Curry, recalling his army days in the desert – 'Impacted dromedary droppings crackling merrily away, sending a fountain of bright sparks winging into the velvet skies'.

The plays recall Byrne's youth working in the A.F. Stoddard carpet factory in Elderslie, where it was the slab boys' job to grind mounds of coloured powder on slabs and to glue the results to patterns from which the carpets would be woven. 'It was truly the most numbingly boring job in the entire universe,' Byrne wrote. 'A Technicolor hellhole. So much for my wanting to pursue an artist's life.' Other real-life experiences found their way into the plays. Byrne's mother was schizophrenic, as is Phil's. 'She wisnae that bad, for her that is,' Phil tells Spanky following an incident. 'Aw she did was put in the Cooperative's windaes and run up the street wi' her hair on fire.'

The Slab Boys was the first play in the trilogy, followed by *Cutting a Rug* and *Still Life*. The story as a whole details Phil's sacking from the factory and his later rejection from Glasgow School of Art, the annual staff dance, at which Hector stabs himself, and, years later, following Hector's death, a meeting between Phil and Spanky to discuss old times. As with Byrne's other major piece, *Tutti Frutti*, the trilogy was sad and sour in equal measure, a dream of rebellion and escape rendered in shades growing progressively darker. Before it did so, though, *The Slab Boys* wove itself into the city's tapestry, with a comedy that fizzed like Sasparilla and stood out like raw sienna on a sardine and chutney sandwich.

JOHN SMEATON
(baggage-handling vigilante, 1976–)

Like some dusty hula-hoops that lean against a pile of Osmond LPs, the celebrity of John Smeaton is but a sad and tender memory now. Yet once it seemed so vivid and vital. For a spell, Smeaton simulated Sir Harry Paget Flashman of the George MacDonald Fraser novels, a figure who deployed violence in a manner that enhanced his own greater glory. In the process he gave to the world a strain of Glasgow patois that mystified all who heard it, excepting Glaswegians, who were so delighted that they bestowed upon Smeaton the status of comedic folk hero.

And so, let us unfurl once more ye tattered scroll of antiquity and recite again ye tale of John Smeaton, the man who raced towards his own destiny threatening to kick its head in. An agreeable and phlegmatic soul, Smeaton had performed since 1995 one of those jobs we seldom get to see; he removed baggage from the holds of long-haul flights and placed it for collection on carousels – speaking officially, he was a Senior Ramp Assistant. Supervising his ramps on the morning of 30 June 2007, Smeaton was taking a cigarette break outside the check-in hall of Glasgow Airport when his trained and expert eye couldn't help but register something amiss. A green Jeep Cherokee, loaded with propane gas canisters, it transpired, was being driven towards the glass doors of the hall. There was a collision and the burning Jeep was evacuated by its driver and passenger. It was at this point that Smeaton considered it civic to step in. Some are born great; some achieve greatness; and some have greatness run towards them, screaming about Allah.

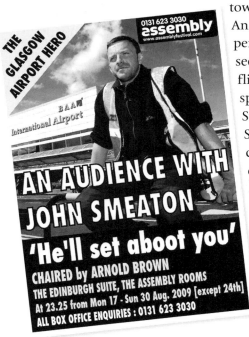

THE GLASGOW AIRPORT HERO

0131 623 3030
assembly
www.assemblyfestival.com

BAA
International Airport

AN AUDIENCE WITH JOHN SMEATON
'He'll set aboot you'
CHAIRED by ARNOLD BROWN
THE EDINBURGH SUITE, THE ASSEMBLY ROOMS
At 23.25 from Mon 17 - Sun 30 Aug. 2009 [except 24th]
ALL BOX OFFICE ENQUIRIES : 0131 623 3030

THE SAYINGS OF SMEATON

IF THE LAW FALLS, WE ALL FALL.

YOU SEE A GUY IN FLAMES LYING ON THE GROUND AND PEOPLE ARE HOSING HIM DOWN. YOU DON'T EXPECT TO SEE THAT IN A DAY AT WORK. ESPECIALLY AT GLASGOW AIRPORT.

HE GOES STRAIGHT FOR THE POLICEMAN AND I'M LIKE, NO, NO CHANCE, THIS ISNAE HAPPENING. I THOUGHT, WE'RE UNDER ATTACK HERE. IT'S YOUR CIVIC DUTY, YOU'VE JUST GOT TO GET IN AND DO IT. IT'S YOUR LUCK AND, LUCKILY, MY LUCK WAS IN.

AND SO I DECKED THE GENTLEMAN...

NEW YORK, MADRID, LONDON, PAISLEY... WE'RE ALL IN THIS TOGETHER AND, MAKE NO MISTAKE, NONE OF US WILL HOLD BACK FROM PUTTING THE BOOT IN.

THEY CAN TRY AND DISRUPT US BUT THE BRITISH PEOPLE HAVE BEEN UNDER A LOT MORE THINGS THAN THIS.

YOU COME TO GLASGOW BUT GLASGOW DOESN'T ACCEPT THIS. THIS IS GLASGOW, YOU KNOW, SO... WE'LL SET ABOUT YOU, Y'KNOW. THAT'S IT.

What occurred in the minutes ensuing remains a source of contention. Some claim passers-by aided Smeaton considerably in his onslaughts upon the barbecued Islamists. But, certainly, it was Smeaton to whom the cameras were drawn. Reporter after reporter heard him deliver what was essentially the Glaswegian equivalent of the St Crispian's Day speech from *Henry V*, a beginner's guide to what the Glasgow citizenry would bear, and, more pertinently, what they wouldn't. Supercharged with shock and adrenaline, Smeaton coined one luminous phrase after another, like a warrior Bard of the Ramp Assistance realm. In the ensuing days news networks flew in, cocked their heads to one side, smiled indulgently and struggled to penetrate Smeaton's opaque colloquialisms. A channel from Australia subtitled him. His was a have-a-go-hero story, but on a geopolitical scale, with a hint of Groundskeeper Willie thrown in.

In the days following, the Smeaton bandwagon gathered speed. A tribute website was set up, featuring a fund for those who wished to buy Smeaton a drink. The *Wall Street Journal* put him on the cover. He appeared before the crowd at Ibrox Stadium, home of his beloved team Rangers, and was given a column in the Scottish edition of the *Sun* newspaper. He was invited to mark the sixth anniversary of the World Trade Center attack and met New York's mayor, Michael Bloomberg. He received a standing ovation at the Labour Party conference, and received a Pride of Britain award and a Queen's Gallantry Medal. *Time* magazine named Smeaton among its People Who Matter of 2007. He appeared, inevitably, in a one-man show at the Edinburgh Fringe, and in 2009 stood (unsuccessfully) as an independent in the parliamentary election for Glasgow North-East.

Though Smeaton remains a well-regarded figure in the city, there is no denying that his fame is a complicated thing. A measure of popular admiration for Smeaton's actions at Glasgow Airport co-exists with a disbelieving delight that a Glaswegian working man could become a global hero. The very unlikeliness of the idea renders it too silly to take completely seriously. Smeaton acknowledged as much, of course, and strove to treat the entire matter lightly. Yet there is no gainsaying the comedic impact of his first appearances on camera, described in *Time* magazine thusly: 'It was the high-seriousness with which Smeaton fielded reporters' earnest questions on June 30 that has truly elevated him to comic status,' wrote Eben Harrell. 'With the faux-authority of his orange worker's vest, he gives an account full of dramatic pauses and the inflated diction of a policeman giving evidence: "I saw a man egress the vehicle," he explained to one reporter. In the event's aftermath, Smeaton's unblinking gravitas became pure British satire – he is the David Brent of airport security.'

SONIA BYTES
(internet cookery programme, 2010–)

Sonia Bytes is an intensely, if unintentionally, hilarious online cookery show which must not be missed but, equally, and paradoxically, must not be seen either. Like the destruction of Sodom, *Sonia Bytes* is so terrible it will turn you to a pillar of salt. And then Sonia will use you to season her risotto.

The Sonia in question is Sonia Scott Mackay, a Glaswegian social gadfly whose 2009 stint as a contestant on Channel 4's *Come Dine with Me* convinced her of one thing: that discussing the culinary arts on camera was just the thing for anyone as vital, smouldering and photogenic as she.

Thus *Sonia Bytes*, a cut-price camcorder approximation of a Nigella Lawson show, shot in a G-Plan kitchen somewhere, we're guessing, in Giffnock. Sonia's schtick is that she's something of a saucy, sexy dominatrix, a belief sustained by two facts: that a) she wields occasionally a riding crop and b) has not been scarred in an acid attack. To underline her conviction she is accompanied on screen by a mute slab of gym-bunny beefcake, wearing little more than a starched butler's collar. His eyes beg for death, either Sonia's or his own – one doubts he is fussy. At the outset of each episode Sonia makes an announcement: 'I cook, he cleans, you watch!' None of these commands seems reasonable. Sonia ploughs on nonetheless, with her Bellini pancakes, her Pavlovas or her Moroccan meatballs. In each case, extreme suggestiveness is deployed as frequently as possible. The internet has brought many, many bounties. But it brought *Sonia Bytes*, too.

Saucy innuendo in Sonia's Bytes.

THE STEAMIE
(play, Tony Roper, 1987)

In the theatre and on television, *The Steamie* has become the defining portrait of the city's sepia era, a set text of Glasgow sentimentalism. Tony Roper's comedy – produced for Wildcat, then adapted for Scottish Television – meditated on bygone days and dear happy ghosts, on a soft-focus Glasgow where aproned wives goaded feckless, half-drunk husbands, boys in back courts raided middens and a locked front door got you reported for crimes against neighbourliness. Custom-built to squeeze out tears of remembrance, *The Steamie* was warm but bittersweet, like bathing in mince and tatties as the rent collector peered through the letterbox.

Set in the 1950s in a communal washhouse or steamie, a kind of council-provided launderette in the age pre-dating domestic facilities, Roper's play is essentially a series of conversations between four women as they undertake the final wash of the year and prepare for their Hogmanay celebrations. The women discuss their children and husbands, the eccentricities of their neighbours, the hopes and dreams of their younger selves, and the hardships of their lives today. 'Hearts are worn on rolledup sleeves,' wrote Jack Tinker, veteran theatre critic of the *Daily Mail*. It can be inferred that the characters are representing four stages in the life of the same woman: Doreen, the hopeful newly-wed (played in the television adaptation by Katy Murphy, previously Miss Toner in *Tutti Frutti*); Dolly (Eileen McCallum), more realistic and phlegmatic; Magrit (Dorothy Paul), edging towards cynicism; and Mrs Culfeathers (Sheila Donald), elderly and defeated.

As with its strain of humour, the very concept of *The Steamie* was born of adversity, sort of. Roper had intended to write a drama set in Glasgow's shipyards, then discovered Bill Bryden's *Willie Rough* (1975) had beaten him to it. Undaunted, he noticed the audience for community theatre was female, principally, and older. The shipyard play was moved to a milieu such audiences might recognise. It was propitiously timed, as Glasgow sought a new post-industrial identity and began to feel just a little teary about the old one. *The Steamie* quickly entered the Scottish theatrical repertory, as one long sigh for a Glasgow washed away like stains from a sheet. The play is revived frequently and, directed by Roper himself, undertook a sizeable tour for its twenty-fifth anniversary.

STILL GAME
(sitcom, 2002–2007)

'Nobody knows anything,' opined the screenwriter William Goldman, striving to summarise an abiding condition of cultural production – that stars, directors and scripts guarantee nothing, should the fickle finger of fate elect to point in the opposite direction; that productions which should be massive hits can unceremoniously bomb, while, sometimes, the least likely prosper.

The truth of this has been borne out, gloriously, by *Still Game*. Most writers would expect jeers were they to pitch a comedy where two bad-tempered pensioners kill time on a rain-soaked housing scheme, with only trips to the mini-mart for light relief. Greg Hemphill and Ford Kiernan, however, earned their indulgence with the success of *Chewin' the Fat*. They went on to justify it with a show that spun gold from dross that, like the work of Ivor Cutler, concerned itself with how little we change on our journey from childhood to senescence.

Starting life as a stage play, and with its central characters appearing occasionally in *Chewin' the Fat*, *Still Game* dealt with the lives of Jack Jarvis and Victor McDade, two bunnet-wearers in their early seventies, now retired from their blue-collar jobs and living in a tower block in the (fictional) Craiglang area of Glasgow. Accompanied by friend and contemporary Winston Ingram, the men confront the many and various vicissitudes of advanced age: the advisability of Viagra, developing a crush on the woman who runs the charity shop, hearing only rarely from offspring, poverty, electricity fraud and widowhood. Despite the show's heavy use of colloquialisms, its writing was of sufficient quality to secure it a place on the national network from its fourth series on. It looks unlikely that Hemphill and Kiernan will make any further episodes, but they know at least they created a landmark on the panorama of the city's comedy, with a series that could discuss sudden death and wee brown loaves with equal bittersweet sincerity.

THE REVEREND OBADIAH STEPPENWOLFE III
(performer, 2003–)

One of the most remarkable Glaswegian stand-ups of recent times, the Reverend Obadiah Steppenwolfe III seems the result of a curious fankle in the space–time continuum. In the accepted contemporary manner his comedy is brutal, a police identity parade where sexism, sodomy and paedophilia assume their usual places; few stag parties or student socialities would leave a club feeling the Reverend had short-changed them or fell short in his ability to dispatch jaws floor-wards. Yet the lines are delivered by an old-fashioned, variety-era comic character. The comedian takes the stage not as himself but as a fictitional entity, a costumed alter-ego. Technically, then, there isn't much to distinguish the Reverend from, say, Francie and Josie, or even from Big Beenie, the G.I. War Bride, created by Tommy Morgan. Well, actually, there is: neither Francie nor Josie ever told an audience member 'Hey, you've got what my gran'pappy calls a four-cock mouth . . .'

Devil's advocate – the blasphemous Rev. Obadiah Steppenwolfe III.

The Reverend is the creation of one Jim Muir, former call-centre worker turned writer and performer, and co-conspirator of Frankie Boyle, with whom an urge to appal is shared fraternally. Though Muir continues to perform as the Reverend, of late it's seemed the character has been sacrificed rather on the altar of Boyle's success. A portfolio of spinoffs – a Steppenwolfe sitcom among them – failed eventually to materialise, though Muir was a frequent presence on Boyle's *Tramadol Nights* series for Channel 4 (2010). It may be that Boyle serves now as the standard-bearer of the pair's comedy, that they are essentially a two-for-one deal, the indulgence afforded by Boyle's considerable mainstream success.

Equally, however, it may be that Muir's always volatile attitude to performance sees his interest on the wane. Muir has always been a genuinely awkward and saturnine quantity. 'It's a very fake sort of profession,' he says. 'Everyone is performing the same stuff, rubbish about their girlfriends, and writing their ad-libs before they go on stage. I had one gig to go and then I was planning to give up. Then I remembered Obadiah.'

In Aviator shades and a suit several shades whiter than his soul, the Reverend possesses a mind that moves in mysterious ways, musing on the exorcisms, conversions and blackmail plots that have featured in his shameless life. Part Jimmy Swaggart, part Keith Richards, redolent of Jack Nicholson visiting Lourdes with the world's worst hangover, the Reverend is a vile but charismatic maniac, preaching in a molasses-thick Southern accent his sermons of guilt-free degradation. Female hecklers are always welcome. 'Hey,' he's been known to say, 'you're what Jack the Ripper would call two nights' work.'

This patron saint of the damned is a human laboratory and unfussy sexual pioneer, devoting his ministry to single mothers and the recently widowed. Moving among the churches, missions and hermaphroditic massage parlours of the Deep South, the Reverend has yet to take a drug he didn't like or meet a sinner with whom he couldn't sympathise. 'In stand-up comedy,' Muir says, 'it's called Walking the Room. When you start to bomb, as the Reverend often does, you go into this new frame of mind. You think, well, if you hated that, here's another half-hour of stuff you'll hate even more.

'And because the Reverend is a character, audiences feel he isn't quite real and that it's fair game to go at him constantly. One aspect of doing the character is that you spend more time coming up with anti-heckler lines than actual material. My mind has become like the drop-down menu on a computer: if you're being shouted at by a guy with red hair and glasses, the brain runs through its program and finds the insults the Reverend has for red hair and glasses. My wife hasn't come to any of my shows for a few years; she just doesn't like to see what goes on up there.

'For me the Reverend is an exercise in positive thinking. Ten years ago I could barely leave the house. Now, the Reverend infects me; he does me a lot of good. I'm a more confident, outgoing person because of the Reverend. Anything he can do or say, I can too.' The thought is not an entirely happy one.

I used to be a sodomite, and the Bible says that any man who lays with another man should be stoned – well, drugs certainly help.

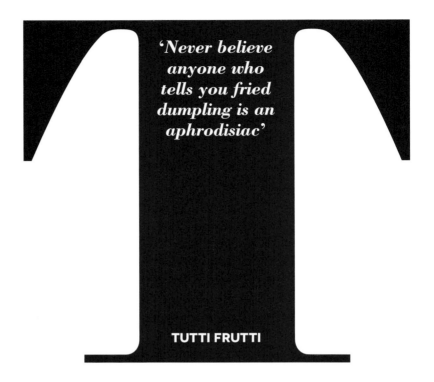

'Never believe anyone who tells you fried dumpling is an aphrodisiac'

TUTTI FRUTTI

TEACHING
(profession, c. 1900–)

Formal education in Glasgow has long been fraught with difficulty, occasioned by the typically Glaswegian presumption that to pursue knowledge is to engage in an activity that is inherently elitist and

The kids are alright.

less than egalitarian. This might explain the following, a list of euphemisms used among teachers in Glasgow to suggest the true meanings behind report-card summaries.

Born leader – runs a protection racket
Easy-going – bone idle
Good progress – you should have seen him a year ago
Friendly – never shuts up
Helpful – a creep
Reliable – informs on his friends
Expresses himself confidently – impertinent
Enjoys physical education – a bully
Does not accept authority easily – Dad is in prison
Often appears tired – stays up all night watching television
A solitary child – he smells
Popular in the playground – sells pornography

THAT SINKING FEELING
(film, 1980)

'There must be something more to life than committing suicide,' decides Pete in the opening scenes of *That Sinking Feeling*, Bill Forsyth's no-budget feature debut. The viewer is invited to doubt it. Forsyth's film is set in one mean city indeed; not violent as such, but derelict and dirty, blighted by unemployment and a constant haar. The solution, Ronnie concludes, following a vain attempt to choke himself to death with cornflakes, is crime, by thieving from a nearby warehouse 90 stainless steel sink units. 'Sixty quid times ninety,' Alec calculates. 'Hey, that's over a hundred quid.'

With their 'ill-gotten drains' the gang will be set to join the consumer society and avail themselves of everything the damp and heartless city denies them: high-end hi-fi, holidays to Grangemouth, all the cornflakes in Christendom and a car more luxurious than one propped up on bricks on a patch of waste ground.

But first the robbery must pass off successfully. Which is when the problems begin. Vic schemes to dupe the nightwatchman by disguising himself as a cleaning lady, a mission he takes to with worrying sincerity, abetted by Wal, who, it turns out, makes a very beguiling lady indeed. Pete's chemistry experiment, meanwhile,  creates a sleeping potion that stupefies the van driver ('How much d'ye think we'd get for his kidneys?'). And, after the robbery, the gang is left with the dilemma of how to turn their purloined sinks into hard cash, leading to a scheme to raid the local Irn-Bru factory.

Although its humour was gentle and unassuming, the film's effect was convulsive. It led Forsyth towards *Gregory's Girl* and, with it, the first stirrings of a film community in Glasgow, spawning *Heavenly Pursuits, Restless Natives* and *The Girl in the Picture*, each a homage to Forsyth's warm and scrupulously observed slapstick. 'The action of this film takes place in a fictitious town called Glasgow,' went the title card of *That Sinking Feeling*. 'Any resemblance to any real town called Glasgow is purely coincidental.' Coincidental maybe, but sublime certainly.

TONGS, YA BASS!
(gang slogan, 1961–)

Described as Glasgow's unofficial motto in the 1960s and 1970s, this phrase is one of the most identifiable nuggets of Glaswegian slang or street-speech, the ultimate rhetorical flourish in asserting a gang's pre-eminence. Not conspicuously comic, you might think. But this is to overlook one thing; the often hilarious mismatch between civic Glasgow and the torrid, wayward city it is meant to coordinate (*see* the Wombles).

Pat Lally would one day become leader of Glasgow City Council, but in the 1960s he owned a menswear outlet in the city centre. Exhibiting the go-ahead spirit that would later define his administrative reign, Lally had developed an idea for a new product line. It had been inspired by a street gang in the Calton, a gang that had formed seemingly spontaneously at a showing of *The Terror of the Tongs*, a 1961 Hammer film depicting the Triads. The film's popularity having inspired the provocative cry 'Tongs, ya bass!', and with the main gang in the Gorbals having in response formulated the ingenious 'Cumbie, ya bass!', Lally moved to capitalise. In 1967, he introduced to his shop a blood-red tie bearing the motto 'Ya Bass'. Below was a heraldic shield of crossed swords.

Lally's future colleagues in the City Council were horrified, as were the police. They pleaded with him to withdraw the line but to no avail. The ties, Lally told the *Evening Citizen*, were 'frivolous and anyone who thinks otherwise is adopting pompous and moral attitudes'. He even received a measure of support from the legal establishment when a Glasgow lawyer argued during a gang trial that 'Ya bass!' was in fact a polite phrase of French origin.

On a related note, the Cumbie, named for its place of origin, Cumberland Street in the Gorbals, had a youth division, a kind of Boy Scout Cumbie, known as the YYC (Young Young Cumbie). It had its own theme song:

> *Standing on the corner on a Saturday night*
> *Up came some bams who wanted a fight*
> *Ah pulled oot ma razor as quick as a flash*
> *And shouted Young Cumbie, Young Cumbie,*
> *Young Cumbie ya bass!*

TOPONOMY:
the scientific study of placenames, their origins, meanings, use and typology

Elsewhere, it is argued that the essence of Glasgow's comedy, its true wellspring and motherlode, resides in its readiness to address the plasticity of language. This is exemplified in the legendary tale of the Glaswegian constable who drags a comatose inebriate from Sauchiehall Street to Hope Street in order to book him, the initial address being beyond his capability to spell. Glasgow's humour abounds in puns, paradox and colloquial invention, in understatement and exaggeration, in the dovetailing of abstruse metaphor with violent injunction – in the sheer malleable, bendable and breakable wordiness of words.

We look in such a regard particularly to Stanley Baxter, whose *Parliamo Glasgow* reincarnated everyday Glaswegian as a wholly new, almost Mediterranean patois. Or even towards the Piranha Brothers, Doug and Dinsdale, in the *Monty Python's Flying Circus* sketch, who combat their waning influence as underworld hoods with verbal dexterity. 'I've seen grown men pull their own heads off rather than see Doug,' claimed 'associate' Luigi Vercotti. 'He knew all the tricks: dramatic irony, metaphor, bathos, puns, parody, litotes and . . . satire.'

Place-names that possess amusing overtones come in two kinds; historical and contemporaneous. The former comprise place-names that were perfectly innocent once but which became funny (or sniggersome at least) with the passage of time; names that were coined prior to the moment when certain nouns and verbs became weighed down by dubious connotations. Into this category we are compelled to place, say, Cockermouth, the market town in Cumbria. Once, this name would have been purely topographically descriptive, indicating the confluence of the rivers Derwent and Cocker. In the modern age, though, it assumes the air of some deranged injunction.

The British Isles contain many such examples, of place-names that once were perfectly innocent but then found themselves in bad company, the rug of propriety pulled from under them: Thong in Kent and Slack Bottom in West Yorkshire, the river Piddle in Dorset, Sandy Balls in the New Forest. Glasgow contains a particularly infamous specimen – Mountblow, an unglamorous sector of

Clydebank that one morning awoke to discover it had somehow become pornographic.

But Glasgow's verbal resourcefulness, its linguistic dexterity, is observed best in one area particularly, in the place-names of the city – or, more precisely, in the names the people of Glasgow bestow upon its places. Most place-names, of course, are the work of those who live, or have lived, in that place. Councils choose street-names to commemorate notable local events and personages; or the purpose of a place becomes immortalised in its name, as in Petticoat Lane or the Royal Mile.

Glasgow, however, seems singular in the alacrity with which its people rename places that possessed perfectly serviceable names to begin with. Its map becomes merely a provisional thing, a first draft. Eventually, in the mind at least, many real names get crossed out and replaced with alternative names, names that fizz and crackle with the punning mischief of the Glasgow argot.

The Armadillo aka the Clyde Auditorium (concert venue)

Designed by Norman Foster and opened in 1997, this venue by the river is intended mainly for the older fan of popular music, i.e. the ones who needs a seat, and a drink at the interval. You may see the likes of Leonard Cohen, Brian Wilson or Paul Simon here; or Chris de Burgh, if you plan inadequately. Dubbed the Armadillo for its clear resemblance to the South American mammal, the design of the building is in fact intended to appear as a series of upturned ship's hulls, in reference to the Clyde's shipbuilding heritage. Now iconically Glaswegian, the Armadillo appeared on the city's riverscape in an episode of The Simpsons, though Groundskeeper Willie was nowhere to be seen.

The Big Red Shed aka the Scottish Exhibition and Conference Centre (all-purpose venue)

Sited on what was once Queen's Dock, and right next door to the Armadillo, the SECC is a Pentagon-like fortification where fun fairs, conferences and trade shows are held, and where international rock acts perform in conditions that evoke the fall of Saigon. This functional aspect, and the hue of the venue's corrugated outer cladding, quickly gave the building its nickname when it opened in 1985. Absolutely nobody enjoys going there. Ever.

Clatty Pat's aka Cleopatra's Discotheque, Great Western Road (nightclub)

Despite closing in 2005, Clatty Pat's lives in fond memory. A nightclub in the city's West End and favoured particularly by nurses and police officers, Clatty Pat's was famed for the cheapness of its alcohol, its mainstream music policy and for its patrons' relaxed attitudes to amatory pluralism. It was said few could leave Clatty Pat's without having secured a partner or a phone number, though the claim rather fails to take account of the evening of my thirty-first birthday. Clatty, incidentally, is a colloquial term, meaning dirty. The club was refurbished and in 2006 it reopened as the Viper, though its seedy, soggy-carpeted youth-club charm was lost forever.

Castle Greyskull aka Ibrox Stadium (football ground)

Dismissive epithet by which opposition supporters refer to Ibrox Stadium, home ground of Rangers F.C., the first British side to reach a UEFA club final and the most decorated team in world football history. The reference derives from the 1980s cartoon series Masters of the Universe, though its precise relevance remains obscure.

The Clockwork Orange aka the Glasgow Subway (public transport system)

Glasgow's fifteen-stop underground rail system opened its sliding doors in 1896; it is the third oldest subway system in the world, after those of London and Budapest. The system underwent a major upgrade in the late 1970s and upon reopening was dubbed the Clockwork Orange. Beyond its derivation in the 1971 movie by Stanley

Kubrick the origin of the term is in doubt. Some maintain it was of newspaper coinage, others that it was first used by the then chairman of British Rail, Sir Peter Parker. Glaswegians use the name sardonically only. The clockwork element refers to the subway being smaller than most, its tracks being of an unusually narrow gauge.

'Every Glaswegian feels he has his own Hornby train,' noted the Glasgow chronicler Cliff Hanley. 'We've got the biggest model railway in the world.' A certain controversy has long attached to the system's colour scheme, orange being associated strongly with the city's Protestant heritage.

Death Row aka the Three Judges, Dumbarton Road (public house)

Legendarily, an area of this Partick bar where the clearly inebriated were obliged to sit if they wished to continue being served alcohol.

The Glitterdome aka Celtic Park (football ground)

Derogatory epithet used particularly by supporters of Rangers F.C. referring to the home stadium of Celtic F.C., Glasgow's second major football team. The name alludes to the Torbett controversy of the 1990s, when Jim Torbett, manager of the Celtic Boys Club, was imprisoned for indecent conduct relating to three of the team's young players. Conflating this episode with the fate of Gary Glitter, the 1970s pop performer later jailed for underage sex offences, the nickname seeks to inflame the opposition's understandable embarrassment regarding the matter. Inter alia: the Paedodome, the Cesspit, the Piggery and Torbett Towers.

Giro Bay aka Inchmoan island, Loch Lomond

For Glaswegians the majestic Loch Lomond, twenty miles north of the city, is the world's grandest backyard paddling pool; a stunning and rugged region that many in the city know more intimately than their own urban neighbourhoods. Scarcely surprising, then, that the area has witnessed several revisions in its nomenclature. A notable recipient was a sandy cove on the isle of Inchmoan. The spot is so beloved of youths from the nearby – and most downwardly mobile – hamlets of Alexandria, Balloch and Renton, that now it is known to Glaswegians as Giro Bay, a Giro being the unemployment benefit cheque with which these youths subsidise their noisy and noisome al fresco parties on the island's tiny beach. So prevalent is the name that in 2011 the Loch Lomond tourism authority were obliged to pulp 3,000 copies of a navigational chart which referred inadvertently to Giro Bay.

Hill 60 aka Queen's Park (scenic viewpoint)

Appearing frequently in film and television productions, particularly Taggart, the views from the highest point of Queen's Park on the city's Southside are totemically Glaswegian, taking in the Clyde Arc, the Gothic needle of the university and out to the Campsies beyond. There is something mordant, though, in such a picturesque spot being known locally by the name British soldiers in the First World War gave to a commanding vantage point near Ypres.

Lally's Palais aka the Royal Concert Hall (theatre)

Pat Lally was the leader of Glasgow District Council from the late 1980s. He was determined Glasgow's year as Cultural Capital of Europe in 1990 should leave behind a tangible legacy and focused his energies on securing the city a new concert hall, despite, as Ruth Wishart wrote, 'financial planning which seemed to have something of a back-of-an-envelope feel'. The similarity of Lally's surname and the French term for a grand building proved too good to resist.

The Pots and Pans aka the Britannia Panopticon (theatre)

Children often featured among audiences at this Victorian-era music hall theatre in the Trongate. Their inability to pronounce Panopticon led to the venue's alternative name.

The Sarry Heid aka the Saracen's Head, Gallowgate (public house)

A pub name with origins lost in antiquity, but commonly taken to refer to the medieval Crusades, the Saracen's Head, dating from 1755, is known colloquially by the effect its wares can induce, i.e. a 'sorry' or hungover head. This may have something to do with the East End pub's signature beverage, White Tornado, reputedly a blend of fortified wine and methylated spirit. Please promise you'll never go. 'A popular place for cocktails of an evening' as Billy Connolly puts it in his 'Crucifixion' sketch.

The Squinty Bridge aka the Clyde Arc (road bridge)

Opening in 2006 the bridge connects the area of Finnieston to Govan and is known for its striking curved steel arch. Its fate in Glasgow was sealed, however, as soon as it became known that, for aesthetic reasons purely, the bridge would cross the river not perpendicularly but at an acute angle.

JEFF TORRINGTON
(author, 1935–2008)

Perhaps the only major Glaswegian comic novel to date, *Swing Hammer Swing!* took Torrington three decades to write. The delay was occasioned by two things: by Torrington's day job at the Linwood car plant near Glasgow, and by the scale of his writerly ambition. A heady brew of Nabokov, Kafka and Camus, Torrington's prose fizzed with tragicomic glee in a masterly work focusing on *flâneur* and layabout Tam Clay as the Gorbals readies itself for wholesale demolition. Before the hammer swings, Clay moves through a vanishing world of shops, tenements, pubs and alleyways, peopled by the richest of characters. Marbled with desperate, poignant comedy, *Swing Hammer Swing!* made the local universal, giving it the scope of a Glaswegian *Ulysses*. The following excerpt is from chapter three, when Clay tries to raise a few shillings by selling his typewriter.

The shop was crammed floor-to-ceiling with junk. Every nook and cranny had been utilised to accommodate the domestic fall-out which had resulted from that most disastrous of community explosions – the dinging doon of the Gorbals. Leaving in their wake the chattels of an outmoded way of living, whole tribes of Tenementers had gone off to the Reservations of Castlemilk, and Toryglen, or like the bulk of those who'd remained, had ascended into Basil Spence's 'Big Stone Wigwam in the Sky'. To be found in this shop with its pervasive stink of Time-rot were their old zinc tubs, their steamie prams, their wringers and their scrub-boards, their quaint old wirelesses, wind-up gramophones, dusty piles of 78s, EPs and LPs, twelve-inch tellies, wally dugs, wag-at-the-wa's, brass fenders, fire-irons, fretworked pipe-racks, marquetry pieces, box cameras and speckled photographs scattered as far and wide as no doubt were the people they depicted, cartons stuffed with picture postcards, old music sheets and books, hundreds and hundreds of books, every domestic prop you could think of, aye, and including not one but at least half a dozen kitchen sinks.

Into this shop too, like so many stale pizzas, had tumbled wall plaques which showed every sentimentalised rural scene imaginable. Ours had been 'The Watermill', though its stream had been diverted after Da Clay'd vented his spleen on it with a flying boot (a great spleen-venter was my old man). The leader of the 'Ducks in flight' had winged

on for many a year with a broken neck caused by – who else – Vic Rudge, when he'd taken a potshot at it with his Webley air pistol. Those selfsame ducks might very well be here as might also my old bike, a royal-blue'n white Argyle with a wee kiltie on the handlebar stalk. With some rummaging I might even be able to howk out those stookie ornaments Ma Clay'd been so fond of: Boy with Cherries, for instance. Poor bugger, he was always getting his conk knocked off before he'd a chance to sample the fruit. 'Tantalus' I'd nicknamed him, being at that time a raggedy-arsed kid who mainlined on bookprint.

'Don't put it there – you'll scratch it!'

The typewriter, about to mate with its dim reflection on a dust-streaked table, was hastily transferred to the lid of a travel-weary trunk. The shop's owner, a crabbit wee nyaff came over now and, looking aggrieved, rubbed a finger across the table's stourie surface. If I'd scratched it I'd make good the damage, he warned me, which was really rich

Jeff Torrington, author of the Gorbals' greatest eulogy.

considering the tabletop already had more scrapes and blemishes on it than there were on my Jimmie Rodgers record collection. Muttering under his breath he fixed his querulous glance on me. 'You, is it? And what rubbish are you trying to unload this time?'

The old yap bent to give the machine the once-over. He poked at it with a finger, mainly in the arc of the ribbon spools but never pressed a key which was about as nutty as buying a car solely on the design of its ashtrays. He straightened. When he spoke his voice was loused up with catarrh and a crack ran through all of his words.

'What's this, then?'

When I told'm he snapped. 'Aye, I didnae think if was for sweepin' carpets! But what'm I supposed to do wae it?' Again I told'm. 'Buy it?' he squawked. 'I thought maybe you wanted it rebuilt.'

'It's a fine auld machine,' I assured him, then slipped in a quick commercial which glossed over the typewriter's crucial lack of the letter I. 'I'll give you a wee demo if you like.' Adjusting the creased sheet of paper I knelt beside the chest and briskly typed: 'The fast brown dog jumps over the lazy fox … Now's the hour to come to the help of the party …'

'There, how's that?'

He shrugged his skinny shoulders. 'Hanged if I know. Havnae got on ma reading specs.' He tugged now from his pants pocket a hankie, so clatty it would've been the talk of the steamie. Raising the pestilent rag he proceeded to snort his brains into it. When the messy job was done and his sight had been partially restored he looked cross to find me still there. 'Better chance of sellin' a cracked chantie. Who'd want a typewriter aroon these parts?'

What a question. A blizzard of authors was sweeping through Glasgow. To get into the boozers you'd to plod through drifts of Hemingways and Mailers. Kerouacs by the dozen could be found lipping the Lanny on Glesca Green. Myriads of Ginsbergs were to be heard howling mantras down empty night tunnels.

'I thought maybe a ten-spot,' I said, as in the classical manner I assumed the stance of the black-belted Haggler.

'Ten bob for that rubbish! You're off your trolley, sonny.'

My Haggle-Master wouldn't be chuffed with me. Recklessly I'd exposed myself to the Haggler's prime foe – the non-Haggler. Mindless of tradition, ignorant of the rules of engagement, the subtle testing of balance until the fulcrum of compromise had been attained, the auld bugger'd simply waded in and fetched me a boot in the cheenies. Turning now he peered into the backshop gloom then shouted, 'Alice, come ben a minute.'

After a few moments a peelly-wally lassie of around fourteen, a comic in one hand, a half-gnawed apple in the other slouched into our presence. She wore a skimpy mauve dress and a nasty line in facial acne. There was a blue slyness to the eyes that slid from me to my 'fine example of British craftmanship …'

'What d'you want, Gramps?' she asked through a gobful of mushed apple.

'You say you get typing at school? Right, have a bash at this thing, then.'

She wasn't overkeen (me even less so) but Gramps insisted. The girl sighed then placed the half-chewed apple on Biffo the Bear and kneeled before the machine. Very self-consciously she adjusted her skinny fingers on the guide keys. I leaned over her. 'If it helps just copy what I've typed.' But with a nervous gulp she began to rap out something entirely different: 'Of all the f shes n the sea the merma d s the one for me.'

She tried again with identical results. Next, with a glance up at me, she struck a rapid tattoo on the i key: the amputated leg kicked impotently.

'Well?' her grandfather queried.

The girl rose. 'It's alright, I suppose, considering its age.' Her mouth sappy once more with pulped apple she turned mocking blue eyes on me.

'A pound.' the junkman offered.

'A fiver, surely.'

'Thirty bob.'

'Four pounds, then?'

'Two, no more.'

I sighed. 'Okay, but it's daylight robbery.'

The old man, still grumbling under his breath, creaked off into the backshop where presumably he stashed his loot. His granddaughter grinned at me then, pausing only to spit out an apple seed, said, 'You'd better give me five bob or I'll tell'm …'

Swing Hammer Swing!, Jeff Torrington, Vintage 1993

TOUGH HIPPIES
(youth tribe, 1968–1978)

Although the name was never adopted formally, the Tough Hippies were familiar participants in the street theatre of Glasgow for many years; added to which, they possessed the most amusing youth tribe slogan ever heard.

Their origins lay in the rock and pop scenes of the 1960s, and the stylistic shifts undertaken. Glasgow favoured the raw, primitive sound of R&B, as exemplified by the Rolling Stones and the Animals. The prevailing sartorial style was just as functional, made up of jeans, sweaters and button-down shirts – all of which suited the no-nonsense scheme kids who followed it. As the decade progressed, things grew more feminine, passing through a Flower Power phase then taking on a markedly Californian aspect featuring sandals, kaftans, beads and flowing hair. It all may have sat well on the Beatles but not so much on the Glasgow lads who, with opportunistic guile, had assumed these flamboyant styles just to keep up. By the close of the 1960s, Glasgow boasted a makeshift youth tribe all its own, the Tough Hippies; under-educated and coarse young rockers obliged to adopt the more refined trappings of a gentler movement.

So counterintuitive were the Tough Hippies that one even made it into a memoir, *Eel Pie Dharma*, Chris Faiers' 1990 account of his youth on the Thames island, a haven for jazz and Mod aficionados. 'Almost all the hippies in Eel Pie were non-violent, the exception being Scotch John,' Faiers wrote. 'Scotch John had grown up in the Gorbals, the toughest part of Glasgow. Before becoming a hippie, he had been the foreman of a construction crew, and in this tough environment Scotch John had become a master of "the Glasgow bop". The Glasgow bop is a spin-off from soccer playing, where experienced players field the ball with "headers" off the strong bone structures of their foreheads.

'To perform the bop, John would grab an opponent by both shoulders, and then smack the victim's nose with his forehead, usually breaking their nose and making a bloody mess of their face. Scotch John had a personality as aggro as the staunchest skinhead, and stories were told of his walking into the Twickenham skinhead pub, the Bird's Nest. Most of us would scuttle past the Bird's Nest on the far side of the street, and a few Eel Piers had been roughed

A gang of tough hippies, Stockwell Street, Glasgow 1974.

up and dumped in the Thames by the Bird's Nest regulars. So when Scotch John sauntered into the busy pub, he was followed by a tail of amused skins into the washroom. BOP BOP BOP BOP! and it was all over. After Scotch John's foray into skinhead turf, most of us were treated with more respect by the skins, as they probably couldn't tell the rest of us from Scotch John, who had the standard shoulderlength black hair and beard, bellbottom jeans and a leather-fringed jacket.'

Back in Glasgow, meanwhile, associates and former members recall the Tough Hippies had their own distinctive *cri de coeur*: 'Eat yer acid like a man, ya bastard!'

MALCOLM TUCKER
(character, *The Thick of It*, BBC, 2005–)

To those who speak television fluently, Malcolm Tucker is what is termed a Breakout Character. These begin their lives humbly, as just another face among the ensemble; another name on the cast list; another mouth with lines like 'George, did you speak to Colin?' Occasionally, though, as the writing of the show progresses or as the public watch and respond, a curious alchemy can occur. The

show's creators come to appreciate that Character X possesses something special, something not apparent on the page, something that needed to get up on its hind legs. The show in question starts off with Character X contributing merely their tuppenceworth; and, soon, they're paying the salaries of all involved, from Spock on *Star Trek* to The Fonz on *Happy Days*.

Malcolm Tucker in the political satire *The Thick of It* is such a Character X. More precisely, he's a Character XXX. Not since Alf Garnett in the 1960s has a television character become so adored for swearing so profusely and profanely. This is what Tucker, played by Peter Capaldi, does; he swears. However, his swearing isn't merely Tourette's syndrome, Millwall-supporting, thumb-slammed-in-car-door swearing. It is swearing of a different calibre; a sort of psychotic and wildly imaginative swearing – Brueghel swearing; elaborate, richly detailed and bearing constantly an undertone of nightmare.

Tucker is head of communications in a lightly fictionalised version of the Blair administration. His role is essentially one of perpetual crisis management, as ministers and members of parliament become embroiled in slanging matches, dodgy deals and PR fiascos, each depicted with a Handicam naturalism and a verisimilitude in direct proportion to its hilarity. 'I just wanted to say to you by way of introductory remarks that I'm extremely miffed about today's events,' Malcolm tells a female minister, 'and in my quest to try and make you understand the level of my unhappiness I'm likely to use an awful lot of what we could call Violent Sexual Imagery . . .' Tucker is a kind of volatile deity. Unyieldingly, he scourges his penitents with threats of cruel and unusual retribution. Even his surname sounds like swearing.

Common misapprehension has it that Tucker was modelled upon Alastair Campbell, head of communications in the Blair administration from 1997 until 2003. The comparison has something to it: Campbell has Scottish roots and a reputation for verbal thuggery. Capaldi insists his inspiration lay elsewhere; not in Whitehall but in Hollywood, where his short film *Franz Kafka's It's a Wonderful Life* was an Oscar winner in 1995. 'You could see people at ICM in Los Angeles – malevolent forces in Armani suits – barking the foulest and most terrifying of obscenities down the phone at people,' Capaldi told the

Radio Times. 'Harvey Weinstein and the team at Miramax were long celebrated for Malcolm-like behaviour. That was the model I took.'

Needless to say, Malcolm's appearances are thrilling. Tucker is a walking taboo, the unthinkable in a Paul Smith suit; a shiver constantly seeking a spine to run down. He is also, unequivocally, the star of the show. This wasn't always the case. When the half-hour comedy began its run – on BBC Four, in May 2005 – Tucker was less central. The blunderings of Hugh Abbot, mild-mannered Secretary of State for Social Affairs, were the focus, such as his doomed attempts to connect with popular culture. 'You've got 24 hours to sort out your policy on *EastEnders*, right?' Tucker told him 'Or you're for the halal butchers.'

In fact, early reviews concentrated on the show's creator Armando Iannucci rather than on Tucker, perfectly understandably given Iannucci's track record on such shows as *The Day Today* and *Knowing Me Knowing You*. That had changed by series two in October 2009. *The Thick of It* had graduated to BBC Two and something had clearly happened with Malcolm. To make the show work in the broadcasting mainstream, a pantomime baddy of Basil Fawlty proportions was required. So the show went gay for Tucker. It began catering to his merest whim, like the occasion he forced researcher Ollie Reeder to go on an errand. 'If you don't go and get me some cheese,' Tucker shouts 'I'm gonna rip your head off and give you a spinedectomy.' The plots – like the arrival of overpromoted female minister Nicola Murray, who becomes a candidate for Prime Minister by accident then makes a disastrous appearance on BBC 5 Live – became pretexts with the purpose of provoking Tucker, of prodding with sharpened sticks his numerous Achilles' heels. 'You breathe a word of this, to anyone, you mincing fucking cunt,' he tells a Tory researcher, 'and I will tear your fucking skin off. I will wear it to your mother's birthday party and rub your nuts up and down her leg whilst whistling "Bohemian" fucking "Rhapsody", right?'

Tucker's bewitching horror was such, in fact, that Iannucci was obliged to clone him. The *doppelgänger*'s name was Jamie MacDonald, Malcolm's second-in-command, played by Paul Higgins, and he was, if anything, even worse than Malcolm, though every bit as Glaswegian. Jamie was the iron fist within Tucker's iron glove. 'I am gonna have your guts as a skipping rope,' he tells policy wonk Julius Nicholson, 'then rip your lungs out, sun-dry them and turn them into a little fucking waistcoat.' Jamie appeared for the first time in episode one of series two, then took bigger roles in the show's stand-alone specials *The Rise of the Nutters* and *Spinners and Losers*, battling a tide of calamity which forces the resignation of the Prime Minister and sends Malcolm's enforcer into new paroxysms of unholy vengefulness. 'I will remove your iPod from its tiny nanosheath and push it up your cock,' he tells backbencher Ben Swain. 'Then, I'll plug some speakers up your arse and put it onto shuffle with my fucking fist. And every time I hear something I don't like, which will be every time that something comes on, I'll skip to the next track by crushing your balls.' Even Tucker is appalled. 'This is crazy fucking stuff, Jimmy Boyle stuff.' Jamie is undeterred. 'From now on, it's a proper fight, a pub fight – Motherwell rules. Tom is gonna get a pint glass in his fucking eye. And a pool cue up his arse. And another pool cue in his other fucking eye.' A little of Jamie went a long way, though. He appeared in the film *In the Loop*, was rested for the show's third series then vanished.

Jamie, though, was a sidelight to the show's main event, Malcolm Tucker. In considering Tucker's impact it is impossible to overstate the contribution made by Peter Capaldi, the actor who incarnates him. Any old scenery-chewer could have a stab at Tucker but it is Capaldi's particular vulpine spareness that makes the character work, the sense that there is little to him but the job; that he has adapted to it physically, become leaner to ensure the swiftest access to the ongoing. 'Christ, Malcolm, how can you appear out of nowhere in a building made entirely of glass?' a minister asks him. His face simplified itself into a binary code or a theatre mask; switching between Old Testament rage and an icy crocodile grin.

By the end of series four Tucker was in opposition and mired deeply in a Leveson-style enquiry that results in his arrest. Shorn of his influence, Tucker had become a sad figure, plotting petty, malicious triumphs and atoning for his past hubris. Echoing the axiom that all political careers end in failure, Capaldi took the hint and announced in March, 2013 that he would not play Tucker again: 'It was difficult to know where to go with Malcolm next,' he said 'I felt I would rather end it now than see him wind up as a diminished character. It's best to go out at the top.'

Tucker's death knell was sounded, temporarily at least, in August 2013 when it was announced Capaldi would assume the role of Dr Who.

The Wit and Wisdom
of Malcolm Tucker

'Come the fuck in or fuck the fuck off.'
Malcolm's salutation to those knocking on his office door.

'It's damage control, OK? We put out the story the way we want it before Hewitt fucks us up the bugle.'
Malcolm attempts to thwart a rival.

'N.M.F.P. Not My Fucking Problem. I quite like that. I'll use that quite a lot today.'
Malcolm's acronym of the day.

'How much fucking shit is there on the menu and what fucking flavour is it?'
Malcolm assesses what the working day holds in store.

'Oh, I'm terribly sorry, you won't hear any more swearing from us. You MASSIVE, GAY SHITE! FUCK OFF!'
Malcolm attempts to modify his behaviour.

'Did you ever travel, like, a 100 miles per hour head-first through a tunnel full of pig shit?'
Malcolm prepares a minister to be interviewed by Jeremy Paxman.

'How dare you. How dare you! Don't ever ever call me a bully. I'm so much worse than that . . .'
Malcolm gets his role straight.

'There is a fucking glacier of shit at DoSaC! I need you over there with a blowtorch right fucking now!'
Malcolm summons assistance.

'Come on, people, let's get going here! I've got a to-do list that's longer than a fucking Leonard Cohen song.'
Malcolm's morning pep talk.

'Do you know 90 per cent of household dust is made of dead human skin? That's what you are to me.'
Malcolm is displeased when a colleague rejects his job offer.

'You step out of line they'll be all over you like a pigeon on a chip.'
Malcolm advises Nicola Murray to be wary of the press.

'You are a human dartboard and Eric fucking Bristow is stepping up every day flinging a million darts of human shit right at you.'
Malcolm's guide to the press continues.

'Fuck me! This is like a clown running across a minefield!'
Malcolm catches Nicola's appearance on Radio 5 Live.

'I'd love to stop and chat but I'd rather have Type 2 diabetes.'
Malcolm's method of minimising social chit-chat.

'Au contraire.'
Malcolm responds to Jamie's claim that he 'couldn't organise a bum rape in a barracks'.

TUNNOCK'S
(confectionery manufacturers, 1890–)

'Invention,' Willie Wonka told visitors to his Chocolate Factory, 'is 93 per cent perspiration, 6 per cent electricity, 4 per cent evaporation and 2 per cent butterscotch ripple.' The numbers add up to 105 per cent, but they established the way sweet factories would evermore be seen; as places at a slight angle to reality, where eccentric perfectionists labour over extravagant creations to the joyful amazement of young and old alike.

And this is a not inaccurate description of Tunnock's, the sweetmeat laboratory that has been amusing, tickling and delighting Glaswegians since Victorian times.
Somehow, Tunnock's has conspired to make the baked good unfailingly cheerful and, particularly in recent times, emblematic of the city. A string of notoriously naff television commercials from the 1970s on only deepened this fondness. Today, ennobled further by the tributes of artist Gillian Kyle, Tunnock's and its range of tea-accom-  panying products represent the music-hall and variety traditions of Glasgow in wafer form, as reminders of simpler times.

The bulk of the company's output – the Snowball, the Tunnock's Tea Cake, the Caramel Log and the Caramel Wafer – was dreamt up in the early 1950s, an era when trad jazz and Coronation chicken had put the city in a bring-it-on kind of mood. And, ever since, these products have not changed in appearance, content or spirit. They are always crispy, chewy and wrapped in cartoonish Art Deco with a rosy-cheeked lad on the front. The Caramel Log and the Tea Cake are fixed points in a changing world, among the few non-negotiables in the packed lunch of existence.

Joyously, the company runs public tours of its production plant in Uddingston. They are wildly popular and oversubscribed. Should you wish to inspect the Tunnock's operation, apply now and they might be able to fit you in next summer. It is one of the oddest, most charming operations currently extant, the last great survivor of the Victorian business world, overseen by the toweringly central, Wonka-like king figure of Boyd Tunnock, the septuagenarian grandson of the company's founder, the type of kindly paternal overlord who in the olden days would build his workforce villages and holiday resorts. A former rally driver, yachtsman and Church of Scotland elder, Tunnock refuses to take life at the pace you'd expect of a man with a reported fortune of £30m. The factory covers 300,000 square feet and employs 550 staff, all of whom seem hopelessly devoted to Boyd and the Tunnock ethos.

TUTTI FRUTTI
(television series, BBC Scotland, 3/3–7/4/1987)

Our scene opens on a windswept Glasgow cemetery, the Eastern Necropolis, where an ill-assorted crew move in gloomy procession towards an open grave. As the formalities proceed a mini-cab pulls up hurriedly and a sizable man wearing a sky-blue suit clambers out. The mourners look on as the man attempts to pay his fare, but his pockets contain just four crumpled dollar bills. Under withering glances he makes his way to the graveside where a priest is delivering the eulogy for one John McGlone, lately departed in a car accident. In the near distance the floodlights of a football ground lower. The service concludes and the mourners move off, all except three middle-aged men in jeans and leather jackets. In tentative three-part harmony they perform a touching 'Three Steps to Heaven', the Eddie Cochran hit from 1960. And so begins the silver jubilee year of the Majestics, Scotland's greatest rock'n'roll combo.

The recent and long-awaited release of *Tutti Frutti* on DVD confirmed one thing in particular; that memory hadn't been playing tricks; that the six-part BBC Scotland show really was as remarkable as legend had come to suggest. Following a brace of screenings in the late 1980s *Tutti Frutti* slipped into a black hole of television history, from which it did not emerge until August 2009. The reason turned out to be delightfully reminiscent of Eddie Clockerty, the penny-pinching manager of the Majestics: the BBC had declined to pay Little Richard a $5,000 fee levied when the singer discovered the show's title song had had its lyrics altered. During the resulting absence the show became rather fabled, a passage intensified by the BBC's reluctance to identify the reason for its disappearance. *Tutti Frutti* gathered the allure and esteem of some lost classic that lived only in fond memory – despite sitting on the same shelf in the same BBC archive that it always had.

Perhaps the most remarkable aspect of *Tutti Frutti* was that the show won a national network screening. Those who have worked in Scottish television comedy have long nursed a grievance in this regard, feeling their work gets a prejudiced reception from station controllers in London. Most of the time these prejudices are justified. Exceptions aside, Scottish television comedy is stridently and impenetrably local, a collection of accents, attitudes, in-jokes and colloquialisms whose effectiveness decreases in proportion to distance travelled away from the geographic source. Scottish television comedy has always struggled to get its passport stamped: how much would, say, *The Karen Dunbar Show*, with its gallery of Glaswegian grotesques, mean to a resident of Dumfries, let alone Henley? Very little. Scottish television humour relies upon its recognisability for its effect, which is precisely why it is so stubbornly non-exportable.

It takes writers of singular talent to overcome this, and John Byrne staked his claim as one of the few in Scottish television, first as a scribbler of jokes for *Scotch & Wry* then as writer of *The Slab Boys*, a trilogy of stage dramas based on his youth working in the carpet factories of 1950s Paisley. The trilogy was made into a BBC series and later staged on Broadway, starring Sean Penn, Val Kilmer and Kevin Bacon. All this, of course, ran in parallel with Byrne's career as a portrait painter and theatre designer of international stature.

Common misconception has it that, in addition to its acknowledged virtues, the show introduced a grateful world to Robbie

Coltrane and Emma Thompson. This is not entirely true. By 1987 both were already familiar television faces; Coltrane via the BBC Scotland sketch shows *Laugh??? I Nearly Paid My Licence Fee* and *A Kick Up the Eighties*, the BBC 2 show *The Young Ones* and such films as *Mona Lisa* and *Absolute Beginners*; and Thompson via *The Young Ones* and *The Comic Strip Presents* . . . Rather, it was the sway of Bill Bryden, film producer and at the time BBC Scotland's head of drama, that got the show made and on to the network, his standing, and his faith in Byrne, being sufficient to secure a commission for a series with much against it, not least its dark outlook and the fact that it posited a man of Coltrane's size as a romantic lead.

Speaking of whom, the man in the sky-blue suit, we discover, is Danny McGlone (Coltrane), younger brother of the deceased 'Jazza', drawn back to Glasgow with some bad grace from his new base in Manhattan. The arrival of Danny is the true brushstroke of genius in Byrne's celebrated script. Ostensibly, the show concerns itself with the travails of a washed-up one-hit 1960s show band as it attempts to celebrate its twenty-fifth anniversary with a doomed tour round the less salubrious venues of Scotland ('After all, this is the band that played to standing-room-only audiences at the Deep Sea Ballroom in Buckie on two separate occasions, 25 years apart,' said Byrne). But, really, *Tutti Frutti* has its crosshairs focused on targets of greater consequence. The show was made, we must remember, long before defunct rock and pop groups adopted the now common habit of reforming themselves following decorous periods of inactivity. The show anticipated what lay in wait for them when they did: the terrible modern moment of realising that the follies of youth will go on recurring in later life.

Tutti Frutti was a show in which Time skulked round every corner, waiting to batter the unwary with a deftly wielded tambourine. Each and every character lived in the shade of what went before, and what wouldn't go away. Danny and his artschool contemporary Suzi Kettles (Emma Thompson) lament their stillborn careers in fine art. Guitarist Vincent Diver (Maurice Roëves) is stabbed by a hitherto-unsuspected lovechild on the streets of Buckie. The band chooses to ignore that its Teddy Boy stylings are now hopelessly *passé*, just as its manager Eddie Clockerty (Richard Wilson) won't accept the time-warp that is his menswear outlet Manhattan Casuals. Marriages and family ties are regretted; Suzi Kettles is stalked by her estranged husband, a psychotic dentist.

All that Jazza – Robbie Coltrane as depicted by John Byrne in *Tutti Frutti*.

Emotional gangrene festers. Rust never sleeps. A pall of disappointment hangs over everything. And such inevitably is the fate, the writer suggests, of those refusing to put away childish things.

Byrne is no nihilist, however. As a tragicomic study of grotesquely extended adolescence *Tutti Frutti* is leavened by its women, each of whom stands by her man, no matter how risibly he behaves. Noreen sees past Vincent's low sperm count and his dalliance with the 'munchkin' Glenna, who in her turn sees past Vincent's boorishness. Suzi Kettles sees past the domestic abuse she has suffered. Miss Toner forgives the deviousness and penny-pinching of Eddie Clockerty. Even Aileen McAteer, wife of drummer Bomba, overlooks her husband deploying her babies' romper suits as noise insulation. A 'highlight' of the Majestics' stage show was their version of the Everly Brothers song 'Love Hurts'. An exemplary piece of popular entertainment, *Tutti Frutti* set about proving that claim, with a flair that commends it to the ages.

'Something weird's going on here'

The Glasgow Smile: When did you first meet John Byrne?

Robbie Coltrane: I first met him in 1977, when I joined the Traverse Theatre. I joined, and then *The Slab Boys* came along. I don't think John particularly wanted me for *Slab Boys* but I was part of the company. And that was just fantastic. I hit it off with John very quickly; I knew his artworks. God, it was so funny that play – it was just a joy to do. It was the hit of the Edinburgh Festival – nobody could get in. Just lines and lines of people wanting to get in. At one point we thought we'd maybe do two or three performances a day just to get the people in. There's a suicide attempt in *Slab Boys*, too. It's typical John Byrne: it's hilarious, then somebody tries to kill themselves.

TGS: Was *Tutti Frutti* fun to make?

RC: Most of the time, yeah. We did get a lot of bloody street abuse, because they couldn't cut off streets. We had to do a lot of things again and again and again because people think it's funny to toot their horn and shout abuse at you. That we could have done without. And it was bloody freezing in the van because they took the window out, to film through. Driving in winter in Glasgow with nae windscreen – that was no fun. It was bloody freezing, I remember that.

TGS: Did you lobby for the release of *Tutti Frutti*?

RC: Emma and I tried to buy it off the BBC. We thought, 'Well, if you're going to bugger about and not give any explanations as to why it's not been on, then just sell it to us.' We thought it was a very important piece – not just because we were in it but because it was the first series that was incredibly funny and also very serious. People think of that as the norm now but nobody had ever done that. I remember at the time the BBC saying 'Somebody commits suicide in this – is it a comedy or not?' and John replied, 'It's a comedy and somebody dies. In other words, it's like real life.' And now you've got *Clocking Off* and umpteen shows where it's perfectly acceptable to

be funny and tragic at the same time. But *Tutti Frutti* was the first.

TGS: What was the reaction when the series was broadcast?

RC: I got a great letter from George Harrison, which said, '*Tutti Frutti* is exactly what it's like being in a band and I rather like the way you played the guitar as Big Jazza – you are fab.' So I phoned my sister and said, 'Annie, I've just got a letter from George Harrison saying I'm fab', and she more or less swooned at the other end of the phone.

TGS: Does any particular scene stay with you?

RC: I don't really think that way. But I was in London at the time playing Samuel Johnson on stage and I went to this friend's duplex in Brixton; they were watching *Tutti Frutti*, I went out onto the balcony because I hate watching myself, it was a very hot night, everybody had their windows open and all you could see was *Tutti Frutti* on all the tellies. I thought, shit, something weird's going on here.

TGS: The case is made often that the series launched your career.

RC: I don't know, you'd have to ask other people. I think it was very much seen as a one-off. I didn't get offered musicals or a lot of leading men parts. It got me out of the alternative comedy thing, that's for sure. People realised I was an actor which is what I'd been saying for years, you know. I'm not a bloody comedian. I do comedy but I also do other stuff.

TGS: What do you remember of the critical reaction?

RC: There was a lot of, frankly, racist reaction down south. There was a guy in one of the big English papers who said that it would probably win a BAFTA for the best Foreign Language Comedy. But people in Aberdeen have no trouble understanding *EastEnders* …

'A perfect piece of work'

Emma Thompson

The Glasgow Smile: How did you feel when *Tutti Frutti* returned on DVD?

Emma Thompson: It was always a mystery to me why it hadn't come out. All I can say is that it was one of the finest scripts that I've ever had the privilege of working on, and I think that the finished product was perfect. It was a perfect piece of work. It was one of those things where every actor was cast right, where the script was genius . . . every word, every syllable. It taught me an awful lot about screenwriting, really.

TGS: Do you remember your first impression of John Byrne?

ET: I remember it so well. It was in Edinburgh at the Festival, and I was doing Footlights so I would probably still have been at university so it must have been between 1978 and 1981. We had been invited to a meal in quite a posh house, one of those beautiful Edinburgh houses with the high ceilings and the front rooms, a townhouse. Anyway, we were kids and this very distinguished, very thin man with a big beard and a lot of hair tied back in a ponytail and a piercing eye, a hawkish piercing eye, was introduced to me and he couldn't have been nicer. I've never known a more gentle, kindly person. Really extraordinary. John, to me, has always epitomised a particular kind of wildly developed gentleness.

TGS: Was Suzi Kettles a creation of yours, or Byrne's?

ET: Well, her character was very, very clear – because of the writing. You knew exactly who she was. She was gallus, and could be a right old bisom but she was also really bright and really good fun. I'd been trained up like crazy to sing in *Me and My Girl* so singing that stuff was no problem 'cause there was no high stuff, it was really just backing vocals. We had such a laugh. God, we had such a good time doing that stuff, and then playing at the Pavilion. Imagine. I've got a great black and white photo of us all on the stage. It was the most fantastic bloody ending. Brilliant.

TGS: It was a drama about male inadequacy, wasn't it?

ET: What John understood so well is Scotland, of course – *Tutti Frutti* is very much about Scotland, what it will put up with, and the tragedy of that, when there's such genius in the country; and the inhibitions, and the misery. There's nobody more fucking joy-sucking than an old Scot, those old men who hate pleasure in all its forms. It's bad down here, too. Down here in London it's exactly the same thing but it's a bit more pathetic – in Scotland there's a brutality to that kind of anti-joy conservatism that really gets me down. That's what the show was about, men and their pathetic capacities for emotional understanding. Yet they want it; McGlone attempting to cheer Vincent up after Glenna's suicide but getting it wrong – that's a very funny scene, the Christmas wreath with the wee Robin on it. So, I understand why so many Scottish artists and actors leave – they have to, because they can't get any air, they feel stifled. There's tremendous rage in Scotland, I think – and that is one of the things you see in *Tutti Frutti*.

Few writers have captured the rough music of Glasgow speech as effectively as John Byrne, as demonstrated by this sampling of dialogue from *Tutti Frutti*.

'It's a home from home. Ninth Avenue is just like Sauchiehall Street on a Friday night. The *Five Past Eight Show* is playing on Broadway. And what is Greenwich Village if it isn't just a bit of the Barrowland with tackety boots? You'd love it!'
Danny tries to convince Suzi to live with him in New York.

'There's nothing funny about it. I don't know if you've ever been sexually abused, had your head sat on and your dental plate stolen but it's no laughing matter, I can assure you.'
Suzi recalls the less glamorous aspects of being an air stewardess.

'Two hooses, Fud. I mean, even Elvis never hud two hooses.'
Bomber considers the extravagance of Vinnie's adulterous domestic arrangements.

'Jerry Lee Lewis got thrown out of this country for havin' a child bride. But at least he didn't duet with her on "Great Balls Of Fire".'
Bomber reacts badly to suggestions of Glenna becoming vocalist for the Majestics.

'Janice, will you come down and put this merchandise in a poke for this gent.'
Eddie Clockerty oversees Manhattan Casuals' unique customer service.

'Remind me never to order Chicken Harry Lauder in a Greek restaurant again.'
Suzi regrets her lunch.

'Never believe anyone who tells you fried dumpling is an aphrodisiac.'
Danny regrets the night before.

'You can have tea, coffee, Coke, Tab . . . or porridge. There's a machine in the tape store.'
George MacDonald Fraser welcomes the Majestics to Radio Buckie.

'You *would* think that – you think Roy Castle's funny.'
Miss Toner berates Eddie Clockerty's defence of Glenna.

'It's better than being a jumped-up haberdasher that reckons a prawn cocktail in a Wimpy bar is a pretty lavish introduction to London nightlife.'
Miss Toner reacts badly to Clockerty's claim that she is gallus.

'What's Polish for showbusiness?'
Miss Toner searches the newspapers for a review of the TV documentary on the Majestics.

'That's hellish – can you not pick them up and suckle them, Janice?'
Eddie reacts badly to the volume of Bomba's twins.

'I got you a table for two at that dump where I got the food poisoning.'
Janice arranges Eddie's lunch schedule.

'I've never felt so low in my life, not even when my mother dropped dead at the kitchen table and never finished butterin' my playpieces.'
Danny regrets his break-up with Suzi.

'What do you want to me to do with the ones that haven't any grooves on them? I'll put them beside the pile that haven't any holes in the middle.'
Miss Toner inspects a delivery of the Majestics' souvenir album.

'I've no offspring I know about, except for a big lassie wi' specs that turned out to be the Butcher Quine of Buckie and stabbed me in the vitals by way of saying, Hello, Dad.'
Vinnie reflects on fatherhood.

'No one swings harder than bombed intellectuals'

THE UBIQUITOUS CHIP

THE UBIQUITOUS CHIP
(restaurant, 1971–)

The guidebooks tell only half the tale. It is true that the Ubiquitous Chip is a Glasgow institution, a restaurant with an international profile. For three generations it has been the destination of choice whenever a member of Glasgow's *petite bourgeoisie* is marking a birthday ending in a zero. In the restaurant's interior courtyard, under a Botanic Garden of unfettered foliage, have passed 40 years of wedding breakfasts, Valentine's dinners, school-teacher retirements and work promotions. No restaurant on earth has witnessed such frequent utterance of the phrase 'Gavin, you deserve it.' The Chip is where Glasgow goes to pat itself on the back, usually with the hand that feeds it.

Yet the Chip also takes a place in the gallery of Glasgow humour (in this context 'the Chip' refers to the establishment's whole being, its two restaurants and three bars, scattered throughout a converted garage in Ashton Lane). The restaurant's very name is an in-joke, in fact, intended to inform diners that the deep-fried staple of the

The Ubiquitous Chip, unofficial embassy of Glasgow's liberal elite.

Glaswegian diet has been extirpated from the menu. The name has become euphemistic. Now it is Glasgow shorthand for a particular social stereotype. The entire city knows precisely what type of person frequents the Chip – the comically self-regarding West End liberal. The Chip has always taken very seriously its lofty and gilded status, as the consulate of the West End's thinkers and artists, and by definition anything that takes itself very seriously is very funny. Nowhere is the essence of Glasgow's aspirational middle class to be found in such intense concentration. The militantly aspirational have proven themselves funny because, inadvertently, they tell us two things: where they are and where they believe they deserve to be.

In essence the Chip is a sort of private members' club for those orbiting the liberal humanities, a sodality of social climbers, autodidacts and wastrels. This tends to give the Chip a dilatory and timeless quality, though it's perhaps more accurate to say that, here, time exerts less sway than it might elsewhere. Young men have grown grey leaning on the Chip's bar as the days pass in a blur of Furstenberg and arguments about J.G. Ballard. The place provides a sense that finally one has found a gathering of like minds and the security is hard to relinquish. Not for nothing did a former columnist of the *Herald*, referring to Wilde's supernatural novella, dub the place 'the gallery where they hang the pictures of Dorian Gray'. The faces may age, but the Chip seems eternal in its ability to act as fulcrum between Glasgow's past and its attempts to ascend the social scale.

Craig Ferguson: The Chip Bar is something of an institution in Glasgow. It is situated above, and affiliated with, a gourmet restaurant called the Ubiquitous Chip, a hippy, dippy and pretentious, but also fantastic, restaurant, which for a long time was the only place in Glasgow where you could get a decent meal that wasn't Italian, Chinese or Indian. It still attracts an artsy, if sometimes pedantic, clientele from the local university and from the BBC station formerly located nearby. The bar itself is known for its Furstenberg lager on tap (thanks especially to the beer's titanic alcohol content) and for its cool, young and good-looking staff, which I suppose I fitted into enough at the time to warrant employment.

I loved working there. No one swings harder than bombed intellectuals. People in the bar business were even more forgiving of drunken behaviour than those in the music business.

from *American on Purpose* (Warners, 2009)

UTILITIES: THE PLUMBER TAPE
(recording, *c.* mid-1980s)

Now available on YouTube but at one time a legendary and elusive artifact heard only by those in the know, the Plumber Tape is a four-minute nervous breakdown that captures the Glasgow temperament at its most comically vicious. It is a recording of a telephone conversation between an operator at a Glasgow City Council emergency hotline and a council tenant whose flat has flooded, thus necessitating the immediate attendance of a plumber. Matters are soured further by the absence of the key that would grant access to the appropriate stopcock. With mounting fury, the caller questions the operator's competence, to say nothing of his parentage, with a psychotic commitment that exists in stark and hilarious contrast to his anonymous nemesis, who exhibits all the empathetic urgency of a sleeping pensioner. 'Just get a fucking guy here tae get the water oan and don't get fucking wide,' the caller advises. 'As soon as we can get it on for you we'll get it done, OK?' the operator replies. This leads the caller into quasi-philosophic realms: 'How the fuck d'ye no' have the key?' he asks. 'We don't have the key,' replies the official, redundantly. 'Ah'm asking you nicely before I get upset,' continues the complainant, revealing that, somehow, he has further reserves of upset to call upon. The operator reiterates that nothing can be done immediately, due to the non-availability of workmen. 'You've no' got the fucking men?' demands the caller. 'WHERE ARE THEY, THEN?' For a further three minutes the discussion seesaws alarmingly, between the passive aggression of the council man and the active aggression of the caller, before culminating in the latter's abject capitulation: 'Tomorrow at the earliest?' he mulls at the top of his lungs. 'Right. Fuck off, ya prick!'

Had the Plumber tape made its appearance in the modern day, the complaining caller would no doubt become some kind of celebrity, with his own breakfast show on commercial radio, a column in a daily tabloid and a fortnight at the Edinburgh Fringe, possibly in tandem with his telephonic opponent. The pair might reconcile cheerfully to honour their four minutes of confrontational badinage, with their verbal jousts transformed into catchphrases, like 'WE DON'T HAVE THE KEY!' As it stands, the tape is a horrible account of an unstoppable force meeting an immoveable object, and a reminder that hell truly is other people.

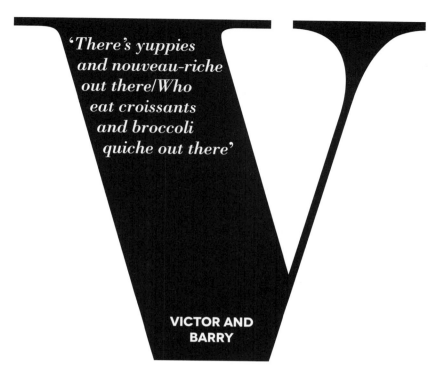

'There's yuppies and nouveau-riche out there/Who eat croissants and broccoli quiche out there'

VICTOR AND BARRY

VICTOR AND BARRY
(double act, 1984–1988)

Putting the GLA into glam and something equivalent into spoof, Victor and Barry remain the best loved exponents of a genre we don't see that much of: Glaswegian camp.

In this, the city has bucked the trend for as long as a trend's been there to be bucked. A strand of the camp has been detectable in British humour forever, since Shakespeare wrote his first bit with cross-dressing. Camp humour in Britain tends also to localise itself. Lancashire has produced Alan Bennett, Victoria Wood and the emotional car wrecks, backstreet divas and middle-aged mothers' boys of *Coronation Street*; in London's East End the drag tradition shakes a tail-feather still; Kenneth Williams took polari, or gay slang, on to tea-time radio. Glasgow, however, just isn't having it; Glasgow's got football training and a few pints with some pals from the Kwik-Fit garage. The glitzier end of the spectrum is somewhere Glasgow ventures but rarely. Several reasons may be suggested: the city's Presbyterian inheritance, the stricter strictures of incomers

Act One Productions Present —
In Association with The Kelvinside Young People's
Amateur Dramatic Arts Society

The Victor & Barry Show

A Pot - Pourri of Words & Music
Brought to you
straight from the Heart
of Glasgow's
KELVINSIDE!

From AUGUST 20th to SEPTEMBER 1st (exc. Sun)

At 10.30 p.m.

At the HARRY YOUNGER HALL
LOCHEND CLOSE
CANONGATE
EDINBURGH

Tickets — £1.00 from Fringe Box Office
or at Venue

WHAT THE CRITICS SAY ....

"Victor & Barry are to Kelvinside what the Champs Elysees
are to Venice" — Ophelia Wishart (miss)
"Puts the 'A' in Showbusiness" — Wet End Times
"The earth moved" — Renee Roberts (mrs) Leading lady
in this years production of "Hello Renee"

from the Highlands and, most obviously, Glasgow's reputation as an industrial cauldron. Whatever the reason, the city's humour has tended more towards the raucous than the outrageous. Its true subject is Glasgow and its audience is Glaswegians, of each and every age.

Fittingly, Victor and Barry (played respectively by Forbes Masson and Alan Cumming) were naughty but in the nicest way possible. Indeed, those of advanced years could have seen them as nothing more than nice young men going about their business. It took an attuned sensibility to see the point Victor and Barry were making; that after industrial decline and the rise of the service industries Glasgow would adjust, however reluctantly, to new realities, to the fact that the hard man was being supplanted by *le bourgeois gentilhomme*. During the transition, Victor Ignatius MacIlvaney and Barry Primrose McLeish were happy to act as templates. As fixtures of the Kelvinside Young People's Amateur Dramatic Art Society, the pair were advocates of poise and refinement, ambassadors from a future Glasgow of their dreams. As charming as they were, though, Victor and Barry were never really particularly funny; they themselves were the joke, but their act was basically a Glaswegian rewrite of Dame Edna Everage or Hinge and Bracket, centred on Victor and Barry's delusions of their own megastardom. They did, however, give us the anthem that is 'Kelvinside Man' (p. 115).

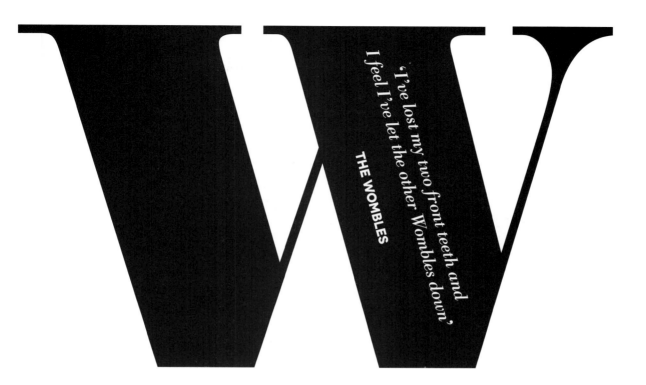

'I've lost my two front teeth and I feel I've let the other Wombles down'

THE WOMBLES

MOLLY WEIR
(actor/comedienne, 1910–2004)

If Glaswegians today remember Molly Weir at all, it will be as the older sister of Tom, the Kendal Mint Cake-chewing TV naturalist, or as Hazel the McWitch in the BBC kids' comedy *Rentaghost*. Some might even know her for an acting career that was strikingly eclectic, with appearances in, among many other films, *The Prime of Miss Jean Brodie*, *Hands of the Ripper* and *Carry On Regardless*.

In the context of humour, though, Weir is noteworthy for her associations with *It's That Man Again* and *Life with the Lyons*, two of the totems of British post-war comedy. Long before any other Glaswegian was working in the mainstream of light entertainment, Weir was blazing the least likely of trails. She had blooded herself in the city's thriving amateur dramatics scene, then in variety theatre. 'My mother told me I sang before I spoke, and I danced before I walked,' she wrote in her 1973 autobiography *A Toe on the Ladder*, 'but in spite of such early signs that I might have a talent for the theatre, nobody, least of all me, could have foreseen that with my unlikely

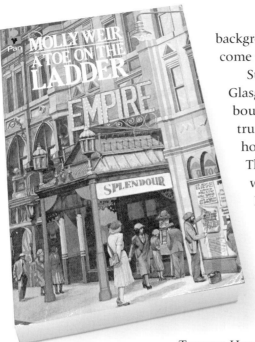

background my dreams of becoming an actress could ever come true.'

Such ambitions took Weir south, in an age when Glasgow's performers seldom strayed beyond the city boundaries. Weir's background turned out to be her trump card. She fell easily into roles requiring a Scots housekeeper type, as she played in *Life with the Lyons*. The show, something of an anomaly on BBC radio, was a slick star vehicle designed for real-life Hollywood couple Ben Lyon and Bebe Daniels. Curiously, at this time Scottish housekeepers were all the rage in Hollywood. Weir was brought in to play Aggie McDonald. 'Why don't you eat civilised food like haggis?' she asked of Lyon. 'What does haggis eat?' Lyon replied. Weir's other hit was *It's That Man Again*, a now incomprehensible madcap wartime comedy built around comic Tommy Handley. Together, the shows established Weir as the doyenne of brisk Caledonian efficiency, a seam she mined until she was of an age to play grandmotherly characters. After suffering a fall, Weir died aged 94 at a nursing home in Middlesex.

THE DUKE OF WELLINGTON
(statue, Royal Exchange Square)

Few sights embody the antic spirit of Glasgow's humour like that presented most weekends by a statue standing just off Queen Street. There is little about the statue itself that is remarkable; it's basically a giant, brassy lump of Victorian military porn that shows the Duke of Wellington (1769–1852), the conqueror of Napoleon, gazing implacably in the general direction of Cruise Menswear.

What makes the statue interesting is something else entirely, to wit the charmingly determined campaign of modification that has been visited upon the thing for several generations now. Pass the statue on a Monday morning and you can all but guarantee that Wellington's head – the head that masterminded the Anglo-Mysore war and was deployed during its possessor's stint as Prime Minister, and that elected to popularise the welly – will be topped off with a fluorescent orange polyurethane traffic cone. Usually, the cone is sitting at a rakish angle; this may be as much to do with wind velocity or pigeon settlement as deliberate choice. Suffice to say that to place the cone atop the Duke's head is no small undertaking. The statue stands on a ten-feet-high plinth, and it's another ten foot before Wellington's crown is reached. Only the young weekend reveller, fresh from the clubs and pubs of Queen Street and en route to the night buses departing from George Square, would be intrepid or reckless enough to attempt it. Yet many evidently do, in the dead of night, unseen by the public, as indomitable as totems from folk myth. The cone is a semi-permanent feature; one that, like the ravens at the Tower of London or the flying of the ensign at Buckingham Palace, is sufficiently occasional to lend its appearance an air of event.

Nobody knows when the tradition was established, though tourism and newspaper sources date it mistily to the mid-1980s. What's certain is how genuinely amusing, how gratifyingly puerile the spectacle can be. The dimension of the cone is suited precisely to the diameter of Wellington's head. A slight hint of self-satisfaction plays about his lips, almost as if this splendid visual joke were his idea all along. His horse, though, is slightly turning its muzzle away to the left, as though rather fatigued by the relentlessness of such japery and attempting to disassociate itself from its master. In all, it's a wonderfully opportunistic piece of guerrilla comedy, an absurdist practical joke in which the grandest of imperial grandeur collides with the commonest of modern banality.

When the statue was erected in 1844 the impressive building behind was the home of Walter Stirling, a prominent merchant. Today it is the Gallery of Modern Art. Few if any of its exhibits, though, possess the fame or significance of the piece of modern art that stands outside.

This isn't to say the famed modification is loved unconditionally by all. In public, the civic side of Glasgow is obliged to frown upon the folk tradition, whatever opinion it may hold privately. In 2005, the City Council finally absorbed the fact that

appreciable numbers of its citizens were regularly climbing to heights in excess of those of double-decker buses while lost in states of gleeful intoxication. It issued a quasi-stern admonishment and Strathclyde Police indicated it would be enforced with prosecutions. Well, it did, sort of. 'Each individual incident would have to be treated on its own merits,' commented Chief Superintendent David Christie, clearly having already imagined the slapstick nightmare into which his officers could soon be plunged. The stricture was relaxed somewhat at the end of 2005 by Stephen Purcell, the new leader of Glasgow City Council, who condoned the statue's comedic alter-ego and reversed the policy of removing cones. Purcell was a preposterously young leader of the Council; he was 37 when he was forced to step down in a blizzard of allegations concerning drug use and links with Glasgow's underworld. He did not reveal, or was not asked, whether he had ever taken part in updating the Duke.

The years since have seen coning become semi-authorised, or at least such a feature of the city's reality that few stop to question how and who might be doing it. It's rather as though the city had its own Traffic Cone Fairy or mad, mischievous Santa Claus, perpetually refreshing its conceit of itself as a socialist city-state where authority and eminence must expect to have their noses tweaked. But there remains a case against coning, and it's put by an organisation named Glasgow – City of Sculpture (CoS), which is staunch in its conviction that coning the Duke amounts to an act of vandalism, backed up by a City Council which neglects its duty of care towards 'one of the finest public sculptures in Europe'. The statue, claims Gary Nisbet of CoS, is now the only public monument in Britain on to which the public is encouraged to climb and deposit objects.

This may be true, but it's scarcely the point. Statues by their very nature are made to be robust. Damage has been done to the Duke over the years, but in most cases it was inadvertent and remedied swiftly. Those remedies were a negligible price to pay against the continuation of a genuine and spontaneous, distinctive and defining piece of civic engagement (albeit an inherently silly one). And continue it does; recent months have seen the image used on lager glasses and smartphone apps. He may yet appear on the city's coat of arms: the bird, the bell, the fish, the tree and the man who popularised the Wellington boot. Like his real-life equivalent, Glasgow's Iron Duke charges ever onward, figuratively if not literally, resplendent in his conical orange headjoy.

RICHARD WILSON

(actor, 1938–)

Wilson's career provides us a helpful litmus test, in that we can infer much from which production a viewer associates with the actor most. We would be gratified were they to cite *Tutti Frutti*, John Byrne's six-part television comedy of 1987, in which Wilson portrayed so memorably Eddie Clockerty, the camel-coated impresario behind a range of fly-by-night enterprises, well described by his secretary as a 'jumped-up haberdasher that reckons a prawn cocktail in a Wimpy Bar is a pretty lavish introduction to London nightlife'. Alternatively, and less discerningly, Wilson's name might conjure *One Foot in the Grave*, the broad BBC1 sit-com that between 1990 and 2000 was very much a national favourite and thereby made Wilson a household name. He played Victor Meldrew, an irascible victim of early retirement, living with his long-suffering wife in the pillowy bosom of middle England. Meldrew became a lightning rod for the myriad vexations of modern life, from traffic jams to jury service, each of which he greeted with what was to become an inescapable catchphrase: "I don't believe it!". Its popularity ended up so wearisome to Wilson he vowed henceforth to utter it only for the benefit of charities. Beyond television, he has enjoyed a career that has been illustrious and varied, appearing regularly with the Royal Shakespeare Company, serving as Rector of Glasgow University, campaigning for the Labour Party and the gay rights group Stonewall and in 2004 receiving an OBE for services to drama.

Grave decisions – Richard Wilson.

IN THE WINGS ...

The wit of Glasgow is unstemmable. It flows like the Clyde but, like the Clyde also, it is littered with stuff that just drifts past, whose presence is fleeting. Some of this stuff is touched upon here: the comics whose catchphrases didn't quite catch on; the sketch shows whose outlines were too faint; the sit-coms, films, plays and characters that came close to the premier league of remembrance.

American Cousins (2003)
Engaging fish-out-of-water romantic comedy by Sergio Casci in which a mob of New Jersey gangsters are forced to take refuge with relatives who run a Glasgow chip shop.

John Barrowman (entertainer, 1967–)
There's gay, like Liberace in a sunhat dancing to hi-NRG disco is gay; and several stops past that there's John Barrowman gay. Born in Glasgow but raised in Illinois, the actor, singer and raconteur has brought new dimensions to the concept of family-friendly flagrancy, with a chirpy comic persona that is half swashbuckler, half San Francisco cruiser.

The Big Tease (1989)
Weak *Spinal Tap*-style fake documentary concerning a Glaswegian hairdresser (Craig Ferguson) who travels to Los Angeles for compete in a championship.

The Book Group (2002–03)
Channel 4 series written and directed by Annie Griffin, dissecting the neuroses of a group of book-lovers in the West End of Glasgow.

City Lights (1984–1991)
Fondly recalled BBC Scotland sitcom set in a Glasgow bank and starring Gerard Kelly.

Tam Cowan (1969–)
Rotund recycler of Christmas-cracker gags via a variety of football-themed outlets.

Dear Green Place (2006–2008)
Poorly received BBC Scotland sitcom starring Ford Kiernan and concerning the madcap, litter-related antics of some Glasgow park-keepers.

Phil Differ (1956–)
Seasoned writer and producer of Glasgow comedy on stage, screen and radio, in *Only an Excuse?*, *Scotch & Wry* and many others.

Electric Soup (1989–92)
Underground comic book of the early 1990s featuring a host of Glaswegian characters and stereotypes, including Wendy the West End Trendy, the Bears fae Brig'ton and Tunnock McNulty.

Flashman (1969–2005)
Plucked from the pages of *Tom Brown's Schooldays*, this character was fixed upon by former editor of the *Glasgow Herald* George MacDonald Fraser and turned into a comically cruel Victorian libertine in a series of best-selling novels.

Willie Gall

In many way the successor to Bud Neill, Willie Gall was a cartoonist on the *Evening Times*, from 1956 until his death in 2006, who took a sideways look, as they say, at the city and its inhabitants: 'Actually, ah've got plenty of hair,' a curiously coiffed man tells his companion, 'but ah suit the toupee better.'

Happy Hollidays (2009)

Another poor sitcom vehicle for Ford Kiernan, broadcast in 2009 and concerning the madcap, litter-related antics of staff in a caravan park.

Heavenly Pursuits (1986)

Made in the wake of the success of Bill Forsyth, this film was an equally aw-shucks look at religious life in Glasgow as a classroom of kids strive to have a local woman elevated to sainthood.

Hello, Good Evening and Welcome (1976–80)

A parliamentary enquiry should investigate how STV got away with such a consistently poor record in producing comedy. One of the channel's few contributions was this fast-moving gags-and-impressions show starring cabaret stalwart Allan Stewart.

Craig Hill (1975–)

Cheerfully camp comic of the 1990s onwards.

The High Life (1994)

Popular BBC 2 sitcom written by and starring Alan Cumming and Forbes Masson, concerning two male air stewards working out of Prestwick Airport for Air Scotia.

Franz Kafka's It's a Wonderful Life (1993)

Oscar-winning short, written and directed by Peter Capaldi, in which an author starting work on his latest opus suffers constant interruption.

Phil Kay (1968–)

Bearded magus of hyperactive stand-up whimsy, usually concerning cheese.

Gerard Kelly (1959–2010)

This energetic performer was a much loved stalwart of Glasgow's pantomime world and appeared frequently on television, notably with Victoria Wood and Ricky Gervais.

A Kick Up the Eighties (1981–84)

Perhaps Glasgow's most overt contribution to the alternative comedy boom was this sketch show featuring Robbie Coltrane and Rik Mayall.

Laugh??? I Nearly Paid My Licence Fee (1984)

Another BBC Scotland sketch show, this one notable for featuring Robbie Coltrane's celebrated character Mason Boyne.

The Live Floor Show (2002–2003)

Weekly BBC Scotland stand-up revue show, notable for giving early television exposure to Frankie Boyle.

Duncan Macrae (1905–1967)

Known best for his comic song 'The Wee Cock Sparra', the craggy and memorably odd Macrae was also among the cream of post-war British character actors, with appearances in *Whisky Galore!*, *Greyfriars Bobby* and *Casino Royale*.

Una McLean (1930–)

Comic actress and embodiment of the indomitable spirit of Glaswegian womanhood, seen to full effect in her portrayal of the fearsome battle-axe Molly O'Hara in *River City*.

Victor Meldrew (1990–2000)

Cartoon curmudgeon played by Richard Wilson in the BBC sitcom *One Foot in the Grave*. Famed for the catchphrase 'I don't belieeeve it!'

Naked Video (1986–1991)

Well-regarded BBC Scotland topical sketch show of the late 1980s that span off and ran in parallel with a radio version, *Naked Radio*. Tony Roper and Jonathan Watson featured.

Orphans (1998)

Memorable tragicomedy directed by Peter Mullan in which three brothers and a sister come to terms with their mother's death. Or don't.

Overnite Express (2003)

BBC Scotland sitcom set on the night buses travelling between London and Glasgow. 'A fetid, rank appropriation of how working-class Glaswegians speak, behave and interact', says someone on the internet.

Paddy's Market (1990)
Tony Roper's ill-starred theatrical companion piece to *The Steamie*, a look at life in the city's now defunct flea market.

The Patter (1985)
Michael Munro's popular dictionary of Glasgow-speak, followed by the sequel *The Patter – Another Blast*. The author was the first to pen a relatively exhaustive survey of Glasgow sayings, aphorisms and patois.

Pulp Video (1995–96)
Yet another topical sketch show from BBC Scotland, this time from the mid-1990s and featuring Ronni Ancona and Greg Hemphill. In some ways the series was the parent of *Chewin' the Fat*.

Soft Top, Hard Shoulder (1992)
Amiable road comedy starring Peter Capaldi in which an ex-pat faces disinheritance if he cannot meet a deadline to travel to Glasgow.

Tinsel Town (2000)
Lurid BBC Scotland series set in Glasgow's club land as recreational drugs took hold. As with *Lip Service* today, only the biting of lips could forestall howls of derision.

A Wholly Healthy Glasgow (1988)
Acclaimed stage black comedy by Iain Heggie, set in the changing rooms of a Glasgow health club.

Dave Willis (1895–1973)
Fondly remembered music hall and film star of the 1930s and 1940s.

THE WOMBLES
(environmental activists, 1968–)

The Wombles, when located on their home turf of Wimbledon Common, have wombled long both underground and overground without fear of reprisal. The same cannot be said about their visits to Glasgow, though. It doesn't do to condone violence, of course, yet it's difficult to hear the tale of one Patrick Scola without a flicker of amusement playing about the lips.

In 1978, Scola was an actor, and his job was to play a Womble. Several years earlier, the popular children's television show was spun off to produce a handful, or a pawful, of pop singles, and the Wombles became the biggest-selling British recording artists of 1975. Therefore, an ensemble to perform concerts was needed. This was where Patrick Scola came in, to say nothing of his five accompanying spear-carriers in furry costumes.

The troupe was performing at the Apollo Theatre in the city when some of its members attended a New Year party in Clouston

Street, in a rather raffish neighbourhood close to Glasgow University. Only the area's seediness could explain why Scola was apprehended later that night, chasing several men and screaming, 'I'll sort you out, you Scottish bastards.' Now, it's just possible Scola's ire had been raised when a fellow reveller scoffed at the importance of recycling glass and plastic separately. Whatever the cause, Scola ended up in the dock, and his brief made a heroic attempt to mitigate. 'My client is a Womble,' he told the court. 'He unfortunately forgot that he came from Wimbledon Common when he drank a Scottish beer.' The real damage, however, was harder to assuage. 'I've lost my two front teeth,' Scola told reporters, 'and I feel I've let the other Wombles down.'

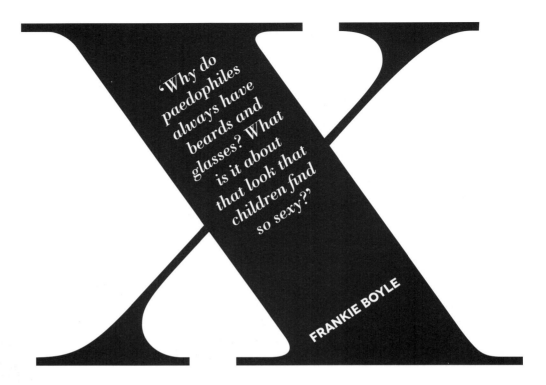

'Why do paedophiles always have beards and glasses? What is it about that look that children find so sexy?'

FRANKIE BOYLE

X-CERTIFICATE: FRANKIE BOYLE
(comic, 1972–)

Now among the most celebrated performers in Britain, Boyle has reaped the benefit of a spectacular blossoming in the status of standup comedy. What is remarkable is his having done so with a style that's as brutal and vulgar as it can be smart and insightful. It's a comedy he described almost exactly when he was describing something else, his native city, as a 'disturbing but strangely loveable place, lurching like an alcoholic from exuberance to unbelievable negativity'.

In the 1980s, we heard with wearying regularity that comedy was the new rock'n'roll. It took nearly two decades for this to come true. It needed a collision of factors: the increase in disposable income occasioned by the demise of the record industry; greying audiences, who preferred to have a seat; a surge in the popularity of sell-through DVDs. Each came to pass, and no longer did stand-up gain its access to the palace of entertainment by means of the tradesmen's entrance.

And no longer is it a form that conducts its business purely in small clubs or student unions. Its leading names embark routinely upon lengthy campaigns around the nation's biggest theatres. In their home towns, a few, Boyle included, can fill 10,000-seat arenas. The proceeds are topped up by best-selling autobiographies and live DVDs. It all creates a momentum that is followed through on news and comment pages, which creates in turn greater audiences for live shows. Altogether, the stand-up comic can ascend to a realm of wealth and influence unimaginable only a decade earlier. For the right kind of performer, comedy truly has become the new rock'n'roll, if what is meant by that is the lucrative, imperial and all-conquering zenith of, say, Kiss or Led Zeppelin.

Boyle is of that number, though the thought might be alarming given the nature of his material. While his persona in performance is amused and inquiring, even genial, he places himself very deliberately at the utmost limits of what is sayable in public. Boyle positions himself as a kind of malevolent schoolteacher, bullying his subjects to think more critically about the world confronting them. His sets are a charnel-house of contemporary dysfunction. His ruminative one-liners provoke a kind of appalled amazement, a disbelief that the worlds of celebrity and politics can be twisted into such grotesque shapes, as in 'Why do paedophiles always have beards and glasses? What is it about that look that children find so sexy?', or 'Does anyone think Camilla is what Princess Diana would look like if she'd survived the crash?' or 'When Barack Obama was giving his speech after being elected president, he did it behind bullet-proof glass. I thought that was a bit harsh – just because he's black doesn't mean he's going to shoot anyone.' It may end up, though, that Boyle's career will be defined for the worse by a joke he made on his Channel 4 series *Tramadol Nights* in December 2010, concerning the glamour model Jordan and her disabled son Harvey: 'Jordan and Peter Andre are still fighting each other over custody of Harvey – eventually one of them will lose and

have to keep him. I have a theory about why Jordan married a cage fighter – she needed a man strong enough to stop Harvey from fucking her . . .'

On that remark the dust has yet to settle. Similar debates around the boundaries of taste and decency have raged around comics since the 1930s at least, when Max Miller would leave out the final word of saucier routines to thwart the Lord Chamberlain. Such strictures affected Lenny Bruce in the 1960s, Andrew Dice Clay and Jerry Sadowitz in the 1980s, and, at the less fragrant end of the spectrum, Roy 'Chubby' Brown and Bernard Manning.

Taking no prisoners: Frankie Boyle.

For better or worse, Boyle seems of a different order. Two factors have conditioned this – a social context in Britain that, from the commencement of the noughties, has felt febrile to a seemingly unprecedented extent, fraught with concerns connected with Islamist terrorism, disabled rights, the social work agenda and issues around paedophilia. Gradually, British society was being re-tuned to acknowledge the needs of the weak and vulnerable; or to scoff at them, if the crowd had taken a drink. And all this was occurring at the very moment stand-up comedy was undergoing its expansion. Those increased audiences – whether attending theatres, reading autobiographies, or watching panel shows or live DVDs – were primed for a comedy that spoke to these new realities. Culturally, the sails couldn't have been set fairer for a comic like Frankie Boyle.

It was fitting inasmuch as Boyle was a product of the previous burgeoning in British humour, alternative comedy, as represented then on liberal, late-night Channel 4: 'I was really into *The Comic Strip Presents* . . . and *Saturday Night Live*,' Boyle wrote in his bestselling autobiography, *My Shit Life So Far*. 'I seemed to be the only person in school who watched any of that stuff. It's easy to forget that while alternative comedy is now the mainstream, at the time it was a real minority interest.'

Boyle's humour was conditioned equally by his upbringing. His neighbourhood, Pollokshaws, was run-down and scheduled for demolition, and the only solace it offered was the opportunity to enact petty recreational cruelties upon equally hapless schoolmates. Populated by misfits and victims, the Glasgow of the young Boyle was a place that bred a kind of juvenile nihilism, provoked by surrounding oddities: 'We always got our hair cut at this barber called Old Hughie, who was from the Islands somewhere, was always completely pished and had a wooden leg. My mum would sit balefully behind us, encouraging him to take more hair off. She always left bitterly disappointed that we still had a little hair. Pretty much the only cut that would have satisfied her would have exposed a sizeable section of our brains.'

Even by the time of his six-part Channel 4 series *Tramadol Nights* in autumn 2010, the debate around taste and decency was deeply irksome to Boyle. One sketch depicted his view of what would be left were the opposition to get their way, in a parodic BBC drama named *Untitled Street*: 'I've got that thing you asked for,' says one faceless character. 'Adjective, adjective, verb,' replies the other.

Even so, no comic in history, British or American, has forced the issue as assertively as Boyle. He seems almost to work from a check-sheet, one that might have delighted the querulous and prurient youngster he depicts in *My Shit Life So Far*: Abortion? Check. Down's syndrome? Check. Paedophilia, rape and pornography? Check. Running through his comedy is an almost childish glee in the repeated uttering of forbidden nouns, paedophile and its derivatives being favourite. So autistically insistent are these repetitions that the explanation might more properly belong in the realm of psychology than in comedy; in a way, Boyle is the Rain Man of rectitude.

None of which is to say that he is necessarily in the right in adopting his shock-and-awe approach to the impermissible. One persistent critic has been the comic Stewart Lee, who in his series *Comedy Vehicle* (produced by Armando Iannucci) put it like this: 'On the 73 bus I saw a 12-year-old girl call someone a cunt. There were mitigating circumstances, though; her daughter was being extremely annoying. Now, I'm ashamed of having thought of that joke – though I have been advised I might be able to sell it to Frankie Boyle's *Tramadol Nights*. Apparently it has the requisite level of contempt for vulnerable people.'

The arguments around the validity of Boyle's approach will continue to be thorny. It can't be denied he derives satisfaction from the dark ingenuity of his material, from his masterly talent for locating the malignant side of any situation. There is no coherent or comforting overview, as such, and he has no particular political or social agenda, as Lenny Bruce and Bill Hicks had. Boyle's desire, it seems, is principally to elicit the hard cackle, the jeer of derision.

At the same time, he needs to be seen in historical context. Audiences, after nearly 40 years in the game, are more than competent at navigating the geography of a comic's intentions, at unpicking knots of irony, sarcasm, facetiousness and provocation. We might regard the infamous Jordan joke as unforgivable, or we might consider it a characteristically unforgiving way of noting that a publicity-crazed celebrity had made a disabled child a counter in her divorce proceedings. Such insights may not be comfortable; but, then, as Steve Martin so famously said, 'Comedy is not pretty.'

'Someone in the next room...'

The Glasgow Smile: Your schooldays in Pollok-shaws seem to have informed greatly the outlook of your comedy.

Frankie Boyle: It was like a zoo. There were 3,000 kids and we were taught in plywood huts some of the time. It was like getting through prison, all these kids with mental health issues slipping through the cracks. I joined the Latin club solely because it happened in a lockable classroom. We'd be in there having lunch and there'd be kids trying to climb in the windows to get at us.

TGS: You first attempted stand-up as a drunken dare, and your early days on the circuit left you with a drink problem.

FB: I don't really believe in the AA view of alcoholism. The idea that I'm a recovering alcoholic is unacceptable to me. I hate the idea of imprinting people with the notion that they are addictive personalities and will always have a problem. I believe that you are what you're doing at the time. It just crushes people's confidence and makes them more likely to relapse. Studies prove that there's less recidivism among drinkers who take up tennis than those who join AA.

TGS: You must find the extent to which your career took off slightly surreal.

FB: Sometimes I sit in the dressing room before a show thinking someone in the next room is watching a football match really loudly. They aren't – it's just the noise 2,000 people make filing into the hall.

TGS: Is it dispiriting having to defend your comedy?

FB: These are jokes, they're not pledges in a manifesto; they shouldn't have to be justified. The only limitations are whether it's funny and whether it's telling people to go out and kill. If someone tells me a joke is unacceptable I say, well, listen to 3,000 people laughing at it – it's clearly not unacceptable.

TGS: What keeps you going, besides the vast acclaim, popularity and riches?

FB: You hear sculptors argue that, to them, the statue is inside the block of marble and they just have to get rid of the waste material. It's the same for me with jokes. Someone attacks Glasgow Airport and I think to myself, there will be five definitively funny jokes within that event and I won't rest till they come out. The worst feeling is when you don't have The Joke on something, you just have A Joke.

ACCORDING TO BOYLE

'Viagra takes half an hour to have any effect; I often find in that time the woman has managed to wriggle free.'

Gay adoption: 'A great idea – the dads already know where all the best parks are.'

'You'll notice that not many Scottish homes have wind chimes – because it'd be like having tinnitus.'

'John Prescott – you're talking about a guy who can't wear a belt and a tie on the same day – or he'll turn into sausages.'

'Mark Chapman, the guy who shot John Lennon, got refused parole. I think we should let him out – just as soon we get him really, really into Coldplay.'

'We've got David Cameron as prime minister now – a wet-lipped buffoon who looks as though he should be playing trombone in a Lurpak advert.'

'Sex education at my school was a muttered warning about the janitor.'

'Belly-button piercings aren't sexy, men just think they are because they remind them of the staple in a porno mag.'

'You remember years ago when they were making Braveheart, everyone said, "Oh, it's ridiculous that Mel Gibson's playing a Scottish guy, that's not gonna be very convincing." And look at him now . . . an alcoholic racist.'

Andrew Lloyd Webber: 'He looks like he's had his face carved off by a diseased butcher, put in a piñata, beaten with hockey sticks for six hours, and had the resultant slop piped back on to his head like icing on the ugliest cake the world has ever seen.'

'I hate homophobia, it doesn't even make sense. Gay people are a lot cooler than straight people. You never see a gay guy on the golf course – well, not during the daytime.'

'If I had a choice between fucking Susan Boyle and being gang-raped by a gang of squaddies I'd buy the first round of WKD myself.'

Y

KEVIN BRIDGES

'Glasgow was recently voted Europe's murder capital. But also the UK's friendliest city. In the same week! We got our act together pronto'

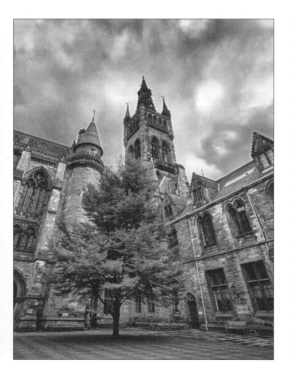

YGORRA
(Glasgow University publication, 1922–1973)

There was a time when our streets would fill annually with callow and loathsome undergraduates who would proceed to perpetrate upon the passing populace elaborate pranks. These saturnalia were known as Rag Week and served the purpose of raising a few shillings for local charities. Famously, Rag Week at Glasgow University was accompanied by a magazine, *Ygorra*, a handbook detailing all that was topical in the academic round, shot through with the wise and insightful attitude to life for which students are so revered. The magazine's title, incidentally, was a phonetic approximation of the phrase 'You've got to' (as in, 'You've got to . . . grow a vile little bum-fluff beard'). Thereby, *Ygorra* anticipated the linguistic mischief of *Parliamo Glasgow* by four decades.

ANDREW YOUNG
(showbusiness journalist, 1929–1998)

A colourful and well-liked character, Andy Young was showbusiness editor of the *Glasgow Herald* for 30 years. His affinity with performers, however, was such that he seldom had the stomach to review their performances critically, preferring to concentrate on features and interviews instead. It was during one such phase, in 1969, that a by now reconsidering Young found himself in Belfast, covering the early stages of the Troubles.

Young duly attended the scenes of conflict, but one condition of his roving brief was that he filed as usual his weekly Glasgow nightlife column. This was proving difficult. In those days, out-of-office reporters submitted text by dictating it down a telephone line to a copy-taker. As Murray Ritchie recounted in Young's obituary: 'His reporting assignments included the Northern Ireland Troubles where he narrowly escaped death when a bomb exploded in a telephone box he had passed moments earlier.' Eventually, Young found a still-functioning box, but on a street where the rebels and the army were exchanging fire. Undeterred, Young entered the box and hunkered down. He lifted the receiver. A volley of semiautomatic gunshots strafed a wall nearby. As inconspicuously as he could manage, Young dialled the number. Outside, several men in balaclavas ran past, screaming. The line to Glasgow buzzed and whirred. A mortar shell burst in the sky. Soldiers appeared on the next corner, readying their guns for action. Young cowered in the corner of the telephone box. After a lifetime, the line was connected. The copy-taker asked the journalist his business: 'This . . . is . . . Andrew Young,' whispered our hero above the noise of nearby gunfire. 'I'm . . . giving . . . you . . . For Leisure and Pleasure.'

YOUR CHEATIN' HEART
(television series, 1990)

'Some are born to sweet delight,' wrote William Blake in *Auguries of Innocence*, 'Some are born to endless night.' Notwithstanding Blake's forgivable ignorance of British television in the years after the 1820s, the line could have been written to summarise the respective fortunes of the two BBC Scotland series written by John Byrne. One of these, *Tutti Frutti*, is kept forever in the gilded locket of memory, a cherished and eternal classic; the other is *Your Cheatin' Heart*.

It is not easy to explain how things turned out like this. Structurally, the programmes were strikingly similar. Each was a six-part dissection of pop obsession in Glasgow: rock'n'roll in the first, country music in the second. Each revolved around spiky leading men with baggage (Robbie Coltrane and John Gordon Sinclair) failing for feisty dames with baggage (Emma Thompson and Tilda Swinton, later to become Byrne's partner). Each was giddy with Byrne's trademark rollercoaster dialogue. Each starred Katy Murphy as a soor ploom and a nippy sweetie. One, though, remained *Tutti Frutti*, the other *Your Cheatin' Heart*.

The former, of course, vanished for more than two decades, the result of some opaque contractual matter relating to music rights. Clearly, the lesson had been learned by the time of *Your Cheatin' Heart*; the music comes not from old recordings but is performed entirely by the cast. This is the first disappointment, but others follow. *Tutti Frutti* is a charming road movie playing out around the holiday resorts of Scotland; *Your Cheatin' Heart* is hung upon a so-what plot involving Barlinnie and drug smuggling, and was set mainly in pubs and nightclubs, and on dark, rainy streets. Coltrane and Thompson were a topflight pairing; Sinclair and Swinton radiate all the chemistry of perpetrator and victim meeting on an identity parade. The rest of the cast is an ever-swelling amoeba of waitresses, barmen, hoods and bagmen. An air of effort and anxiety hangs over everything. Repeated once and never seen again – and requiring only one viewing to understand why – *Your Cheatin' Heart* is historically fascinating but an uncharacteristic misstep from Byrne. Once his rock rolled away, it was crying time again.

YOUTH: KEVIN BRIDGES
(comic, 1986–)

Should you doubt the argument made in the introduction to this book – that Glasgow humour is a mirror rather than a window, concerned above all other things with reflecting back the lived process, the *Weltanschauung* of being Glaswegian – consider the work of Kevin Bridges. He is virtually the Platonic ideal of a Glasgow comic, historic or modern. His experience of the city is the first principle of every routine he performs.

Partly, this is a function of his precocity; Bridges flourished at a preposterously young age, dictating that he had not lived long enough to know of much, beyond his own upbringing. Equally, his background gave him his subject: life on the periphery, the rough opportunism of those social classes with their noses pressed against the glass. A typical Bridges routine concerns, and to a degree delights in, the disruptive energies of those who've been excluded from the post-1990 reboot or renaissance of Glasgow – the neds, the wide boys, the NEETs; the tribes who scoff at any notion of bourgeois propriety. In Bridges' routines, these tribes set about getting their own back, by means of drink or drugs, derision and disobedience. His is a comedy of petty anarchies, about which his attitude is one of scandalised amazement. His interest in and insight into the actual matter of daily social life in Glasgow is but the latest example of a tradition, an aesthetic, a mission which reaches back to the days of Tommy Morgan and Lex McLean, to Francie and Josie and *Parliamo Glasgow*.

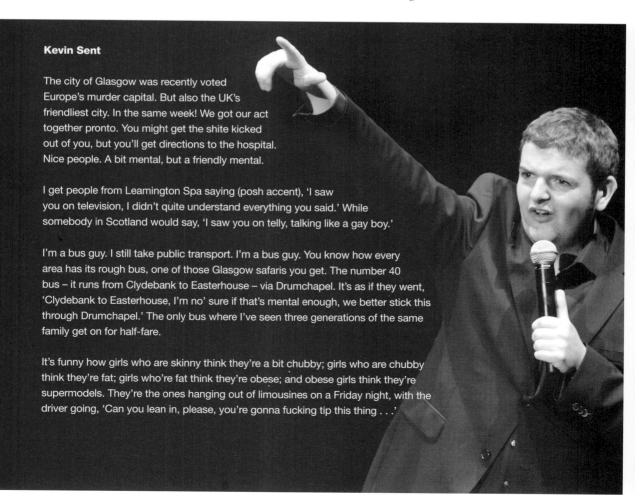

Kevin Sent

The city of Glasgow was recently voted Europe's murder capital. But also the UK's friendliest city. In the same week! We got our act together pronto. You might get the shite kicked out of you, but you'll get directions to the hospital. Nice people. A bit mental, but a friendly mental.

I get people from Leamington Spa saying (posh accent), 'I saw you on television, I didn't quite understand everything you said.' While somebody in Scotland would say, 'I saw you on telly, talking like a gay boy.'

I'm a bus guy. I still take public transport. I'm a bus guy. You know how every area has its rough bus, one of those Glasgow safaris you get. The number 40 bus – it runs from Clydebank to Easterhouse – via Drumchapel. It's as if they went, 'Clydebank to Easterhouse, I'm no' sure if that's mental enough, we better stick this through Drumchapel.' The only bus where I've seen three generations of the same family get on for half-fare.

It's funny how girls who are skinny think they're a bit chubby; girls who are chubby think they're fat; girls who're fat think they're obese; and obese girls think they're supermodels. They're the ones hanging out of limousines on a Friday night, with the driver going, 'Can you lean in, please, you're gonna fucking tip this thing . . .'

'Hey, you. Has Jimmy "Chainsaw" McPhee been in tonight?'

NOT THE NINE O'CLOCK NEWS

ZENITH
Not The Nine O'Clock News (BBC sketch show, 1979–1982)

Representing the return to British television of a university wit tradition slumbering since *Monty Python's Flying Circus, Not the Nine O'Clock News* was a BBC 2 sketch show of huge popularity in its day. Billy Connolly not only married one of the show's stars, Australian comedienne Pamela Stephenson, he appeared in a number of sketches, including this classic from 1980.

Interior pub. Enter two men, a bearded, dangerous-looking individual (Billy Connolly) and his rat-like lieutenant (Rowan Atkinson). Connolly addresses the barman (Mel Smith) in a Glasgow accent made of sandpaper.

Connolly: Hey, you. Has Jimmy 'Chainsaw' McPhee been in tonight?
Barman: Naw.
Connolly: What about Big Jock, the Kneecruncher?
Barman: Naw.
Connolly (rat-like companion whispers in his ear)**:** Whit aboot Stick-the-boot-in-his-head-and-ask-questions-later McDonald?
Barman (thinks): Naw.
Connolly: Hacksaw Haggarty, the Hen-choker?
Barman: Naw.
Connolly (exhales and begins speaking in a camp lisp)**:** Can I have a Campari and soda, please?

INDEX